ORGANISATIONAL

CHANGE &

DEVELOPMENT

AN AFRICAN PERSPECTIVE

First published in 2015

ISBN: 978-1-86922-540-7
eISBN: 978-1-86922-541-4 (PDF eBook)

Published by Knowres Publishing (Pty) Ltd
P O Box 3954
Randburg
2125
Republic of South Africa

Tel: (011) 706-6009
Fax: (011) 706-1127
E-mail: orders@knowres.co.za
Website: www.kr.co.za

Printed and bound: Mega Digital (Pty) Ltd. Parow Industria, Cape Town
Typesetting, layout and design: Cia Joubert, cia@knowres.co.za
Cover design: Marlene de Villiers, marlene@knowres.co.za
Editing and proofreading: Mandy Collins, mcollins@icon.co.za
Project management: Cia Joubert, cia@knowres.co.za
Index created with: TExtract, www.Texyz.com

ORGANISATIONAL CHANGE & DEVELOPMENT

AN AFRICAN PERSPECTIVE

by

Dr Rica Viljoen

KNO RES
PUBLISHING

2015

ENDORSEMENTS

When I read the book *Organisational Change and Development – An African Perspective*, by Dr Rica Viljoen, my heart leapt with joy to know that the experiences of people like Rica and Loraine Laubscher have been documented to enrich the lives of people in our country. They show us how to adapt to the ever-changing environment in South Africa, sharing the true meaning of organisational change through their knowledge.

I've been privileged to work with Rica over the past 20 years. I have first-hand experience of the impact her methodology had on individuals and teams, and in organisations. To have had both her and Loraine as mentors and having been able to be taught by them has had an impact on me as an individual, but also on organisations with which I associate.

The methodology of inclusivity and spiral dynamics gave me the necessary tools and knowledge to translate and connect with employees in a more effective way and with far more insight into the challenges that they experience. The true meaning of spiral dynamics and the knowledge imparted to me by Rica and Loraine gave me the ability to apply it in my daily life when I deal with people. It has always proved to be correct and in line with the situations that I've had to face. I would recommend this book to each and every person.

Organisational development is to an organisation what breathing is to a human. Change at a personal level is inevitable for me to develop and grow in order to reach my own capacity through work opportunities given to me within an organisation. Change in an organisation is the only way of delivering exceptional results from the very start. This is done by diagnosing what needs to change, and by applying strategic planning and creating change in organisational culture through focused OCD interventions.

Evaluation of one's personal growth forces one to make changes that might not be comfortable, but that are necessary to understand and explore one's own capacity. This could be as a specialist in our own field or in our overall approach to perform at our best through taking up our role in the organisation.

Organisational development can be seen as the essential part of creating the 'vehicle' to make things happen, and of creating a more productive individual. It does this by defining and developing the individual into an integral part of the organisation, which benefits the organisation's need to grow and sustain itself.

This book can assist both organisational development practitioners and leaders to implement an integral inclusivity strategy that will manifest in organisational and personal benefits.

Rene de Beer, Group Human Capital Officer, Renlyn Group (Pty) Ltd

The story of me is the story of OD (Organisational Development).

When an OD process is implemented in an organisation it tells the story of change. It is the story of change, new growth, becoming better.

The focus of the story is the journey of the organisation through three destined domains of reason, namely organisation, teams and individuals. However, there is second story. This story is not always told. It is not always there when OD is implemented. The story is of the ME.

As an organisation goes through change, so does the person, the ME. This does not refer to individuals as elements of the organisation but to the ME. As a person, each of us as the individuals in the organisation must go through an internalised change process, our own OD journey. Very simply, I refer to this internal change journey as learning. And, in my opinion, without learning, the internalised change process that each individual must go through, there is no OD story.

In implementing an OD process, the teller of the OD story must know where the organisation is going, what it will look like when it gets there and how it will behave once it is done. That story can only be told if the story of ME is interwoven into the story of OD.

If you are, or should be a teller of OD stories or learning stories, reading a book like this will provide you with valuable insights to the worlds of change, dynamics, growth, learning and most of all, organisational development.

Cliff Brunette, Learning Experience Specialist

The true impact of any OCD (Organisational development and change) intervention lies in the authenticity of such a process. Through authentic intent in any OCD process the potential sacredness of such a process can be revealed and experienced as a once-in-a-lifetime opportunity for real transformation. However, such transformation then becomes an alchemical process by which those involved can never be reverted back to their original form.

A pre-requisite for the success of these OCD interventions lies first in the correct diagnosis of what should be done and continuous re-evaluation throughout the process. The sacredness of such a journey is respected through the integrity of the OCD practitioner, proper boundary management of the entire process on all levels, and staying true to the intent of the process.

The outcome is then not only improved workplace culture on an organisation, team and individual level, but that people have reported how their entire lives have been transformed and impacted to a point of no return. Stories of improved quality of life, being able to be a better father to their kids and becoming leaders who are willing to look beyond the obvious issues and to make tough decisions have been told. OCD then does not represent a profession only, but also a responsibility towards humanity and a greater purpose in life.

I have been privileged enough to witness and learn from a true master in OCD interventions. This journey can be regarded as sacred. Most of these teachings have been captured in this book and will transform the way you see OCD forever.

Ansuné Coetzee, Organisational Change and Development Practitioner, Mandala Consulting

DEDICATION

This book is dedicated to:

Yvonne Nell, my first human resources manager, for teaching me about consistency and about having difficult conversations in a direct manner and with confidence, and being just. You were an important role model early in my career.

Gayle Piek, a respected colleague and dear friend, who believed in me before I did so myself – for teaching me to see things for what they are, for sharing numerous ideas, conversations and memories with me, and discovering the writings of Jung together. You wisely led me to the field of organisational change and development, and supported me unconditionally.

Wimpie du Toit, a seasoned human resource executive, who not only simulated my thinking, but also enabled a lovely space for me to reflect and write. I will keep my promise to document the stories, typically only spoken.

Thank you

ACKNOWLEDGEMENTS

First and foremost, I would like to thank my family, Hein, Stefan and Ruan for standing beside me throughout my career, and always being supportive of my need to travel and do organisational change and development work.

I would like to acknowledge the contribution of all the participants in the interventions that I have facilitated over the last two decades. Your stories co-created the insights that informed this book.

During the late 1990s, we did numerous adventure training interventions. These were deeply facilitated. My first team-building session was extremely difficult to facilitate. A team with challenging personal dynamics came for a high-rope session. Being well-trained, yet very inexperienced, I wanted to work purely – to follow theoretical frameworks, yet facilitate the session dynamically. The head instructor of the adventure-training course, Leon Lategan, offered his facilitation assistance. Quite arrogantly I responded that I could do this on my own. At the end of the day I was in tears, and pleading with him to assist. The words: "I don't want to facilitate alone..." still ring true today. Together, we dealt with more than 150 two- or three-day sessions. Some of these were very difficult interventions like conflict resolution sessions during the integration of the different defence forces. Thank you, Leon, I learned a lot from you, and respect you as facilitator and philosopher.

Over the years I've had the honour of facilitating with different subject matter experts. Here I need to acknowledge Dr Lorenza van Schalkwyk, Dr Willem de Jager and Francois Steyn, who did marvellous organisational change and development work in the organisation where I was employed. Professors Frans Cilliers, Pieter Koortzen and Michelle May influenced my personal facilitation style significantly. Marius Pretorius annually hosts the Robben Island Diverse Experience (RIDE). This is a very challenging, yet profoundly meaningful psycho-analytical event that not only can prepare organisational change and development consultants to work from this theoretical stance, but also prepares line managers to experience how power dynamics, diversity factors and boundaries impact on human behaviour at work. Thank you all for your investment in my personal development.

Drs Jopie van Rooyen senior and junior opened up a lucky packet of surprises for me. I immersed myself in the work of Jung, and came across personality types. You enabled me to understand how people differ, and how they are similar. I have integrated personality type into my daily practice. When I enrolled to do my master's degree, Dr Jopie (Jr) told me about the Bar-On EQ-i that was not available in South Africa at the time. I imported a version of the instrument from MHS in America. The insights gained here led to a career change. I left banking, and formed Mandala Consulting, a niche organisational change and development house based on Jungian principles. Today, I still use the EQ-i to do pre- and post-intervention analysis at individual and group level.

Stratified systems thinking as explained by Eliot Jaques (1972) formed a key part of my exploration into understanding the phenomenon of social life in organisations. These explorations led me to Bioss, and for the last decade I have been an associate and a CPA practitioner. Thank you to Piet Calitz (for our thought leadership), Lisa Ashton, Ruth Pienaar and Jaques Haworth for all the wisdom shared.

My doctoral study focused on organisational transformation through inclusivity and was undertaken at Unisa under the study leadership of Professor Lize Booysen (whom I respect deeply, and still consult with and view as a mentor today). The theoretical underpinning of this book has its roots in my thesis.

A selected few HR practitioners were exposed to the thinking of Loraine Laubscher through the transformational unit of the organisation where we worked. We all read the 1996 book *Spiral Dynamics* written by Don Beck and Chris Cowan. It had a remarkable impact on me, and left a deep mark. However, I found it conceptually difficult. Deliberate attempts to understand it better led me to a journey that would place me on a totally different route. I met Loraine Laubscher, the lady who explained spiral dynamics in Africa in 2009. Our paths never diverged. I attended a course she presented, and became her academic supervisor for her PhD, which at age 82 she passed with flying colours at the Da Vinci Institute for Innovation and Technology. Concurrently we co-authored five chapters in text books on the application of spiral dynamics in Africa. I also met Dr Beck several times, and was accredited by him in the use of spiral dynamics technology. He and Loraine are indeed inspiring people.

The Da Vinci Institute for Innovation and Technology, by name Professor Bennie Anderson, allowed me academic freedom in the role of senior lecturer and later head of faculty of Management of People to test my assumptions even further and to develop my ontological stance and theoretical frameworks. I am still actively involved in lecturing and leading studies at the institute.

Dr Albert Wort appointed me as visiting scholar at the University of Johannesburg a few years ago. Dr Adri Drotskie, with whom I had worked closely at executive level in an organisation before, and who was then the head of the MCOM programme at UJ, introduced us. Working in the Department of Industrial Psychology and Human Resources assisted me to engage with world-class scholars and to contribute academically. Three years ago Professor Theo Veldsman appointed me as senior research fellow, and currently I am working closely with Dr Magda Hewitt in the leadership and emerging markets field.

I also worked closely with Professor Willem Schurink, who taught me a great deal about qualitative research. In particular, his understanding of auto-ethnography, life-history research and personal narratives assisted me in my personal purpose in life, namely, to record the stories of voices not previously heard.

Through the Da Vinci Institute for Innovation and Technology relations were formed with Professors Ronnie Lessem and Alexander Schieffer. This co-operation led to the integration of integral theory and research in my personal practice, the formation of the Mandala Centre for Integral Development and a book published through Ashgate on Inclusive Organisational Transformation. The integral methodology has philosophical congruence with spiral dynamics, and hopefully this relationship will further the development of this field of study.

Numerous business leaders and human resource and organisational effectiveness executives allowed me to work in their space. A sincere word of thanks to Dawie Strydom, who first gave the Benchmark of Engagement a chance. Since then, this instrument has been used as basis for multi-cultural research in 42 countries.

Italia Boninelli, in her current role as executive vice-president: People and Organisational Development, AngloGold Ashanti, has been most helpful in the research phase of this book. Not only were strategic thoughts shared on the future of this field of study, but in-depth understanding of the complexity of strategic organisational development became evident.

Dawie Mostert, senior vice president: Organisational Effectiveness of Sibanye Gold, should also be acknowledged here. His maturity, systemic thinking and willingness to allow soft organisational change and development work in a traditional 'hard' environment are remarkable. Johnny Lanchester and dear Melody Perumal are playing a significant role in this remarkable transformational journey.

Although the list of exceptional leaders can hardly be saturated here, the integrity, humaneness and steward-leadership of Adri Vermeulen, currently Managing Director of PPS in Namibia, should be highlighted. Adri has been working with the strategic process described in Chapter 12 with exceptional business success for the largest part of the decade. Adri, not only got the DOING right, his BEING is inspirational.

The book was peer reviewed by highly respected academics. Thank you Professor Elana Swanepoel of Unisa, for your practised eye, sharp mind and dedication to the development of others. Dr Mary-Anne Harrop-Alin, of the University of Johannesburg, thank you for being colourful, gentle, yet firm and kind, yet insightful. Dr Marthie de Kock, of the Da Vinci Institute for Innovation and Technology, thanks to you too. You are mature, thorough and consistent. Without the guidance of all of you, the book would not have been the same.

Ansuné Coetzee joined Mandala Consulting three years ago. In her, I found a person with integrity, a kindred spirit and a valued business partner. Your contribution to our practice is significant. Thank you Ansuné for ensuring that I have time to write. This leads me to my writing partner and friend, Jan Nel. Without him I cannot document what I think. We need to write more, Jan, there is work to do.

To the reader, the OCD practitioner or business executive, thank you for picking up this book. The field concerns itself with humans. Your life stories make the theory in print come alive; your narratives provide rich context for the work described here. OCD practitioners believe they are successful when business leaders believe they have done it on their own. We are because of you.

FOREWORD

Have you ever thought about the experience of a butterfly in its cocoon? How wonderful it must feel to fly free; you can fly free too if you wish. I love rainbows; how they dance and scatter their colour across the blue sky; just as magical as the stars that splash themselves in infinite numbers.

This poetry forms the epilogue to Rica Viljoen's Organisational Change and Development from an African perspective. In my foreword I want to reflect on, most especially, the significance of such a South African perspective on so-called OCD. The comment, "I love rainbows" gives the game away. It was Archbishop Desmond Tutu who coined the term "rainbow nation" to describe his beloved South Afirca.

Uniquely then, South Africa is a "window on the world", for us[1] a window on integral *worlds*, that is north and south, east and west, as we[2] originally depicted in *African Management* in terms of a so-called *South African Business Sphere*. Of course, pride of place in such a transcultural and indeed transformational 'rainbow-like' consideration of not only individuals and organisations, but also, and especially, whole societies, must go to *Spiral Dynamics*, and that masterful tradition of America's Graves, Beck and Cowan[3] on the one hand, and South Africans Rica Viljoen and Loraine Laubscher[4] – now also extended to the fellow-authors of the book – on the other hand.

Let us now position all of these in historic OCD perspective. The *organisation development* movement was born, like most matters managerial in America, in the 1950s and 1960s, with the seminal work of Chris Argyris[5], on *Personality and Organization*, together with the conflicts that need to be overcome – OD-wise – between them, and the even more seminal work in the 1960s by Argyris's compatriot Warren Bennis[6], on *Organization Development*.

In that classic work Bennis compared and contrasted bureaucratic versus *democratic* management. In fact the two doyens of American management thinking then "lost the OD plot", as far as we are concerned, and fell in love with leadership and learning instead, with a due emphasis now on the individual rather than the organisation. For me this was a backward step.

In the wings, in fact, now in the 1970s and 1980s, were a Hollander, a Canadian and South African, Bernard Lievegoed – *The Developing Organisation*[7], Elliot Jaques – *Requisite Organization*[8], and Albert Koopman – *Transcultural Management*[9] in turn, all of whose work appeared in the Blackwell's book series we developed in the 1990s on *Developmental Management*. While Lievegoed, as an anthroposophist and a psychiatrist, introduced the now well-known *stages* of organisation *development*, from pioneering to differentiated, to, most importantly for OD purposes, *integrated*, Jaques introduced the whole notion of organisational *stratification* in now seven such layers. What South Africa's own Albert Koopman did, uniquely and appropriately to his land of birth, was to focus on the particular, organisational and societal contributions of the 'north' and the 'south' to development as a whole, the one (north) focused on 'making profit' and the other (south) on 'profiting society'.

In my view, the distinctive contribution of *Southern* Africa generally, and Viljoen and Laubscher specifically, to the OCD field is, is to interlink, developmentally, self, organisation *and* society in an overtly *transcultural* guise, befitting of South Africa as a *rainbow* nation. In fact, it is such a societal, as well as organisational, concern, that has brought together our[10] Trans4M under the guise of our *integral Enterprise*, and their mandala, into a Mandala Centre for Integral Development, that interlinks our integral and as such, societal concerns.

Beck and Cowan's[11] *Spiral Dynamics: Mastering Values, Leadership and Change*, that came out in the 1990s, again under the rubric of our *Developmental Management* series, was uniquely concerned, from the outset, with societal as well as organisational dynamics. Such a 'rainbow-like' – beige, purple, red, blue, orange, green (first tier); yellow, turquoise (second tier) – perspective on cultural 'memes' has, interestingly enough, been transformed by Laubscher into *human niches*, which gives such a spiral even more of a societal orientation. Indeed, Beck and Laubscher played a seminal part, alongside Mandela and De Klerk, in masterminding South Africa's extraordinary transition in the 1990s.

Interestingly enough, though not yet with the same degree of success, given the turbulent situation in the Middle East, Beck and Lebanese-American Elza Maalouf[12] have attempted in the new millennium to promote the same kind of Co-*Emergence* in Israel and Palestine, together rather than apart.

Retracing steps then, what I am arguing is that Graves, Beck and Cowan, Laubscher and Viljoen, Maalouf and also her husband Said Dawlabani[13], as well as recently Nichols Beechroft[14] in *The New Magna Carta: A Psychiatrist's Prescription for Western Civilization*, have taken a 'societal' turn against the developmental tide, and the predominating influence on such, for them as for us, highlighted in my forthcoming *Integral Advantage: Emerging Markets and Societies*[15] is predominantly S*outhern* African. For while Laubscher and Viljoen are South African, and I am Zimbabwean, Beck has been profoundly influenced, over the past two decades by Southern Africa.

Let me finally put all of these into perspective OCD-wise. In the new millennium Harvard Business School Professor, Rakesh Khuran[16], an organisational sociologist of Indian origin, wrote his seminal work *Higher Minds to Hired Hands: The Social Transformation of American Business Schools and the Unfulfilled Promise of Management as a Profession*, where he maintained:

Eventually business schools began responding to the clarion call for developing leaders, not managers. In the 1990s, for example, Harvard shifted from its emphasis on general management to "educating leaders who make a difference in the world". One of the central features of a bone fide profession, for Khurana, is a coherent body of expert knowledge built upon a well-developed theoretical foundation. The renowned American business executive and writer Chester Barnard in fact observed in the 1930s that the "Great Man" view on leadership generated "an extraordinary amount of dogmatically stated nonsense". Leadership, as such, lacks a usable body of knowledge to go with it.

As far as I am concerned, this recent pre-emphasis on leadership, as well as entrepreneurship, whether economically or socially oriented, represents an 'infantilisation' of the prior, evolving field of management and organisation. What Viljoen and Laubscher have so successfully done, together with their fellow South African authors, and standing on the shoulders of giants Graves and Beck, is to further evolve OCD, societally now so to speak, and indeed transculturally, thereby doing justice to their 'rainbow nation'. As such they are furthering the societal, as well as individual and organisational, shared cause of our Mandala Centre for Integral Development, through perhaps what should rightly be termed OSCD: Organisational and Societal Change and Development.

Ronnie Lessem, Trans4M
March 2015

References

1. Schieffer A. and Lessem R. (2014 *Integral Development: Realizing the Transformative Potential of Individuals, Organizations, Societies.* Farnham. Gower.
2. Christie P., Lessem R. and Mbigi L. (1993) *African Management : Philosophies, Concepts and Application.* Johannesburg. Knowledge Resources.
3. Beck D. and Cowan C. (1995) *Spiral Dynamics : Mastering Values, Leadership and Change.* Chichester. Wiley-Blackwell.
4. Viljoen R. (2015) *Inclusive Organisational Transformation : An African Perspective on Human Niches and Diversity of Thought.* Farnham. Gower.
5. Argyris C. (1965) *Personality and Organization.* New York. Harper and Row.
6. Bennis W. (1969) *Organisation Development.* New York. Addison Wesley.
7. Lievegoed B. (1990) *The Developing Organization.* Chichester. Wiley-Blackwell.
8. Jaques E. and Clement S. (1991) *Executive Leadership.* Chichester. Wiley-Blackwell.
9. Koopman A. (1991) *Transcultural Management.* Chichester. Wiley–Blackwell.
10. Lessem R. and Schieffer A. (2009) *Transformation Management : Towards the Integral Enterprise.* Farnham. Gower.
11. Beck D. and Cowan C. (1995) *op cit.*
12. Maalouf E. (2014) *Emerge: The Rise of Functional Democracy and the Future of the Middle East.* New York. Select Books.
13. Dawlabani S. (2013) *Memenomics. The Next Generation Economic System.* New York. Select Books.
14. Beechroft N. (2015) in *The New Magna Carta : A Psychiatrist's Prescription for Western Civilization.* Creative Space Independent Publishing Platform.
15. Lessem R. (2015) *Integral Advantage: Emerging Markets and Societies.* Farnham. Gower (forthcoming).
16. Khurana R. (2007) *From Higher Aims to Hired Hands: The Social Transformation of the American Business Schools and the Unfulfilled Promise of Management as a Profession.* New Jersey. Princeton University Press.

TABLE OF CONTENTS

List of figures

List of tables

ABOUT THE EDITOR

Dr Rica Viljoen, the editor's, research, teaching and service activities reflect her interest in multi-national leadership, inclusivity, organisational change and development and sustainability. Her research has been published and presented internationally, and reached more than 42 countries. She is head of the Department of the Management of People Faculty of the Da Vinci Institute for Innovation and Technology. Rica is a Senior Research Fellow at the University of Johannesburg. As a master OCD practitioner she focuses on large-scale organisational change and development. She is the managing director of Mandala Consulting, a niche organisational change and development company that specialises in transformational processes, organisational research and spiral dynamics.

Dr Viljoen's corporate career was in banking, where she held an executive organisational change and development role. She is accredited with numerous professional bodies such as the South African Board of People Practices (SABPP), the Institute for People Management (IPM), the Institute for Management Consultants South Africa (IMCSA) and the American Psychological Association Division 13 (APA). She worked closely with Dr Loraine Laubscher on integrating African spiritual consciousness with mainstream scholarship. Together with Professors Ronnie Lessem and Alexander Schieffer she started the Mandala Centre for integral research. She recently published a text book, *Inclusive Organisational Transformation*, through Ashgate Publishers.

ABOUT THE CONTRIBUTORS

Dr Loraine I. Laubscher was granted her Ph.D in 2013, at the age of 83. She has spent her lifetime applying, explaining, teaching and researching the thinking that produced her thesis – Human Niches Spiral Dynamics for Africa. Over the years, she has explored and described the core intelligence and deep thinking systems that flow beneath our belief systems.

Dr Laubscher specialises in integrating First and Third World cultures in the global workplace. She is recognised as a pioneer in South Africa, connecting with the natural intelligences of indigenous people and in accessing those intelligences in the design of living environments, governance systems, and negotiation strategies. She worked for years in the mines (gold, platinum and coal), in township communities and in production-oriented industries. Some of the papers that Loraine presented are an indication of her interest in change leadership. She continues to pursue this interest as is evidenced by her contributions to a number of books that Dr Rica Viljoen is writing on Inclusivity and Integral Thinking.

Dr Laubscher has presented at numerous international conferences, coached various industry leaders and politicians and continues to lecture and conduct workshops to facilitate and develop an in-depth understanding of spiral dynamics theory on diversity management. She is currently in the process of developing a unique assessment to describe African spirituality in the workplace.

Dr Anna-Rosa le Roux is a registered industrial psychologist and has built a career in consulting psychology weaving corporate and consultation experience together in organisations in the Middle East and Africa. She holds post-graduate degrees in psychology specialising in the organisational change and development domain with expertise in strategy facilitation, organisational design and structuring, team alignment and effectiveness, integrated wellness solutions and leadership development and coaching. She is currently the head of Organisational Effectiveness at Woolworths Financial Services.

Dr Le Roux served on the executive councils of organisations such as the Society for Industrial and Organisational Psychology of South Africa (SIOPSA), The Association of Change Management Professionals, Africa (ACMP Africa). She is an honorary vice president of the International Society for Coaching Psychology (ISCP) and part of the International Steering Committee of the First International Congress of Coaching Psychology (ICCP). She has represented South Africa in Coaching and Consulting Psychology in the UK, Spain, Australia, France, Italy and North America.

Dr Adri Drotskie has been the MBA Director of Henley Business School South Africa since 1 February 2015. She has years of corporate and academic experience, working for Transnet (eight years) and Absa Bank, a member of the Barclays Group (10 years), and is a senior lecturer and Head of the MCom (Business Management) programme at the University of Johannesburg (seven years).

Dr Drotskie is a strategist by profession, with skills in strategy development and implementation, action learning, scenario planning and systemic thinking. She has strong leadership and management skills and has experience in managing large teams, but she has also lectured on post-graduate programmes in contemporary management, history and philosophy of management, international business, strategic marketing and strategic management. She holds a Ph.D from the University of Stellenbosch, with the title Customer Experience as Strategic Differentiator in Retail Banking.

Tonja Blom's career is in the field of organisational change and she is employed by one of the biggest auto-manufacturing companies in the world. During 2007 and 2008, while being employed by a multi-national company in the Slovak Republic, she witnessed the severe impact of change at a national, organisational and local level. Individuals, organisations and the economy were forced into major changes related to ideologies, systems, procedures and habits. This required individuals and organisations to deal with change. Some failed miserably to cope outside their comfort zones.

In many ways, these changes were similar to those as experienced in South Africa post-1994. After returning to South Africa, she became involved in HR system implementations in a global manufacturing organisation, which again confirmed the extent to which individuals struggle with change.

Blom is currently in the process of completing a DBL focusing on organisational change and leadership. She became involved in TRE® (Tension and trauma releasing exercises) as a result of the increased stress and tension individuals experience when confronted with organisational change. She has completed TRE® level I, and will complete level II with international accreditation during April 2015.

GLOSSARY

AI	Appreciative Inquiry
AK	Applied Kinesiology
AL	Action Learning
APLA	Azanian People's Liberation Army
BeQ	Benchmark of Engagement
CE	Chief Executive
CEO	Chief Executive Officer
CPA	Career Path Appreciation
EFF	Economic Freedom Front
EQ-i	Bar-On Emotional Intelligence Quotient
Exco	Executive Committee
GPMC	Greater Pretoria Metropolitan Council
HR	Human Resources
HRM	Human Resource Management
KPA	Key performance areas
KPI	Key performance indicator
MK	Umkhonto WeSizwe
IDP	Individual Development Plan
ISIS	Islamic State of Iraq and al-Sham
IO	Industrial and Organisational Psychology
LGI	Large Group Intervention
OC	Organisational Change
OCD	Organisational Change and Development
OD	Organisational Development
MBTI	Myers-Briggs Type Indicator
RIDE	Robben Island Diversity Experience
SANDF	South African National Defence Force

ABOUT THIS BOOK

At the beginning of my organisational change and development journey, the story below was told under an old oak tree to a group of practitioners by Bruce Copley. I have been searching for the original story ever since. All that I could find was that it was an old Indian story that was retold from generation to generation. As a storyteller, narratives grow on me, and take on a life of their own after they have been repeated many a time through numerous interventions. This is my version of this story.

Long long ago,
Maybe today, maybe tomorrow
There was a man who had returned from the war in a terrible state
His wife was so in love with him
She allowed him to be pre-occupied, and he was actually quite rude to her
All for the sake of love (as he explained to her)

After she had tried everything that her elders had taught her to win over the man,
She decided to set him free to go and sort himself out.
One night she sadly told him:
Please go away, and find your Truth for yourself!

The man left the very next day on his quest.

He walked all the way to the South. He did not find Truth.
He walked all the way to the North. He did not find Truth.
He walked all the way to the East. He did not find Truth.
He walked all the way to the West. He did not find Truth.

Quite disillusioned, he decided that there was nothing left for him to do,
but turn back and go towards his home.
After months of walking along streams and climbing hills
he came to the summit of the very last mountain,
and there at last he found TRUTH.

She seemed to be a sage old lady.
Her face was cut with wrinkles.
Her hair was thin and wispy,
but her eyes were bright and sharp.
A mole, as big as a coin, covered part of her mouth
in which she had only one tooth left.

The man spent a year and a day listening to the wisdom of Truth.

On the last day of his visit,
He spoke to Truth and acknowledged the wisdom he had gained.

He asked her what he could do in return for the insight she had given him.

Truth reflected for a long while (as all clever people do)
Then, with a crooked finger in the air she said in a clear voice...

"Tell all the people that you meet that I am young and beautiful!"

This story deals with the universal truth that there are different perceptions and different interpretations due to different questions of the existence of different people. This statement is true of the topic of organisational change and development as well. As a master organisational change and development consultant who has been actively working in this field of study for more than two decades, I was a bit wary that my own views on the topic would be too cemented.

An inquiry was conducted into the field. Numerous senior executive human resource practitioners, line partners, CEOs and organisational change and development consultants were asked about their conceptualisation of the field of study. What became evident was that there are as many interpretations and applications of the topic at hand as there are practitioners. Furthermore, the sample group largely equated organisational change and development with organisational design – which theoretically is inaccurate.

Where the book initially started off in an attempt to produce a scientific/practitioner's body of knowledge for organisational change and development consultants, the purpose quickly deepened and a very sacred intent crystallised. The Ghanaian people have a saying that when an old person passes on, a library burns down. Organisational change and development can be compared to this old person. Not only has the field of study eroded over time, it is practised in such a fragmented way by individual practitioners that the deep ontological philosophies that underlie this enabling discipline have become mechanistic.

The purpose of this book became clear – it will attempt to remember the old ways, to present the integrated systemic nature of the field of study by tackling the topic in a multi-faceted way, and will deal with all the facets of the evolving practice of organisational change and development.

An attempt was made here to present a comprehensive approach to the topic, to anchor practitioner methodologies and approaches in theory and to consider alternative ways of optimising individual, group and organisational behaviour. Specific energy has been expended on positioning inclusivity as a radical organisational change and development methodology, integrating spiral dynamics insights into traditional approaches, weaving integral theory into transformational thoughts, and anchoring the field of study in deep behavioural theory and psychological practice.

Readers are invited to suspend their own assumptions as to what organisational change and development is about, and to travel to the corners of the world, as presented in this book, just as the man in the story above does, in an attempt to find their own truth.

1

GENERAL ORIENTATION

1.1 Introduction

This book on organisational change and development (OCD) explores how the changes in the new world of work, the implications of the new sciences of how social systems adapt and the rising levels of awareness impact on business leadership. Adaptive intelligence in individuals, groups, societies and organisations becomes increasingly important.

Through the optimisation of individual functioning, leadership capacity can be built, and ultimately business decision-making can be optimised. Focused OCD interventions can significantly contribute to enhancing individual dynamics, to increasing functionality in teams and rewiring organisational strategies, structures and practices, to ensure congruence between what is happening inside the organisation and outside the system. An in-depth understanding of the social containing system in which the organisation is operating ensures relevant and appropriate reactions to external impacts.

The *doing* (strategy) and the *being* (values) should be translated in such a way that human energy to perform in the system is wired around these aspects. The knowing of the impact of self on others enhances sustainability. It is the task of OCD practitioners in the new world of work to enable systems to unleash this human energy for organisational benefits.

The book is designed to capture leading-edge thinking about OCD in organisations as it merges with traditional African wisdom. Currently, OCD practices differ from company to company and from practitioner to practitioner. In some cases OCD focuses on organisational effectiveness. In other organisations it is practised as a highly individualised craft and often influenced by the ontology of the individual practitioner. In an attempt to provide a solid conceptualisation of the field of study, a framework of inclusivity that can be followed, case studies and OCD methodologies, this book strives to combine some of the practices into an inclusive ontology.

1.2 Background

Africa is a continent of many peoples. The diversity dynamics introduced by various factors such as tribes, nationalities, gender, age and other diversity of thought aspects such as personality type, intelligence and worldview result in a complex, self-adapting environment. The promise that underpins the valuing of diversity may manifest in new social, economic and political models for the future.

OCD practitioners play an important role inside organisations as strategic partners, enablers, inspirational leaders, thought leaders and group process facilitators. The manner in which the OCD practitioner co-constructs organisational strategy, architecture and culture is reliant on the systemic interplay with other strategic functions such as learning, development, communication and human resources.

Efficient OCD practices can revitalise relationships within the workplace, communities and ecologies. This book aims at providing a solid theoretical and empirical grounding from an OCD stance and perspectives to the field of workplace spirituality. OCD methodologies that can result in inclusivity from across various disciplines would evoke a view of the potential for a more humanistic and ecological view of life in organisations.

1.3 The field of organisational change and development

Numerous definitions for organsitional development (OD) can be found in the literature. However, most of them are similar in that they agree that OD deals with the following:

- The optimisation of the individual, the group and the organisation – thus, the organisation as a whole.

- The optimisation of organisational climate, health and effectiveness.

- Changes in organisations to make them more effective.

- Interventions form part of the scope of practice.

- Strategy forms part of the scope of the field of study, but also of culture, climate and people optimisation.

- Continuous improvement issues and sustainability of organisations.

Gert Roodt and Chris van Tonder (2008:55) define OD as:

> " ... a scientific discipline and practice field concerned with multi-faceted change processes, primarily of a planned and sustainable nature, with the purpose of enhancing the adaptive and self-renewing capabilities of organisational systems in response to or in anticipation of shifts in stakeholders' needs or demands – as reflected by diagnostic data generated mainly through the application of behavioural science knowledge and technology and interpreted through collaborative sense-making and learning processes, facilitated by change agent(s), and which involves a critical mass of organisational members in a manner that will ultimately contribute to improved individual, organisational and societal wellbeing."

In the development of the field of study the influences of the socio-technical and the socio-psychological management tradition have oscillated, and they have continued to influence the development of OD methodology, Roodt and Van Tonder (2008) explain.

Anna-Rosa le Roux (2008) describes the development of OD in her doctoral study.

She quotes David Bradford (2005:xxvi) who states that OD should introduce processes that are both effective and humane, should also be inclusive in its scope, and ought to take into account core organisational functions if it is to improve organisational effectiveness.

The author, in her doctoral thesis (2008), underlines that if behavioural changes are required, radical organisational transformation is implied. Implementing a new computer system, for example, requires people to act differently. Therefore, behaviours must change. Individuals, and groups should act differently. And the processes that support organisational strategy as well as organisational structures should be aligned to accommodate this change in behaviour.

Human resource practices such as job description, performance appraisals and personal development plans are impacted, so organisational culture ultimately must change. Organisational change (OC), therefore, has OD implications.

In her doctoral study, Le Roux develops an organisational development model to support organisational change and transformation in a dynamic, continuously changing business environment. The literature reveals that there is a tendency to employ universal and generic models to challenges of organisational change, whereas successful OD needs a situation-specific or contextualised approach.

The resulting model deviates from the established perspectives on OD, in that it reflects a hybrid of several fields of study, and resolves organisational change challenges from a systemic perspective. The model will assist South African organisations within this industry to implement their OD interventions within the uniqueness of their organisational settings, their physical locations and the operating contexts of their specific organisation, and within broader industry dynamics that are at play.

The OD model addresses the positioning of OD at a strategic level, and highlights the importance of executive level sponsorship and the contribution of OD interventions to the bottom line. Various elements, reflecting the character of OD, have been heuristically placed in relation to those other elements that are necessary for successful OD implementation, thus creating an empirically validated model for dealing with change and transformation.

The OD model incorporates practical guidelines for implementation within organisations in South Africa. These guidelines can be found in the detail of the open codes. It suggests content considerations to aid the process of effective change.

In most text books and academic journals the fields of study of organisational development and organisational change are being dealt with separately. This division is mechanistic. Organisational change, however, resides in the heart of OD. Therefore, in this book organisational change and development (OCD) is positioned in the elaborative definition thereof. The field of study is enlarged, yet paradoxically, focused on the following:

- Not only optimising individuals, groups and organisations, but societies too.

- Opportunities to impact on business performance, return on investment and ultimately business sustainability through playing an active role in mergers and acquisitions, and radical organisational change such as technological changes and globalisation.

- The optimisation of a multi-cultural workforce.

- The *doing* and the *being* in organisations – the strategic formulation, facilitation and translation as well as the value and behavioural components of the organisation.

- An integration of socio-technical management and socio-psychological management traditions.

- Interventions happen on individual, group, organisational and societal levels in various forms.

- Creating shared understanding, significance in transformational efforts, alignment and ultimately inclusivity.

- It is mandated from the top, and deals with leadership.

- It is concerned with the unleashing of individual and collective voice and therefore rising levels of consciousness.

David Jamieson and Christopher Worley (2006) point out that today's OD practitioners cannot excel at all aspects of OD, and that there is room for some specialisation by specific use of one's previous work life and other academic preparation. Potential partnerships between OD and other disciplines such as IT and engineering, as well as HR to add value to socio-technical process design and organisational leadership should be considered, Le Roux (2008) adds. She argues in her 2008 doctoral study that is not OD's responsibility to take over the work of another functional area, but to identify the cross-sections of OD with other disciplines (such as information technology, marketing or human resources) and apply the principles of OD to provide strategic direction to other fields. At the intersection of several established disciplines, the field of OD possesses more options than many other practice fields, Le Roux (2008) explains.

In an interview with Italia Boninelli, the executive vice-president of People and Organisational Development at AngloGold Ashanti, she explains that the field of study has become increasingly more complex over the last decade. Where traditionally OCD practitioners could concern themselves with internal optimisation, the business reality is increasingly focused around societal needs. To become strategic, OCD strategy and interventions must be linked to the strategic objectives of the organisation and be aligned to external business drivers. Strategic integration includes the external positioning of the organisation in its chosen markets with the choices of internal arrangements of structure, processes, and resources. Translation of strategy, but also values are critical for business success.

Italia Boninelli shares the Burke-Litwin model shown in Figure 1.1. She highlights the centre of the model to be the playing field of the organisational development practitioner. Interestingly, for her, the OCD practitioner plays an influential role in society.

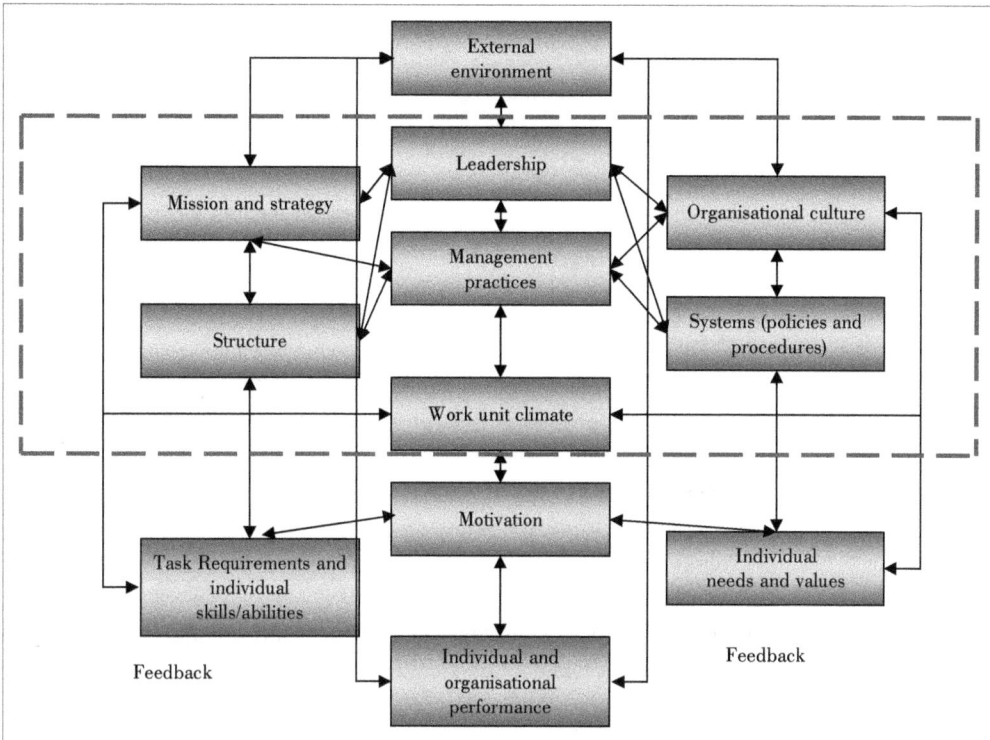

Figure 1.1: Burke-Litwin model, adapted by Italia Boninelli (2015) from Burke and Litwin (1992: p. 524)

1.4 Delimitation

During the interviews that form part of the research phase of this book, it became clear that most participants equate OCD and organisational design. This book makes a very pertinent distinction. It does not deal with organisational structures, work design or job descriptions. The author holds the view that organisational design falls under the umbrella of strategy and in the domain of the chief operating officer, whereas OCD belongs in the human resources domain.

Organisational design deals with hard issues, and OCD deals with the soft issues. In her doctoral thesis, the author distinguishes between the *doing* and the *being* – the what we do and the way we do it, as two different behavioural energies. These are thus two aspects of soft issues. Organisational design deals with configuration issues and with structural concerns, and is therefore out of the scope of this book.

Although there are overlaps between strategic human resources and OCD, there are differences too. OCD is not concerned with recruitment, placement, development, reward and labour relations. However, OCD practitioners can assist their strategic human resource partners to optimise individual, group and organisational behaviour, and can ultimately ensure leadership and internal alignment around organisational strategies and values, and through the process unleash human potential to perform sustainably. By understanding the containing social systemic dynamics, OCD practitioners can ensure optimal external positioning and social responsibility.

1.5 A typical OCD process

A typical OCD process includes the following phases:

Determination: Identifying what is required for each client

Designing: Customising and developing the solution scope

Delivering: Facilitating, delivering or project managing the solution scope

Delineating: Evaluating the progress and assessing the solution as it progresses

Different OCD approaches, methodologies, and alternative modalities that focus on the various parts of the four-phase process are listed below:

Determination: Business culture and climate studies, pre- and post-measures, ethnographic studies, quantitative and qualitative assessments, psychometric tests and indicators.

Designing: Design of an OCD strategy to enhance individuals, groups and organisations in relation to systemic dynamics.

Joint-action planning to design the way to move forward.

Designing of OCD interventions.

Development of course content within our scope of expertise. Inclusive strategic consultation and facilitation on initiatives to be undertaken (HR and OCD), scoping of realistic solutions.

This phase does not refer to organisational design as a discipline.

Delivering: Facilitation (strategy, psycho-analytic, humanistic or Rogerian) Executive coaching, training, lecturing, project-managing parts of or a complete solution scope, supervisory, first-line and executive leadership development.

OCD interventions such as diversity interventions, emotional intelligence development, personality type analysis, spiral dynamics interventions and change resilience capacity building.

Delineating: Evaluating the solution progress through quantitative and qualitative re-measuring assessments and delineating next steps.

Using valid, construct-based assessment tools that are multi-cultural sensitive for pre- and post-intervention analysis and for the quantification of the return of investment of OCD strategies and interventions.

As the field of OCD is concerned with the total organisation, and is typically mandated at executive level, all steps of the 4D-process must be followed.

1.6 Ontological assumptions and conceptual framework

The author adopts an existential phenomenological stance. Subjective human experiences are considered as personal values and worldviews, aspirations, questions of existence, emotions and relationships are reflected. Here, it is accepted that individuals have minds of their own and powerful internal experiences as they function in social settings.

Further, an integral conceptual framework is adapted. Ken Wilber (2010, np) explains that:

> "The word integral means comprehensive, inclusive, non-marginalising and embracing. Integral approaches to any field attempt to be exactly that: to include as many perspectives, styles, and methodologies as possible within a coherent view of the topic. In a certain sense, integral approaches are 'meta-paradigms,' or ways to draw together an already existing number of separate paradigms into an interrelated network of approaches that are mutually enriching."

Although this book is not written from an integral research perspective as described by Ronnie Lessem and Alexander Schieffer (2010), it relies heavily on the four-world model, explained by the authors in their series of books that are published in the Innovation and Transformational Series published by Ashgate Publishers.

This model, which resembles a mandala [a spiritual and ritual symbol in Hinduism and Buddhism, representing the Universe] that symbolises wholeness, presents an integral journey of an individual or society where the proposed process enables individuals to ground themselves in the south, to explore the cultural social setting and philosophy in the east, to apply models, frameworks and theoretical approaches in the west and to apply insights gained by impacting social innovation in their communities.

The book is, however, not presented in this format. OCD processes are designed in this manner. It is not enough to only tell the story of the individual, or the story of the culture, or the story of the literature. The awareness from an integral journey must enable insights that should be applied in the real world enabling transformation.

The mandala is used as a symbol throughout the book. First, it reminds the reader of the importance of integrating projections, and of owning up to the parts of self that we do not like in an attempt to become whole. Second, on a collective level, it reminds us not to polarise mechanistically, but to create organisations and societies that can deal with tensions of diverse views by allowing an integral space.

Third, the integral theory, Jungian theory, human niche theory and inclusivity theory all have niches of holism. Fourthly, Africa is teaching us about the value of forming circles in an attempt to create inclusivity and belonging – the mandala reminds us of that.

Finally, the niche OCD house that the author established adopted this name, and Loraine Laubscher refers to her inclusive problem-solving methodology as people mandalas.

Groups can be asked by OCD practitioners to colour in mandalas in an attempt to arrive in the here and the now. To remind the reader continuously of being mindful and integrated, mandalas that can be coloured in have been added on empty pages. I hope you enjoy this reflexive activity.

1.7 How the book is presented

The book is divided into four different parts. These parts loosely present the four parts in integral research as explained by Ronnie Lessem and Alexander Schieffer (2010).

Part 1 deals with the theoretical foundation of the field of OCD. Therefore, this part is written more academically. Inclusivity, a radical transformational methodology, is positioned as an approach to ensure sustainable organisational change in the new world of work. Similar to integral research, grounding happens in part 1. Other than typical integral research though, the grounding here is theoretical and not personal grounding.

The second part deals with diversity of thought. Here spiral dynamic theory and human niche insights are shared. A specific emphasis is placed on the thinking system that is prevalent in Africa, namely 'Purple'. This thinking system is also dominant in other emerging economies. OCD practitioners should be very aware of how this thinking system functions, in order to assist leaders in organisations to translate organisational strategies and behaviours thoroughly. As the case with integral research, emerging happens by studying the dynamics of the containing social system.

The third part deals with different OCD applications. Here OCD methodologies, schools of facilitation and approaches are discussed. Alternative modalities are presented. Different OCD interventions are introduced. Specific emphasis is placed on the people mandalas methodology as described by Laubscher. In typical integral research, navigation follows the consideration and interpreting of theoretical frameworks. Here, OCD methodologies, modalities and interventions are shared, to enable OCD practitioners to navigate their way through organisational dilemmas.

The last part deals with systemic functional interrelatedness. Here, the measurement of OCD interventions is discussed, which introduces industrial psychology and human resource assessments. The overlap with organisational strategy and strategic architecture is introduced. OCD is also cemented in consulting psychology as a guiding philosophy. Typically, in integral research, the fourth step is to effect and realise the social setting in which the researcher operates. Applied to this book, here OCD as a field of study affects other areas and fields of study.

1.8 Chapter Layout

Inclusivity is presented in Chapter 2, as a radical organisational transformational methodology that translates the *doing* and the *being* in an organisation, ensuring that human energy in the system is unleashed. This energy manifests in levels of engagement that can be wired around strategy and values, the what and how we do. It is argued that there is no other way to align individuals, groups and organisations in the new world of work, thus creating sustainability, than adapting in an intelligent manner through ways of creating inclusivity.

OCD practitioners in the new world of work must have a variety of change models and approaches that they can use as theoretical explanations of how the manifested dynamics occur in organisational systems and teams. Different change models are presented and highlighted in Chapter 3.

As the domain in which OCD consultants involve themselves lies at individual, group, organisational and even societal level, a deep understanding of human reaction to change at different domains is needed. In Chapter 4 different theories and approaches are discussed to ensure depth of understanding of the psychological implications on humans during transformation. Integral research is positioned as a way to amplify previous muted voices, and to facilitate the normalisation of ethnographical experiences during change.

Spiral dynamics or human niches, provides valuable insights into understanding thinking systems in multi-cultural settings. The purpose of Chapter 5 and Chapter 6 is to share insights about the human niche theory. Different thinking systems excel at diverse areas of society and/or life. Understanding diversity of thought adds an insightful perspective to making sense of what is important to individuals, groups and organisations and how social systems adapt to changing conditions. The first tier of the spiral is presented in Chapter 5 and the second tier in Chapter 6.

Inclusivity can be achieved by applying various OCD methodologies such as world café, organisational story-telling, appreciative inquiry, dialoguing and other OCD modalities. Chapter 7 compares different methodologies and critically discusses the application, the benefits and the limitations thereof.

Chapter 8 deals with alternative change and development interventions and modalities such as TRE, laughing yoga, breath-work and art. Ways of weaving alternative modalities into OCD interventions are explored. Specific conditions for doing alternative work in corporate settings are explored. This chapter is co-authored by Dr Tonja Blom.

In Chapter 9, different OCD interventions are discussed. Experiential learning, action learning, large-group events and diversity interventions are considered. The assumptions of different facilitation approaches such as the Rogerian and psycho-analytical schools are presented.

Dr Loraine Laubscher, the co-author of Chapter 10, created a unique blend of process work that oscillates between different thinking systems that create inclusivity in emerging economies. In this chapter the powerful methodology of value circles now called people mandalas, is presented. Case studies are discussed where sustainable organisational transformation occurred using this technique.

OCD interventions focus on enhancing individual, group and organisational effectiveness. In Chapter 11 the importance of congruence of leadership thinking and business realities is discussed. The Benchmark of Engagement Instrument is introduced as a construct-based, multi-cultural sensitive instrument that determines levels of human energy in the system to perform. The instruments discussed here are diagnostic in nature, and therefore can be used to inform OCD strategy and corresponding interventions. It can also be used as pre- and post-measures to determine effectiveness and sustainability of OCD attempts.

So far, the book mostly focused on enhancing individual, group, organisational and societal behaviour. Furthermore, effort was made to explain how human energy is unleashed through inclusivity. This energy must be wired around the organisational *doing*. Chapter 12 is co-authored by Dr Adri Drotskie. The authors weave the link between strategy and OCD and argue that both the *doing* and the *being* are critical elements of OCD strategies.

The book concludes with Chapter 13 that grounds OCD strongly in consulting psychology. The American Psychological Associations Division gives 13 stipulations for the field of study, namely consulting psychology, to be shared. Ethical requirements that should be integrated in individual and organisational practices are discussed. Dr Anna-Rosa le Roux co-authored this chapter.

PART 1
GROUNDING IN THEORY

2

INCLUSIVITY – AN INTEGRAL APPROACH

2.1 Introduction

The objective of this chapter is to weave meta-insights from organisational and social system change literature into a systemic, eclectic framework of inclusivity. In this chapter, systemic relationships on the individual, group and organisational domain are explored in relation with dynamics in the external domain, and a logical argument is built to address the complexities and interrelations of the topic under discussion in an effort to synthesise, rather than analyse, different diversity and adaptability variables.

The reader is reminded of the underlying post-modernistic phenomenological ontology of this book. This implies that there is not only one specific way of interpreting an issue, but that each individual will determine his or her reality through an interplay of diversity factors on individual, group, organisational and contextual factors. The concepts in the framework should be viewed as being similar in nature to a variable. It is not the definition of the author that is important when the framework is applied, but rather, the interpretation of individuals, in groups, in organisations, in countries and the sharing of these insights around the concepts which promise to create higher levels of shared understanding or consciousness. As a transformational methodology, inclusivity is particularly applicable in collective societies such as those found in Africa.

2.2 The concept of Inclusivity

During an in-depth literature review on the topic of inclusion and inclusivity that formed part of the doctoral study of the author in 2009, the concept of inclusion was mostly found in the fields of study of educational psychology and gender studies. Furthermore, inclusion as a concept could be found only in a few academic publications and then, in the context of diversity or organisational climate.

The topic of inclusivity as it presents itself in the field of OCD lacked the sophisticated theoretical development of a mature discipline and thus more exploratory research with the focus on making a contribution to the theoretical body of knowledge is required. Since then, inclusivity as it will be defined here, has been measured in 42 countries in a sample group of more than 55 000 participants. The concept was developed further and published in the book *Inclusive Organisational Transformation* in 2015. In this book, the author discussed the development of the framework as discussed.

Inclusivity can be defined as follows (Viljoen, 2014, p.13):

> "A radical organisational transformational methodology which aligns the doing and the being side of the organisation around commonly defined principles and values, co-created by all."

The definition is supported by the following extension:

> "It is a systemic approach that focuses on underlying beliefs and assumptions, and challenges patterns within the individual, group and organisational psyche to expend energy and engage in a sustainable, inclusive manner with the purpose of achieving a shared consciousness."

In the multi-cultural environment of emerging economies where local and global, and public and private organisations must operate today, inclusivity becomes a non-negotiable pre-requisite for sustained business. It may very well be the new agenda for OCD practitioners in organisations, namely, how to wire the human energy on individual, group and organisational levels around organisational strategy and values. In this book the term OCD practitioner and OCD consultant is used interchangeably.

2.3 Inclusivity and engagement

Inclusivity unleashes **energy in a system**, which may in its turn enable performance, Viljoen (2015) explains. Energy, according to scientific laws, may be classified as positive, neutral or negative. Einstein taught that it is not possible to destroy energy, although friction may cause energy to decrease – the principle of entropy. Energy may, however, be transformed from one form to another.

Engagement is uniquely positioned by Viljoen (2008, p.18) as the output of the human energy in the system to perform. Engagement, as defined here, is the systemic result of the interplay between the individual potential, the group potential and the organisational potential within the context of a specific industry or a national culture.

In a culture of inclusivity the energy in the system may be perceived as positive. Everybody is involved and shares his or her different viewpoints, non-performance is not tolerated and everyone assumes personal authority. There are high levels of support, trust and respect. Leadership may be humane and vulnerable as mistakes may be shared and speedily resolved. The energy in the system is in a virtuous cycle and all the emotions mentioned in this context again reinforce the climate of inclusivity.

In a system in which the energy to perform is negative, a vicious cycle will exist. People will not feel that they are trusted, supported and respected. Therefore, individual defence mechanisms will come into play and group dynamics will become destructive. In-fighting will take place, people will withdraw and power plays and political gamesmanship will be commonplace. It will not be possible to share personal emotions without penalties being exacted, and nobody will admit to mistakes in order to protect themselves. People will tend to blame others for whatever goes wrong.

Carl Jung (1954) stated that a person may fight either the internal or the external world at any one time, but not both worlds together. Thus if a person focuses internally in order to cope, the external work will be neglected. This will manifest in lower levels of customer service and deterioration in the quality of work. Leaders should do everything possible to shorten the period of time during which an individual expends energy on self-preservation or adaptation. Developing change resilience, improving reality testing and influencing current mental models may accelerate this individual change process.

If a system is neutral, the system will be indifferent or apathetic – the individual either does not care anymore, could not care less or has tried too often without any reaction to implement change. Voices are not brought to the organisational table and people do just enough in order to survive.

Specific, focused OCD methodologies and modalities may be applied to build change resilience, adaptive intelligence and inclusivity in social systems. It can enable voice to be released. By focusing on unleashing human energy to perform, OCD practitioners may claim their rightful place as strategic business partners, as their value-add may impact directly on business results.

2.4 Learning and adapting through a culture of inclusivity

Inclusivity offers great potential for organisations as it enables them to use the gifts of their employees effectively. It also ensures the unleashing of the benefits of a diverse workforce. However, there needs to be a clear vision and strategy underlying these efforts, with both a starting point and a re-evaluation point, in order to manage the differences in any environment strategically. A culture of inclusivity in which differences are not only allowed, but also valued and promoted, is a critical pre-requisite for organisational success.

The ability to deal with environmental demands, says Reuven Bar-On (1997) is critical for any individual who wishes to perform in the turbulent environment of today. The development of this ability is important not only on an individual level, but also on a collective level, where it becomes an organisational capability that may become a distinctive advantage if optimised and encouraged.

Continuous learning is critical in adapting to change. Learning comprises not only knowledge sharing, but also the critical processes underlying the continuous development and acquisition of knowledge. Leaders and OCD practitioners should be aware of the theories in respect of adult development such as spiral dynamics (chapters 5 and 6) and apply these theories in respect of the employees.

Organisations should become agile learning institutions. They should learn to tap into all their diverse resources and discover ways to adapt speedily to change while at the same time operating in diverse communities and markets, Peter Senge (1993) explains. Leadership should, thus, ensure the co-creation of an inclusive culture in which individual differences in diversity factors, such as personality, value systems, race, gender and thought processes, are valued.

2.5 Integral inclusivity framework

The inclusivity framework introduced in figure 2.1 presents a practical roadmap for OCD practitioners to follow in an attempt to rewire the human energy in the system to be virtuous. By sequentially focusing on each part of the inclusivity framework, a multi-faceted, integral OCD philosophy can unfold that may enable organisational transformation sustainably.

The inclusivity framework consists of three inter-related, yet distinct parts. The bottom part of the framework deals with assumptions of the nature of the world, especially the world of work and consciousness. The middle part of the framework deals with the dynamic interplay between the individual, group and organisational domains and considers the dynamics of the containing system, namely the social or national cultural dynamics. The impact of leadership, through *doing* and *being* strategies and initiatives, manifests in human energy in the system to perform. The energy can be described in categories of engagement, indifference or disengagement – descriptions of the energy archetypes that will be visible as fractals in all social interactions in that system, for example in performance indicators such as customer complaints or safety indicators. The top part of the framework indicates specific OCD methodologies and modalities that the OCD practitioner can facilitate to optimise behaviour on individual, group and organisational domains, with the intent to create sustainable, adaptable organisations for the future.

Each part of the inclusivity framework will be discussed below.

The bottom part of the inclusivity framework deals with assumptions about the nature of the world – our ontology and epistemology – that is in itself diverse. Here we study the dynamics of the new world of work, the implications of systems theory and rising levels of consciousness. The reasons why we adapt, the essence of change and awareness of adaptation as drivers for a new way of doing things and a new way of being, are explored.

Integral Inclusivity Framework

EQ Journey → Individual presence — Me — Personality, Skills, Intelligences, Human niches, Personal values ← OCD interventions

Storytelling → Emotional containment — We — Stages of group development, "in group and out group" Unconscious mechanics Norms in groups ← Appreciative inquiry

Dialoguing → Organisation Gestalt — They — Culture, worldviews, climate, human niches, strategies, structures, policies, practices ← World café

Knowing — Contribution

DOING — Sustainable transformation

How individuals adapt — Individual presence — Engagement/ Commitment

Call — Co-creation — Emotional containment — Organisation Gestalt — Aparthy

BEING — How groups adapt — How organisations adapt — Disconnect

Becoming

Why we adapt — Essence of change — Awareness of adaption

Dynamics of new world of work — Systems theory implications — Rising levels of consciousness

Nature of the world

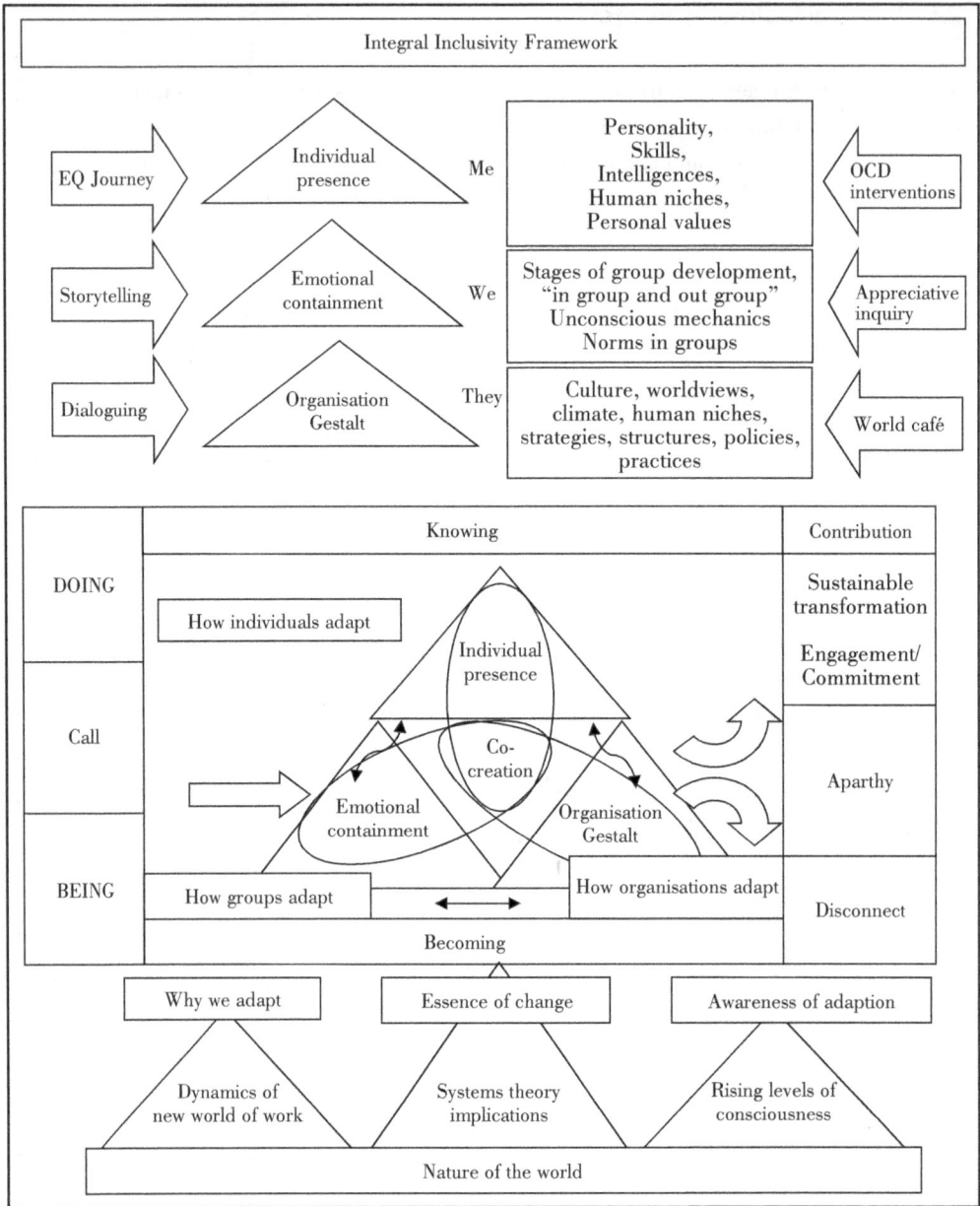

Figure 2.1   Integral inclusivity framework, (2015, p. 284)

The bottom part of the inclusivity framework

The dynamics of the new world of work

The complexity of the external environment and the challenges that confront leadership today cannot be underestimated. Companies must cope with multiple dimensions of change that involve regulation, ever-evolving technology, new competitors and business models, market pressures and constantly changing customer demands.

The future workplace is becoming increasingly diverse as globalisation increases and equal employment practices are implemented on a global scale. The world of tomorrow will be vastly different from the reality of today, and, therefore, new organisational and individual strategies and approaches will be required to deal with this accelerated pace of change.

The adaptive ability of the individual, the team and, ultimately, the organisation to respond quickly to this changing external reality will be the differentiating factor in sustainable organisational transformation.

The first triangle at the bottom left corner of the inclusivity framework represents the dynamics of the new world of work and **the reason why organisations, groups and individuals adapt and change**. Themes in the new world of work include: a shift in the power dynamic away from positional power to personal power; less line authority and more influencing power; fewer direct reports to a more multi-disciplinary team approach, fewer resources more challenges, less stability more freedom and a less homogenous workforce to be replaced by a kaleidoscope of differences in terms of diversity of thought.

As people in organisations and how they informally and formally organise are not similar to 20 years ago, we cannot merely apply old organisational or leadership theory that dated back then to behavioural challenges in social systems today. As organisations, groups and individuals change, so must the leaders adapt to stay congruent, to be relevant and effective.

Systems Theory Applications

Systems thinking theory, as discussed by Russell Ackoff (1994) and Peter Senge (1993, 2003), inform the second triangle in the inclusivity framework. It describes **the essence of change** as systemic, paradoxical, chaotic and complex. It also warns of the resistance of systems in adapting to change.

The traditional systems thinking models of input, transformation and output, were found inefficient in describing human behaviours in organisations. Adult members in organisations will make up their own minds about whether they will implement strategy or not.

Organisations are living systems, Senge (2003) explains. Therefore, in order to understand how decisions are made and strategies implemented within an organisation, it is necessary to acknowledge and understand how both individuals employed in the organisation and groupings of individuals view the system and what their worldviews are.

Systems thinking is underpinned by paradox theory, complexity theory, chaos theory and self-organising theory. In organisational life the day-to-day operations must be maintained while leadership, with the help of OCD practitioners, simultaneously and paradoxically positions the organisation for the future through the implementation of transformational strategies.

OCD practitioners should have systemic problem-solving techniques in their toolkit. One of these approaches is design thinking as described by Ackoff, and being taught by the Da Vinci Institute. Johan Strümpfer facilitates an alternative approach. The author (2014) blends design thinking principles, grounded theory methods and systems thinking in an unique way to determine casualties, to map social systemic dynamics and to reverse engineer the future.

Rising levels of consciousness

Living systems thrive when they balance the need for stability with the imperative to change (Senge, 2003). In order to manage resistance effectively it must be understood in terms of the efforts of people to regain the equilibrium that has been disrupted by change. However, different people change in different ways.

It becomes important to understand the nature of diversity as it pertains to change – the third (last) triangle in bottom of the inclusivity framework. Internationally there are rising levels of consciousness. People are more aware than before. They know their basic rights; they have access to Google, and to communities that do things differently, where they can see other ways of organising. We cannot continue to treat employees in organisations the same way that traditional management did in the previous century. As people adapt and change, including in their own consciousness, leadership must adapt and form new ways to deal with these dynamics.

World events such as the terrorist attacks of September 11, 2001, and the dynamics of the Islamic State of Iraq and al-Sham (ISIS) and Boko Haram bring the complexity of diversity to the fore. Questions like "In what context do the beliefs and convictions of one culture outweigh those of another?" and "How do we deal with the challenges posed by this dilemma?" become critical to explore. In this respect, organisations are also forced to explore the vast impact of diversity issues on their ability to sustain performance.

Conclusion

The dynamics of the new world of work, systems thinking philosophy and diversity dynamics collectively comprise the reason why individuals, groups and organisations must change.

Everything is subject to change. People's lives, the communities and societies in which they live and the organisations in which they work are all affected by waves of change according to Peter Senge and Otto Scharmar, in the book *Presence* (Senge, PM, Scharmar, CO, Jaworski, J & Flowers, BS. (2004)) Some changes are gradual; others traumatic; some are of their own making, many are beyond control. The effects of global recession, globalisation and technology transformation involve changes on an unknown scale and of unknown complexity.

All these changes generate human reactions to change – for individuals, organisations and societies. Christo Nel (2003) believes that organisational transformational strategies have one aspect in common, namely, their impact on human beings. The ensuring of behavioural optimisation during transformational efforts may prove to be a distinguishing factor for competitive organisations.

Different change models in respect of organisations, groups and individuals were described in chapter 3. The middle part of the inclusivity framework in figure 2.1 depicts how individuals, groups and organisations all change in different ways in relation to the social containing system dynamics. The leaders of successful organisations of the future will all manifest resilience to change as a common characteristic. This resiliency will afford leaders the opportunity to analyse the many systems within the organisation and make well-informed decisions in order to move the organisation forward.

Any strategic effort to change the fundamental functioning of an organisation will result in a climate change, as people will have to behave differently and new mental models will have to be adapted. In order to understand the human reactions to change it becomes necessary to explore the essence and dynamics of the individual, the group and the organisational domain. These dynamics, which are discussed in detail in chapter 4, will be summarised in the following paragraph.

The middle section of the inclusivity framework

The diverse nature of the organisation, the group and the individual

The complex, inter-related and multi-faceted relationship between the individual, the group and the organisation create a specific archetype of human energy in the system as discussed in paragraph 2.3. The diverse and dynamic essence of the organisation, group and individual are summarised in the three triangles and the three rectangles at the top of the inclusivity framework.

The individual domain

Jeff Smulyan (2000:43) refers to Chase Kaufman and writes

> ... viewing social change through the lens of individual experience, we are able to move away from infinite generalisations and abstractions and into the realm of individual constructions of meaning. Through the examination of ... individual's lives, we gain access both to multi-faceted meanings of the self-within-the-culture and to a richer, more detailed portrait of the culture which contributes to and is constituted by those meanings.

Each person possesses an individual profile of characteristics, abilities and challenges all of which result from heritage, learning and growth. These factors manifest as individual differences in terms of intelligence, creativity, cognitive style, motivation, and the capacity to process information, communicate, and relate to others. Stereotypes, mental models and worldviews are all ways of making sense out of the non-sense in the external world. These mechanisms fulfil the function of integrating both the perceived and the real issues in the external world. However, this process takes place on different levels of abstraction, preference, intelligence and skill, and is influenced to a large extent by, for example, culture, education, societal norms and practices, and religion.

Human beings may share universal perceptions of primitive environmental stimuli, certain cognitive patterns and the ability to generalise new ways of engaging which, in turn, leads to changes in existing patterns. Thus, human beings definitely understand reality in individual ways, Carl Jung (1954) explained. Human beings unconsciously filter the world through their own worldviews and come to believe that what they perceive is the only reality. As a result of the fact that people are convinced that what they think is true, other perspectives may appear irrational, uninformed and misguided. Based on this experience assumptions are made and stereotypes and generalisations often surface, for example: "She will be too emotional as a leader because she is a woman," or "All black taxi drivers are irresponsible."

Different levels of awareness exist and every person develops different levels of consciousness according to Marion Woodman (1995). In South Africa major efforts need to be made to normalise both the power imbalances and the hurts and anger of *apartheid* so that the true work, namely, that of valuing diversity of thought, may take place.

OCD practitioners can assist line partners in conducting psychometric assessments to describe diversity of thought factors such as personality, emotional intelligence, complexity handling ability and worldview. Chapter 9 deals with different measurement instruments that can be used to inform focused interventions such as individual coaching journeys, emotional intelligence development initiatives and personality type analysis.

The focus of all of these instruments is to enhance awareness of own growth and development areas as well as a celebration of the unique strengths or gifts that are presented by the individual to the organisation. Ultimately, this information can enhance business decision-making as own dynamics become clear, the impact on others is considered more, and the change resilience or grit is built.

Individual behaviour can be optimised through a range of OCD interventions that include personal purpose workshops, personal mastery interventions, leadership interventions, change resilience workshops and diversity interventions. An array of facilitation methodologies such as Rogerian, humanistic and psycho-analytical facilitation can also be meaningful.

The group domain

The basic definition of a group is that the sum of the individual parts must be more than the individual parts itself. This is often not the case. Understanding group dynamics becomes a critical part of any OCD practitioner's scope.

The various group stages that form during group development should be considered. By understanding what behaviours manifest in which state and how conversations shift and develop, OCD practitioners can adapt their intervention techniques and facilitation methods. A facilitator should deal differently with a group that is storming, than with a group that is norming or performing. The adjourning phase of groups should also be dealt with sensitively, as members lose a sense of belonging and leave residues of previous encounters behind, moving forward.

Unconscious group dynamics play a role in the diversity dynamics and should be taken into account by leadership. The work of Frans Cilliers, Pieter Koortzen, Michelle May and Marius Pretorius in this regard is viewed as critical in the development of any OCD practitioner. Psycho-analytical facilitation assists organisations in dealing with power dynamics, splits in teams and understanding the role of boundaries in social systems.

Other teaming interventions may include team-building, team development work, the use of personality type analysis in teams, the sharing of team roles, experiential learning in teams such as low-rope and high-rope activities. Team dynamics can be observed in group decision-making activities, business simulations and strategic planning sessions. If the OCD practitioner consults not only to the task but also to the group process, team dynamics can be optimised. Functional team dynamics are critical for the individual to bring his or her voice to the organisational table.

The organisational domain

Social organisations have a *doing* and a *being* side. The *doing* side concerns itself with strategy formulation and translation, organisational design, strategic architecture construction and business plans and measurable. The *being* side speaks to the soul of a company.

Professor Johann Coetzee conceptualised the organisational soul in his third doctorate, completed at the Da Vinci Institute in 2013. Here leadership intent, values and behaviours manifest in a specific sense or climate. Overtime climate becomes culture – how we do things here. And each organisation is characterised by a unique culture. Professor Petri Schutte (2004) stated that leadership has a 72% impact on culture that has a 24% impact on bottom line. Leadership and culture are thus closely interlinked.

OCD practitioners can assist line managers in determining underlying beliefs in the organisational psyche. A culture study, like the Benchmark of Engagement (BeQ™) can be used to describe perceptions about the individual, the group, the organisation and the societal context in which the organisation functions. This instrument is described in more detail in chapter 11. It is critical to choose an instrument that measures accurately in multi-cultural settings; one that is construct-based and diagnostic in nature. The results of such a measurement can then inform OCD strategy. The translation of culture study results, through joint action planning, can create human energy in the system and can be viewed as an OCD intervention in itself.

Other OCD processes that can be facilitated on the organisational domain include strategic planning sessions such as scenario planning, various diagnostic methodologies, strategy map co-creation and other *doing* interventions as described in chapter 12.

The contextual domain

The dynamics of the social system are described in chapters 5 and 6, which deal with spiral dynamics. Understanding the containing system is critical, as organisations always operate in relation to a specific national context that will impact the way of doing business in that environment. This is presented in the inclusivity framework as the oval in the background of the individual, group and organisational domains.

The diversity in the external environment – South Africa, Africa and the international arena – which arises as a result of the different world religions, diverse worldviews, national cultures, and societal norms, should also be taken into account in transformational efforts. OCD practitioners first should understand multi-cultural dynamics. Second, they must have access to diagnostics to describe social systemic dynamics. Last, by understanding spiral dynamic principles, OCD practitioners can consult on how different people think in their systems – and so inform learning and development journeys, remuneration strategies, motivation efforts, disciplinary approaches, communication strategies and other organisational efforts.

Theory that can be applied to describe the contextual domain is national cultural dynamics as described by Geert Hofstede (1999), Fons Trompenaars and the findings of the Globe studies[1]. In this book, attention is given to spiral dynamics or adaptive intelligences as described by Clare Graves, Don Beck, Loraine Laubscher and the author. Collective societies, which are often a description of emerging economies, require specific OCD approaches such as inclusivity.

OCD practitioners must have contextual dynamics diagnostic tools in their backpacks. Systems thinking and design thinking processes based on the work of Ackoff and Senge can be facilitated. Through co-creating shared understanding of causalities at play in social systems, groups of people can diagnose interventions to focus on leverage points. Systems dynamics and mechanics can inform strategic planning sessions and eliminate one-size-fits-all solutions to systemic problems.

Leadership, the key to unlocking human energy

In the products of the unconscious we discover mandala symbols, that is, circular and quaternity figures which express wholeness, and whenever we wish to express wholeness, we employ just such figures.
Carl Jung (1954)

On the left centre side of the inclusivity framework, the pivotal part that leadership plays is

---

1   Conducted by the Center of Creative Leadership. The Global Leadership and Organisational Behavioral Effectiveness Research project studied differences of culture in various countries. It was basically informed by Hofstede's assumptions.

indicated. Two different energies should be integrated in the individual and the collective leadership psyche – namely the *doing* and the *being*. If leadership only does the *doing*, then only the hard stuff, namely strategy, structures and tasks, will be driven. The unintended impact of this is a productivity or quality-driven culture.

On the other hand, if only the *being* is embraced, consultation will happen and accommodation will be the order of the day – but nothing will get done. A mandala is a symbol for integration of opposites, for wholeness. Leadership must strive to become whole, to claim back the parts that they project on others. OCD processes can assist leaders to develop through personal purpose, self-mastery and other leadership development interventions.

Leaders should provide direction for the organisation – the *doing*. Furthermore it is the task of leadership to optimise individual, group and organisational behaviour in order to achieve sustainable business results. It is also expected of leadership to manage the boundary of the organisation with the external world, while simultaneously optimising the internal reality, aligning this internal reality with external challenges, and achieving this in such a way that it leads to sustainable performance.

The way – the *being* – in which leadership carries out the *doing* leads to sustainability on an organisational level and legacy on an individual level. In this thesis greater emphasis is placed on the *being* rather than the *doing* (although paradoxically both are equally important) as the focus of study is on the process through which leadership tasks are performed and not on the content of the tasks. Therefore, a deliberate effort was made not to include theory on strategic planning and the formulation of strategy.

Two equally important leadership tasks, namely, the *doing* and the *being*, are positioned strategically, thus indicating their influence on the individual in the group within the organisation within the context of the national culture. As an approach to achieving sustainable organisational change the radical, organisational, transformational methodology of inclusivity can be introduced.

Different approaches of leadership have developed over the years and are well documented in literature. Certain of the most relevant theories are summarised in chapter 4. Each theory provides a framework that contributes to the understanding of the world and the behaviour of people living in the world. Most of these models developed from western thought.

The underlying themes of the most recent leadership approaches are both inspirational and authentic. Despite valuable efforts on the part of researchers such as Ronnie Lessem (1993) and Stephan Banhegyi (2006) to promote the acknowledgement of the contribution of African leadership, this acknowledgement is still sadly lacking in the global academic literature. Lessem and Alexander Schieffer (2015) underline the importance of integrating southern, eastern, northern and western leadership philosophies in an attempt to be integral. The four directions of a compass represent four points of a mandala.

All change starts with self-change, Stephen Covey (2004) teaches, and, accordingly, leadership starts from self-leadership and self-discovery, and culminates in the successful leading of others. The essential nature of leadership is that of a catalyst for change. Laubscher (2013) says that OCD practitioners must also have a catalytic nature. They should be able to retain their own identity even when intervening in the dynamics of others, enhancing those relationships.

Human beings, Marrion Woodman (1995) says, actively either build or derive meaning from their experiences. Therefore, everybody actively creates his or her own psychological reality in the context of relationships with others. Leadership is thus both as a complex phenomenon and a profoundly humane exercise.

It is a task of leaders to assist employees to make sense of a turbulent and dynamic context. If leadership is able to understand the psychological and perceptual processes that individuals employ in order to assign meaning to diversity issues, it is also possible that leadership may be equipped to cultivate an inclusive organisational culture that facilitates the understanding and the valuing of diversity among all. OCD practitioners should assist leaders in building change resilience and adaptive intelligence.

A duality faced by leaders is that of simultaneously manifesting caring and enabling while they are also expected to accept and adapt to masculine values, language and norms within organisations. It may be argued that both males and females suppress femininity due to the perception that femininity is weak and inappropriate in organisational life. Sustainability lies in the integration of opposites, Carl Jung explained years ago. Femininity in both males and females should be acknowledged, valued and integrated. The mandala is a symbol of this integration process.

Leadership can be positioned on the periphery of or the boundary between the external and internal environments that must make sense (through the *doing* and the *being*) of the 'non sense' created by the chaotic, external and internal challenges. Through the application on the part of leadership of a methodology of inclusivity (in terms of which individual, group and organisational strategies, interactions, conversations, connections and interventions around crucial, strategic themes take place spontaneously in an ethical, principle based, inclusive, respectful and culturally intelligent manner) transformational efforts may be implemented in a sustainable way.

The top part of the framework

In the top part of the inclusivity framework the diversity factors that are at play on individual, group and organisational domains are presented. Various OCD interventions are indicated in the arrows, to present specific OCD interventions that can optimise behaviours on the various domains. Emotional intelligence journeys, storytelling, dialoguing, world café methodology, OCD interventions and appreciative inquiry are listed as typical ways to enhance inclusivity and therefore rewire organisations around their core purpose. These methodologies, amongst others, are described in chapters 6 and 7.

2.6 Conclusion

This chapter introduced the three-dimensional integral inclusivity framework that can inform an integrated OCD journey in an organisation. A three-day session can be facilitated on each part of the framework. The world is changing and as a result, leadership must change. Changes are systemic as we are dealing with living social systems. Systems thinking principles explain the nature of these changes.

Everybody changes in a different way and there are organisational advantages to the ability to manage diversity in an optimal way. As change resilience is increasingly becoming a core capability that sustainable, global companies strive to develop, it is becoming increasingly important not only to understand how individuals, groups and organisations change, but also how they change in relation to each other. In order to optimise these differences the essence of the individual (diversity of thought due to paradigms which are influenced by personality, different intelligences, stereotypes, worldviews and other factors), the essence of the group (group stages, group dynamics, unconscious patterns and other factors) and the essence of the organisation (climate and culture) should be understood, crystallised and optimised within the context of the industry, country or continent.

Leadership exerts a major impact on the culture and climate within organisations. In order to implement sustainable transformational efforts in organisations the 'what' and the 'way' of the change initiative should be translated throughout the organisation by means of a process of inclusivity. Ultimately, the culture will be conducive, indifferent or destructive – virtuous, neutral or vicious – and this, in turn, adds to the complexity of organisational dynamics. As a direct correlation was found in literature between climate and bottom line and other performance indicators such as productivity, safety behaviour, customer experience and staff satisfaction, companies should expend sufficient energy on optimising these organisational factors and, thus, minimising process losses in human energy.

The process of inclusivity will enable organisations to optimise the gifts of and contributions from a diverse workforce, unleash tacit knowledge which may result in innovation and ensure engagement with organisational strategies and goals. Different OCD methodologies can facilitate inclusivity in organisations. As leadership is the leverage point within the organisation special efforts should be made to optimise leadership behaviour by utilising interventions such as emotional intelligence development which could, in turn, have an exponentially positive impact on the effectiveness of the individual, team and organisation.

The radical organisational transformational methodology of inclusivity may result in sustainable transformation in social systems such as organisations, societies or geo-political regions. Though a systemic, designed interplay between OCD methodologies, such as world café, storytelling, dialoguing and appreciative inquiry methodologies, the energy in a system may be unleashed and aligned, and, in this way, engagement and, thus, commitment, and buy-in into the organisational strategy may be achieved. These methodologies are discussed in chapter 7.

3

ORGANISATIONAL TRANSFORMATIONAL MODELS

"The value of an idea is often directly related to the amount of resistance it evokes."

Manfred Kets de Vries, 2001

3.1 Introduction

The challenges posed to organisations by the new world of work were discussed in chapter 2. Organisations need to adapt to this changing reality to be able to remain in business, and moreover, to excel at it, in order to distinguish themselves from their competitors. Organisational changes owing to mergers, acquisitions, hostile take-overs or internal and external pressures are commonplace.

As organisations undergo a metamorphosis, a complex network of transformations take place, both internally and externally. The author (2009), in her doctoral thesis on sustainable organisational transformation, says that internal transformations that take place must be congruent so that the organisation can be capable of functioning in an efficient and effective manner externally. For example, changing from a hierarchical structure to matrix management, or from a service organisation to a sales organisation, requires behavioural change.

In all the examples mentioned above the organisational culture will also have to be transformed to ensure sustainable change, as new behaviour patterns will be needed and old paradigms transformed into new ones. Any attempt to change culture may be described as a radical organisational transformational effort, as new underlying belief patterns that will result in behavioural change are implied. OCD consultants should support organisations with change management processes if behavioural change is required.

To be able to reap the benefits of diversity as explained in the previous chapter, it is essential that social transformation take place within organisations. Any attempt to instil an organisational culture in which diversity is valued may therefore be classified as an organisational transformational attempt, since the attempt focuses on existing organisational cultural aspects that are changing. The creation of a culture of inclusion, say Frederick Miller and Judith Katz (2002), that leverages diversity, may also be described as a radical change effort. Manfred Kets de Vries (2002) mentioned that dealing with discontinuous change is far more difficult than dealing with incremental changes, and that discontinuous change usually comes at a high price in the form of human capital. Finding innovative ways of engaging diverse voices in the organisation in terms of important things becomes necessary.

The objective of this chapter is to conceptualise the different theoretical perspectives on organisational change that are found in the literature today, as these different perspectives pertain to human reactions to change. These reactions are caused by organisational transformation (on an individual and collective level). Rather than exploring specific in-depth approaches or arguing their applicability or shortcomings, quick fixes are followed and existing (and even dated) models are ignored. As the inquiry into the theme of organisational transformation progresses a framework for exploring cultural changes within organisations will emerge.

Insights derived from a systems-thinking theory as described by Peter Senge (1993) give rise to the realisation that a change in one element of a system will require adjustments in terms of all the other parts of the system to enable the system to function effectively. A transformational effect on a single element of the organisation will lead to failure. Therefore, the implications of systems thinking and the unintended consequences of any transformational effort on people should not be underestimated.

OCD consultants should have an array of relevant change philosophies, models and frameworks in their toolkit to apply to various business realities at applicable moments in time.

In this chapter transformation is addressed from an organisational, a group and an individual perspective. Organisational transformation implies in-depth change in the way that individuals, groups and organisations behave. Organisations and the individuals within these organisations and groups are generally resistant to change. OCD consultants must be able to make sense of the dynamics of organisational transformation by applying a relevant approach, model or framework to the problem at hand. An in-depth understanding of change theory is a pre-requisite for OCD practitioners.

In this chapter some traditional and some recent approaches, models and frameworks are presented. The choice of which approaches, models and frameworks must be introduced were influenced by how often these are currently being used by OCD practitioners in South Africa. The author sent out a public LinkedIn request in this regard. The results of this inquiry, together with what approaches Mandala Consulting, a specialised OCD organisation, has come across over the last two years, influenced the selection of approaches, models and frameworks presented here.

3.2 Change approaches, models and frameworks

The only sustainable source of competitive advantage over time is the ability of an organisation to learn more quickly than its competition, Peter Senge (2003) explains.

Arie de Geus (1997), the pioneer of the organisational learning movement, describes how global organisations affect all areas of life, and reshape social realities owing to the fact that these organisations divide the world into those who benefit from it and those who do not. Margaret Wheatly (2005) points out the important role of communication in the creation of shared learning and visions. All learning integrates thinking and doing, and deeper levels of learning create an increased awareness of the larger whole. This, in turn, leads to actions that increasingly serve the emerging whole. As the external environment continuously changes, organisations shift their own paradigms and learn to align the internal environment with the external reality.

Rapid, surprising change is the 'new normal'. It is essential that organisations be hyper-alert to what is happening around them. They must make sense of this new reality rapidly, and act accordingly. There is a long-term outcome (end-state) to the formulating of strategy. Sustainability in OCD language is linked to a specific time-frame where leadership decides collectively to execute a strategy over time.

The mere fact that a strategy exists, implies change. Therefore the end-state of strategy is characterised by an inherent capacity to adapt and to evolve. This, in turn, implies that self-renewal is inevitable.

The Sigmoid curve (also termed the S-curve) indicates that the way to ensure constant growth is to start a new S-curve before the first S-curve ends. The correct point at which to start the second curve is at a point where there are sufficient time, energy and resources to move the new curve through its initial stages before the first curve reaches a plateau and begins to decline, says Charles Handy (1995). Change is therefore a constant in every organisation.

Jim Collins (2001) warns that companies that fall into reactionary behaviour rather than maintaining break-through momentum will either spiral downward or remain mediocre. In the new world of work it is critical for organisations to build an innate capability of adapting to change and to transform readily when necessary. OCD consultants should assist line management to make sense of the non-sense that changes in the external world create by ensuring responsiveness in the inner world.

Typically, change management efforts form part of organisational transformation and therefore are found in the field of organisational change and development. Change management efforts should encompass much more than merely communication initiatives. These efforts should acknowledge human reactions to change, the amount of energy in the system, systems thinking and underlying mental models within the organisation, says Christo Nel (2003). Lovemore Mbigi (2000) states that organisational transformation is not simply an intellectual journey – it is also an emotional and spiritual journey. The emotional and spiritual resources of an organisation may be accessed through the use of bonding symbols, myths, ceremonies and rituals, explain Danah Zohar and Ian Marshall (2000).

Most managers do not possess the requisite knowledge to deal with complexity, and, therefore, they attempt to reduce complex situations to simple ones, explains Ackoff (2003). This leadership ability, together with personality type, plays a role in the interpretation of organisational challenges and, ultimately, in the specific culture that a leader creates. Elliot Jaques (1997) designed a framework to facilitate the understanding of existing paradigms of global change and the complexities involved in eco-systemic inter-connectedness. This framework provides an open context within which to question, change and design in order to ensure the continuous relevancy of contribution and the competitive appropriateness of an organisation's strategy and operation, according to Lisa Ashton (2007).

Wendell French and Cecil Bell (1999) describe the current trend of many organisations of moving toward a more decentralised, flat and/or team-based structure in which more generalists than specialists are employed. This shift raises the question of how to deal with an increasingly diverse workforce, and how to ensure that a cross-section of different people with different cultures and different perspectives work together effectively. It also poses a challenge to the employees in organisations, as a shift must take place within them. They have to move from the perception that career success lies in the following of a structured career path to the concept of employability in the new world of work in which lateral movements are sometimes preferred to vertical movements.

Environmental changes and the opportunities identified in these environmental changes drive strategy and strategic planning, and these, in turn, drive organisational change. A typical strategic process may include scenario planning – a process describing the most probable way in which the future could unfold. Accordingly strategic architecture must be formulated in such a way as to ensure that the organisation moves from the 'will be' scenario to the 'should be' outcome according to Ackoff's idealised design. During this phase of strategy formalisation the emphasis is on visioning, defining the mission, identifying values, exploring the profit model, organisational structure and the core capabilities that will ensure effective strategy implementation. A strategy map may then be co-created according to which the risks of the chosen strategy may be identified.

Authors that documented this approach include Johan Heroldt, Marius Ungerer and Maurits Pretorius (2000); Robert Kaplan and David Norton (2006); and the author (2009). Different transformational efforts demand different enablement or change management initiatives (see table 3.1).

Table 3.1 Transformational efforts compared (2009).

Type of transformation	Researcher	Scope	Type of change	The what	Change management
Culture change (for example total safety culture or culture climate of inclusivity)	Kuhn (1996); Mihata (1997) Nel, (2003); Wilkins & Patterson (1985)	Radical	Culture	Fundamental change	Critical

Type of transformation	Researcher	Scope	Type of change	The what	Change management
Mergers and acquisitions	Andrade, Mitchell, Stafford (2001); Jovanovic & Rousseau (2002); Shleifer & Vishny (2003)	Radical	Culture, processes, structures	Fundamental change	Critical
New business ventures	Drucker (1987); Hagen (1962); Hamilton (1978); Jones & Clark (1976)	Radical	Culture, processes, structures	Fundamental change	Critical
Business process re-engineering	Champy (1995); Dubois (2002); Hammer (1990)	Radical	Processes	Fundamental change	Critical
Right-sizing	Allan (1997); Newell & Dopson (1996); Smeltzer & Zener (1994); Worrall, Campbell & Cooper (1999)	Job contents	Functional	Employees	Very important
Restructuring	D'Aveni (1989); Edwards, Robinson, Welchman, Woodall (1999)	Organisational	Processes	Reporting structures	Very important

Type of transformation	Researcher	Scope	Type of change	The what	Change management
Total quality management	Deming (1991); Gummer & McCallion (1995); Hill & Wilkinson (1995); Kelada (1996)	Improvement from the bottom of the organisation up	Large-scale systems change	Customer centric	Very important
Automisation	Braverman (1955)	Systems	Procedures	Technology	Very important

It is clear that a holistic and continuous approach to organisational strategy and strategic planning is required. Underlying assumptions and beliefs drive culture, and these, in turn, drive and support the successful execution of strategies. A change in organisational culture would be needed in order to cement both strategy and organisational changes.

3.3 Systemic models of change

Organisational transformation requires change at organisational, group and individual level. In contemporary academic writings, specifically in literature pertaining to recent organisational transformation, a wide variety of models describing organisational and individual change are presented. It is evident that an integrated, holistic approach in terms of transformation should be taken in order to ensure sustainable success. It is important that policies and procedures be aligned with the organisational effort. Models that address the concept of organisational change and the process of change are introduced in this section.

Nature of change

An understanding of the nature of change is critical before specific change models that describe change may be explored as exploration will influence the appropriate transformational strategy. Linda Ackerman (1997) distinguished between three types of change that are presented in Table 3.2.

Table 3.2 Types of change, Linda Ackerman, 1997

Type of change	Characteristics
Developmental	The change may either be planned or emergent; it is incremental (or first-order change). The focus of the change is on the correction of existing aspects of an organisation (such as skills or processes).
Transitional	Seeks to achieve a known, desired state that is different from the existing state. It is episodic and planned (second-order change) or radical.
Transformational	Is radical (second-order change). It requires a shift in the assumptions made by the organisation and its members. Transformation may result in an organisation that differs significantly in terms of structure, processes, culture and strategy from before.

Change is sometimes planned and sometimes it unfolds spontaneously – emergent change, Patrick Dawson (1996) mentions. Another distinction is made between episodic – infrequent, discontinuous and intentional change – and continuous change, which is on-going and evolving, say Karl Weick and Robert Quinn (1999). The principles of complexity theory can be applied to change in today's world of work. Organisational change is neither fixed nor linear in nature, and may be described as emergent and self-organising. Inclusivity, as defined in chapter 2, is positioned as a radical transformational effort, since applying this methodology results in significant changes in organisational strategy and culture.

Ralph Stacey (1996) acknowledges that the majority of literature focuses on long-term planning and strategy, and on equating success with consensus, uniformity and order. According to him the essential management task is that of dealing with unpredictability, disensus, inconsistency and instability.

Stacey compiled the Agreement versus Certainty Matrix (see figure 3.1) on the basis of complexity theory. At the bottom left of the matrix, traditional *decision-making applies. In the chaos area, guess-work and randomness apply. Leaders in the new world of work need to possess the skills to deal with the complexity and lack of certainty that decision-making in this chaos area entails.*

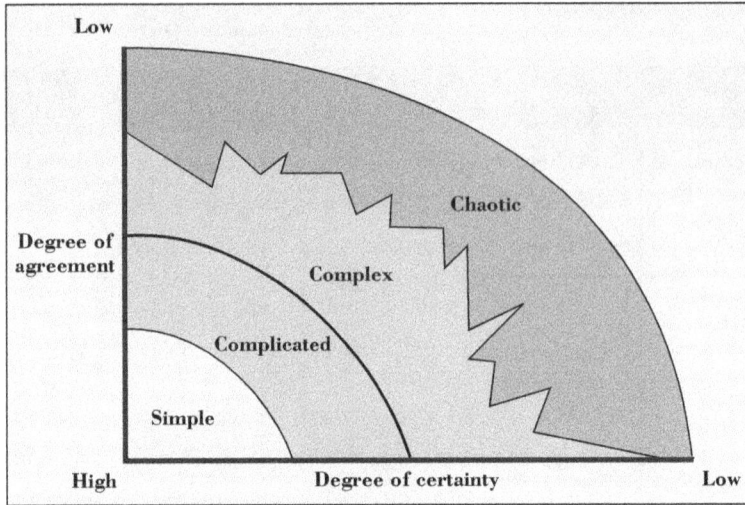

Figure 3.1   *Agreement versus certainty matrix, Stacey (1996)*

Randy Pennington (2003) plots changes along two scales – radical to incremental on the one scale, and core to peripheral on the other. By plotting the nature or essence of a proposed change along these scales it becomes possible to gain insight into the degree of difficulty or complexity of the change effort.

Models that address the concept of organisational change

It is important to ensure cohesiveness between the goals and the purpose of an organisation, the division of labour, the co-ordination between units and the people who will carry out the work. Jay Galbraith (1978) conceptualised this argument in the now familiar star model, which studies alignment between structure, management processes, work processes, people and rewards.

The Seven S-model of McKinsey[2] is a management model that describes seven factors that may be used to organise a company in a holistic and effective way. These seven factors comprise shared values, strategy, structure, systems, style of management, staff and skills, stipulate Tom Peters and Robert Waterman, 1982). This model may be used for guiding organisational change efforts. The model highlights the importance of the people component in business success.

Igor Ansoff (1987) agreed that the drive and skills of key managers are critical, and added that stakeholders, the power structure, culture and the problem-solving competency of managers should be taken into account. Edward Higgins (2005) added the additional factor of strategic control systems, which include performance management, to McKinsey's model as described by Ronald Lippett, Jeanne Watson and Bruce Westley (1958), to form the Eight S-model of successful strategy execution.

---

2   The consulting house

Warner Burke and George Litwin (1992) presented a model that describes how to create first- and second-order change. First-order change refers to situations in which certain features of the organisation change, but the fundamental nature of the organisation stays the same. During second-order change the nature of the organisation itself is transformed.

This model is still widely used in South Africa today. The Burke-Litwin model studies the interrelation of mission and strategy, structure, management practices, leadership, organisational culture, systems and climate. This model also takes into account both individual needs and values, as well as task requirements and skills. The impact of both these aspects on motivation is also considered.

French and Bell (1999) provided synonyms for first-order change: transactional, evolutionary, adaptive, incremental or conditional change. They also provided synonyms for second-order change: transformational, revolutionary, radical or discontinuous change.

Elliott Jaques (1997) described the Requisite Organisation, and referred to a unique, systematically scientific approach to the effective management of work systems, including structure, leadership processes and human resources, as illustrated in Figure 3.2.

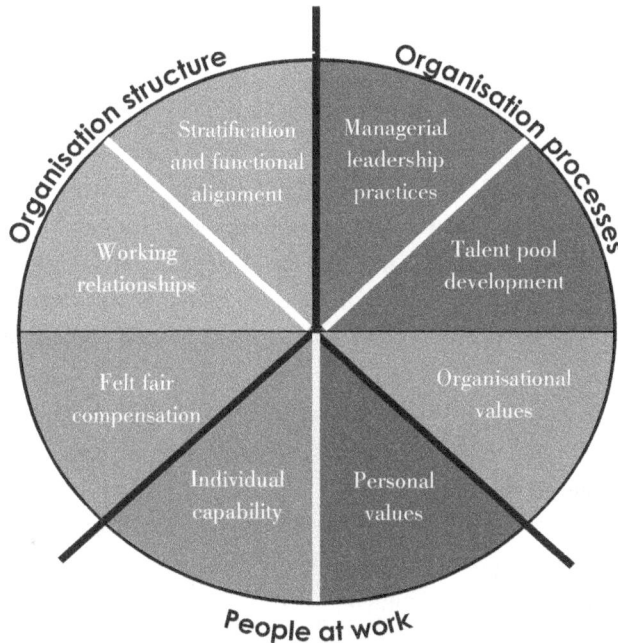

Figure 3.2   Requisite organisation theory, Elliott Jaques (1997)

The Beehive Model (figure 3.3) of organisational renewal is both a theoretical model and an analytical tool in a honeycomb formation, and is used to obtain a snapshot of organisational compliance with the application of either best or poor practices associated with seven individual workplace practices in the contemporary economic climate, according to Mario Dentor and Ernst Bouwer, (2003) and Christo Nel (2003). Business consultation takes place in respect of those areas which have been identified as characteristic of the old economy of work, and joint action planning is carried out in order to improve these aspects.

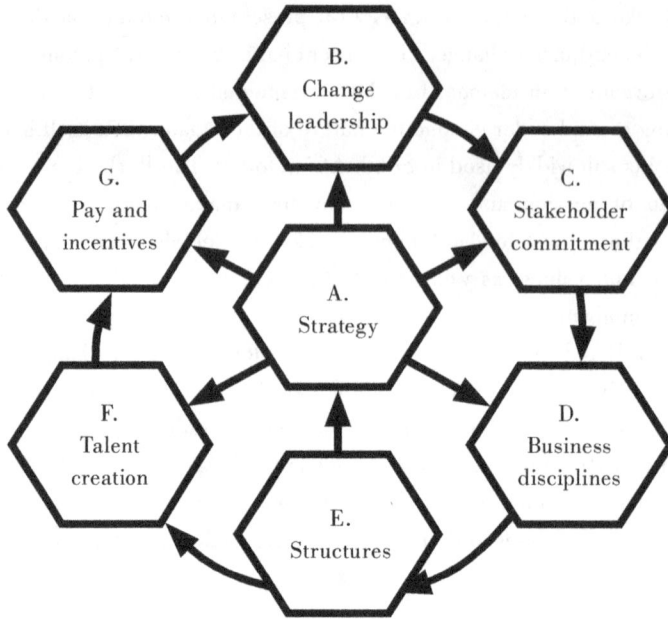

Figure 3.3   The beehive model, Christo Nel (2003)

In the Beehive Model, strategy is presented in the centre of the change model, with the other practices clustered around its formulation and implementation practices. The practices that were explored included the structures of the organisation, the people capacity, business processes, stakeholder commitment and pay and incentives. The unique feature of the Beehive Model, Nel (2003:2) explains, is its inclusion of the practice of change leadership, which refers to "the use of proven leadership and processes for implementing change and turning strategy into operational action that delivers competitive performance".

Mbulelo Mayikana (2003) held a similar view, and stated that change efforts might be measured in terms of the following areas: shared vision, strategic link, shared values, leadership and management style, staffing, skills, structures and systems. Nithin Nohria, William Joyce and Bruce Robertson (2003) examined more than 160 companies over a 10-year period and came to the conclusion that those companies that outperformed other companies excelled at strategy, execution, culture and structure – thus in OCD and OD applications. The author (2015) published case studies in the book *Inclusive Organisational Transformation* to the same effect.

Manfred Kets de Vries (2005) identifies the clinical paradigm, which is based on the following three premises: what you see is not necessarily what you get, all human behaviours, no matter how irrational they appear, have a rationale, and we are all products of our past. He stated that the meta-force that underpins these three premises is the unconscious, and explained that a considerable part of our motivation and behaviour takes place outside our conscious awareness.

The metaphor of an iceberg was used by Senge (1993) to describe the unseen power of underlying beliefs in systems. Wilfried Krüger (2005) also uses this metaphor to explain that, when managing change within an organisation, the management of cost, quality and time – as the obvious dimensions – is visible (above the water line). However, these factors are less important when compared with the more subtle, but profound dimensions that lie beneath, namely the management of perceptions and beliefs, and power and politics. This model is presented in Figure 3.4.

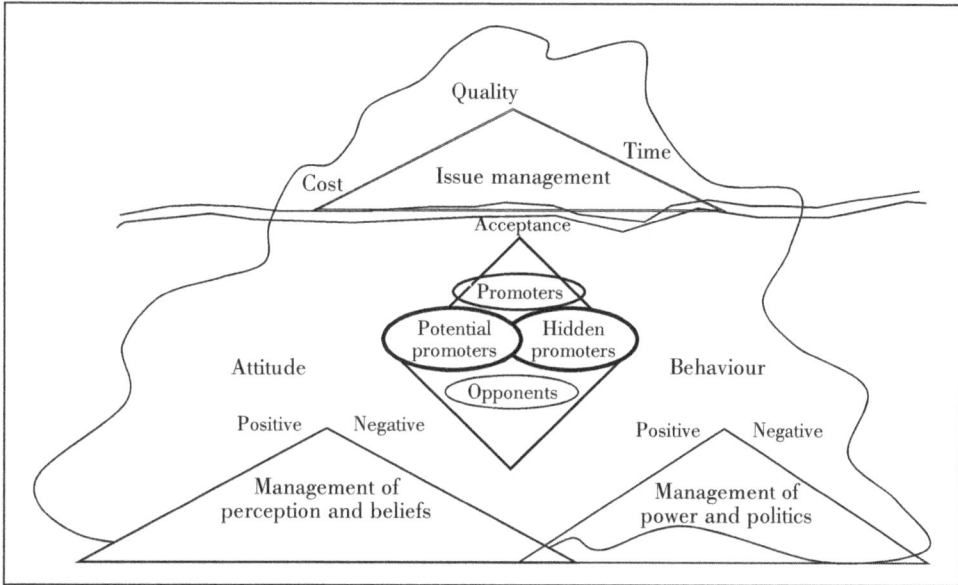

Figure 3.4   Change-management iceberg, Wilfried Krüger (2005)
Source Wilfried Krüger, 2005

OCD practitioners can apply systems-thinking philosophy and principles in their work in that all organisational change efforts must address the underlying beliefs and assumptions to create sustainability.

3.4 Change-process models

In the literature different models are presented that focus on change as a process comprising different phases or steps. Some of the popular models of the past will be briefly discussed.

Kurt Lewin's (1951) *change-management theory* is based on a model of unfreezing, changing and refreezing. For many OCD practitioners this framework still constitutes the theoretical foundation of planned change. Edgar Schein (1987) improved on Lewin's model by specifying the mechanisms at work in each stage. Ronald Lippett, Jeanne Watson and Bruce Westley (1958) expanded the three-stage model into a seven-stage model. David Kolb and Alan Frohman (1970) and Warner Burke (1994) also produced similar models. Although these models are helpful in describing change in isolation it is often not possible within organisations to take such a simplistic view of systemic problems.

The change formula (also known as the change equation) of Richard Beckhard and Reuben Harris (1987) is a simple, yet powerful tool that provides a quick first impression of the possibilities and conditions that are relevant to changing an organisation. **D**issatisfaction, **V**ision and **F**irst steps are needed to overcome the **R**esistance to change within an organisation. This model is presented in Figure 3.5. If any of the three variables, namely **D**, **V** or **F**, is zero or near zero, then the product will also be zero or near zero, and the resistance to change will dominate.

$$ D \; x \; V \; x \; F \; > \; R $$

Dissatisfaction x Vision x First Steps > Resistance to Change

Figure 3.5   Change formula, Richard Beckhard and Reuben Harris (1987)

Ralph Kilmann (1989) specifies critical leverage points for structured organisational change, namely, initiating the programme, diagnosing the problems, scheduling the 'tracks', implementing the 'tracks' and evaluating the results. 'Tracks' refer to focus points for organisational change, namely, the culture, management skills, team-building, strategy structure and reward systems.

John Kotter (1990) identifies eight steps in the change phase model that must be followed in an exact order to ensure sustainability. These steps include: establishing a sense of urgency, creating a coalition, developing a clear vision, sharing the vision, empowering people to clear obstacles, securing short-term wins, consolidating and keeping on moving and anchoring the change.

Frederick Miller and Judith Katz (2002) identified six strategic levers for organisational change, which were similar to the eight steps of Kotter (1990). They also emphasised the importance of the education and accountability of the supervisors, the value of talent, and the need for creating a culture that is supportive of the change initiative.

The systems model of change in Robert Kreitner and Angelo Kinicki (2004), namely, that of input, transformation and output, does not take into account the human impact to the necessary depth. Peter Senge, Otto Scharmar, Joseph Jaworski, and Betty Flowers (2004) in a book on systems thinking called *Presence*, mention that most change initiatives do not fail because they lack grand visions and noble intentions. They fail because people are not able to see the reality they face.

They identified seven core capacities needed for transformation. Each capacity was seen as a gateway to the next activity. These capacities were described in the 'Seven Capacities of the U-Movement'-figure (figure 3.6). The first step to change is to transform perception through the sensing of the new reality.

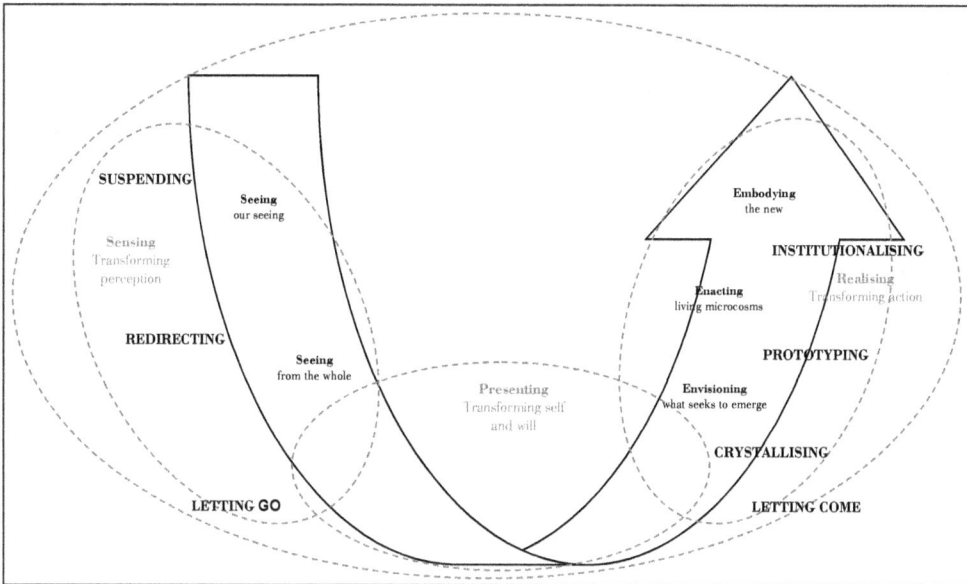

Figure 3.6   Seven capacities of the U-movement, Peter Senge et al (2004)

Otto Scharmer on Presence: human purpose and the field of the future, co-authored by Senge, et al. (2008) describes the core elements of the U-curve as follows:

1   **Co-initiating** common intent: stop and listen to others and to what life calls you to do.

2   **Co-sensing** the field of change: go to the places of most potential and listen with your mind and heart wide open.

3   **Presencing** inspiration and common will: go to the threshold and allow the inner knowing to emerge.

4   **Co-creating** strategic microcosms: prototype the new to explore the future by doing.

5   **Co-evolving** through innovations: ecosystems that facilitate seeing and acting from the whole.

Change agents

Nel (2003) explained the process of change agents within an organisation, and indicated that initially, only a few 'change mavericks' were needed. This approach is displayed in Figure 3.7.

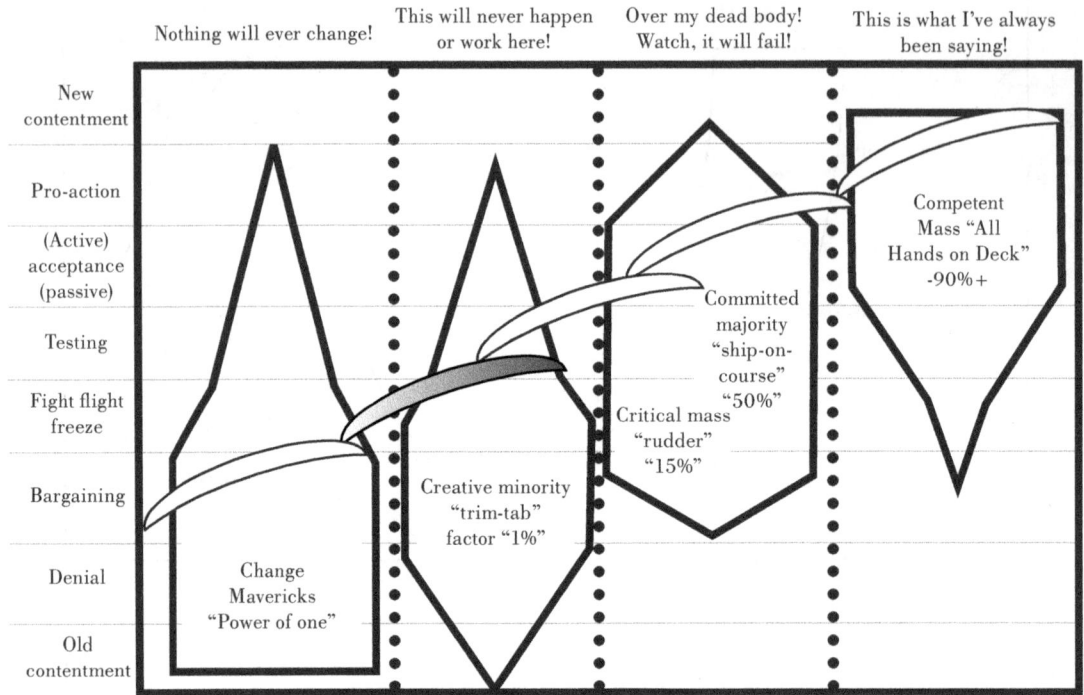

Figure 3.7 The purpose of change agents, Christo Nel (2003)

The maverick qualities of non-conformance, imagination, independence, belligerence and divine dissatisfaction with the status quo were required, say Bill Fischer and Andy Boynton (2005). These mavericks will influence the creative minority, who will, in turn, influence the committed majority, who will then ensure that the mass also buy into the change process.

In the design of an organisational transformational journey the OCD consultant should focus on constructing a change minority that will positively influence the critical mass. In-depth change resilience interventions are the focus of the OCD consultant. The critical mass will provide the necessary momentum that will align the competent mass to engage in the change initiatives and the new way of doing and being. This transformational journey should not be left to evolve by itself. The OCD consultant and the relevant line partners should carefully design it, step by step.

Successful leaders did not simply command strategic change; but, instead, they ensured integration within organisational designs to facilitate the changes. A new business model is needed – a model which provides the framework of and support for each unit, sponsors the changes during the planning process, and promotes the importance of leadership by example during the change efforts. This concept, namely, that of operating models that cement change efforts, does not appear often in recent literature. The paradox that an operating model be implemented in order to ensure that the new reality becomes the new, accepted way (which will once again become relatively fixed) merits continuous focus. OCD consultants can assist in facilitating the co-creation of strategic architecture.

Change is a journey

In effect all the above-mentioned models imply that dissatisfaction must be experienced in terms of the current reality, that a future state should be identified, that change agents should be leveraged, that leadership buy-in should be created, that small wins should be celebrated, and that their efforts should, somehow, be both initiated and institutionalised. A special attempt should be made to ensure the sustainability of the change efforts.

The choice of models can be critiqued as dated. It must, however, be noted that these are still the models that are mostly used in corporate South Africa and Africa today. Further, it is important to distinguish between consultancy-applied models and models that have a deep academic and theoretical underpinning. The author presented models that belong to the last category.

The author (2015) found that it takes between two and five years on average for an organisation to move through a traumatic change. The purpose of focused change-management initiatives is to assist organisations and the people in it, to move faster though the different stages described by the various change models and frameworks. The benefit of well-planned, theoretically anchored, and congruent change-management efforts should be quantified in terms of the time saved on moving through the U-curve of change.

3.5 Conclusion

Situations are not static. Instead, a milieu is active and in constant evolution. Leadership must remain acutely aware of the fact that the most effective answer at the present moment might not be the appropriate response at a later stage. The interplay between the changing external environment and the internal world always leads to continual changes in both worlds. Organisational transformation and the dynamics that surround it, form the base of all efforts of OCD consultants.

Human reactions to change are discussed in the next chapter.

4

HUMAN REACTIONS TO CHANGE

All changes, even the most longed for, have their melancholy; for what we leave behind us is a part of ourselves; we must die to one life before we can enter another.

Anatole France, unknown

4.1 Introduction

In the previous chapter different change philosophies, models and frameworks were presented. From an OCD point of view it is not so important that any specific model is adapted. What is more prevalent is that the model that forms the basis of the transformational journey is a congruent and an applicable one – congruent with the challenges at hand, and applicable to make sense of the challenges at hand.

In this chapter, the individual human reactions to change are discussed. There is an old biblical saying that there is nothing new under the sun. The different models and frameworks presented in this chapter will remind the reader of this saying. Although various authors have described the topic at hand, the underlying themes are repetitive. A change archetype emerges – one where there is a process or journey with a beginning, a middle section, where transition happens, and an end. OCD consultants should support their line partners to understand the normal psychological responses to change at individual level, and insist that the time to move through change is incorporated in strategies.

4.2 Different theoretical approaches to human reactions to change

The secret of change is to focus all your energy, not on fighting the old, but on building the new.

Socrates, unknown

The human reaction to change may stem from the individual, from the organisation or from both. Ben Swanepoel, Heinz Schenk, Marius van Wyk and Barney Erasmus (2003) identify the fear of the unknown, habit, self-interest, economic insecurity, failure to recognise the need for change, general mistrust, social disruption and selective perceptions as factors that may contribute to resistance to change on an individual level. On an organisational level, the following aspects are at play: structural inertia, cultural inertia, work group inertia, threats to existing power relationships, threats to expertise, threats to resource allocation and previous unsuccessful change efforts as organisational factors standing in the way of successful change management interventions.

It has been considered for decades that change has a significant implication on the psyche of individuals and organisations. John Kotter and Leonard Schlesinger (1979) named four reasons underlying resistance to change, namely self-interest, misunderstanding, low tolerance for change and different assessments of the situation. It is critical that OCD consultants have sound academic roots. Today, still, most change initiatives underestimate the importance of the human reaction to change.

In a fable about survival in an ever-changing world John Kotter and Holger Rathgerber (2006) quote the story of penguins in a penguin colony in Antarctica. These penguins face a transformation – their iceberg is melting. The eight steps of Kotter's change process (discussed in previous chapter) are discussed, and emotions in respect of change and uncertainty are shared. This story can be told to a team or organisation that is in the midst of radical transformation. By facilitating an intervention that unpacks the different characters, the steps in the change process and how they relate to the specific organisation, human reactions towards change can be normalised.

Claes Janssen (1996) presents a model for understanding change in terms of moving through psychological and behavioural states. The four-room apartment model of change is illustrated in Figure 4.1. In all change people move from contentment, which is lost, via a period of denial, which is a defence of the old, through confusion, which will come to an end when the insight is gained that the old must be 'given up'. This 'giving up' is the turning point that opens the mind to new possibilities, and hence, there will be a move towards renewal. Manfred Kets de Vries (2001) presents a similar model, namely, the Model of Organisational Mourning. The stages of this model correlate with the four-room apartment model of change, although other descriptions are used to identify them, namely: shock, disbelief, discarding and realisation.

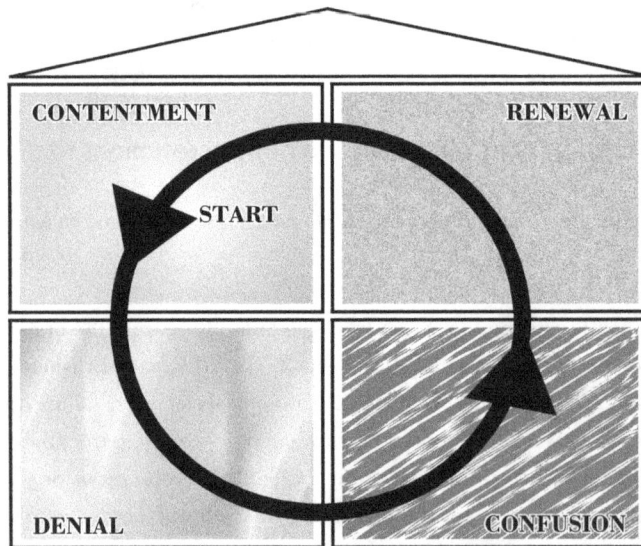

Figure 4.1   Four-room apartment model of change, Claes Janssen (1996)

Willem de Jager (2003) describes the interplay between changes within the external environment and how individuals react to these changes in the internal world. In the Organisational Change Curve Approach (figure 4.2) he explains that during change and transformation, people regress by focusing on the past and denying the change – this agrees with the model of Claes Janssen.

Next, people go through a period of preoccupation during which they wonder where they stand, and how they will be affected. This is normally the stage during which resistance occurs or during which the human response to change is prevalent. This stage correlates with the confusion stage of Janssen (1996).

As individuals and groups enter the exploration and commitment phases they start to look towards the future and possible opportunities the future may hold. Janssen (1996) described this as the renewal and contentment phase.

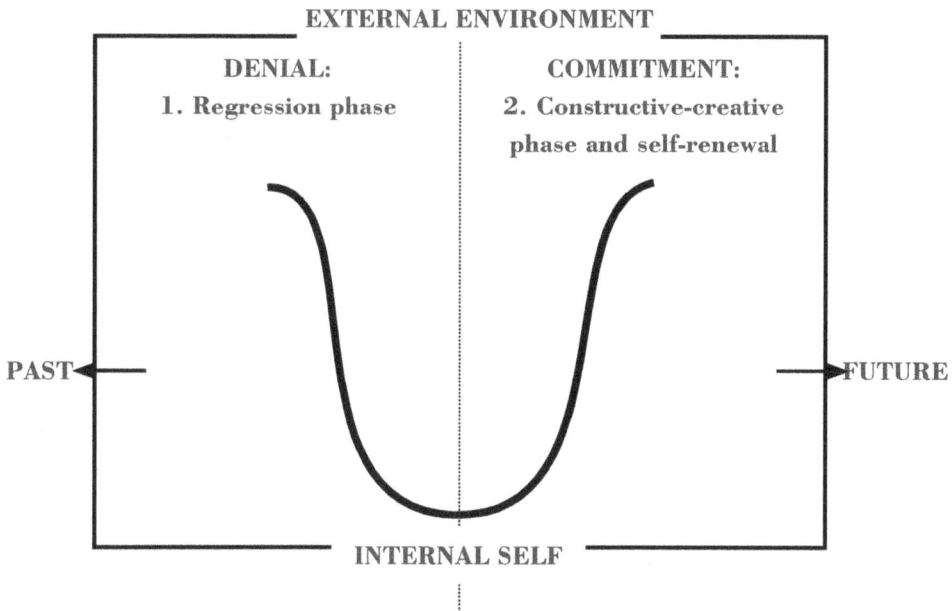

EXTERNAL ENVIRONMENT

DENIAL:

1. Regression phase

COMMITMENT:

2. Constructive-creative phase and self-renewal

PAST ← → FUTURE

INTERNAL SELF

Figure 4.2   Organisational change curve, Willem de Jager (2003)

Kets de Vries (2005) has a similar view, and described his view in terms of the Five Cs of the Individual Change Model. According to this model, individuals move from concern to confrontation to clarification to crystallisation to internalised change. This model is also similar to the change models applicable to organisations which were discussed in the previous chapter.

In order for people to adapt to the change he identifies three internal forces that work with and against each other, namely, defence restructuring (the habitual defences that people use to deal with stressful situations), affect restructuring (the emotions that come to the fore and how to manage them more effectively) and self-other restructuring (alteration of perception of self and others). This model is illustrated in figure 4.3.

The Transition Curve provides an excellent analysis of how individuals deal with personal change, according to John Fisher (2006). This model is an extremely useful reference for individuals who are dealing with personal change and for managers and organisations helping staff to deal with personal change. It explains that, when confronted with change, anxiety will arise. This will be followed by happiness, which will, in turn lead to either denial or fear. Fear will lead to threat and then to guilt. This guilt may turn into hostility or into a gradual acceptance of the change. It is only when the change is accepted that an individual will be able to move forward.

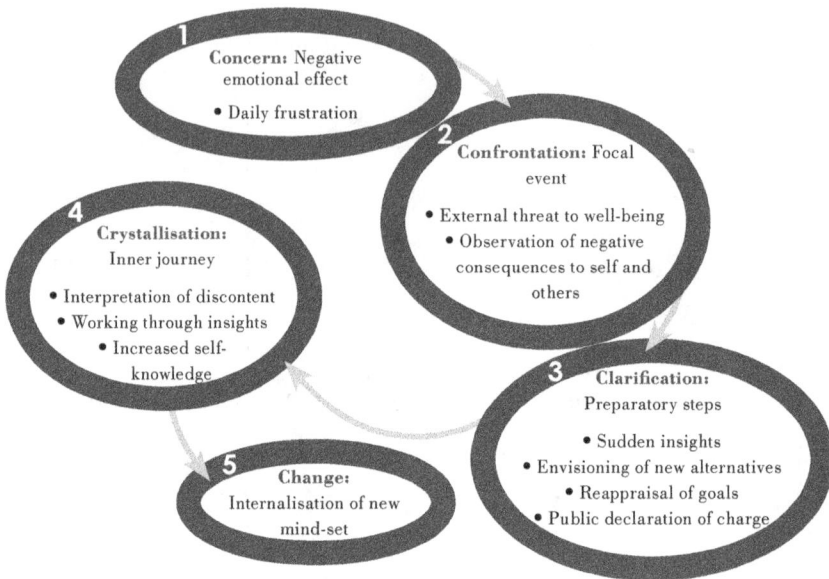

Figure 4.3   Five Cs of the individual change, Manfred Kets de Vries (2005)

Similar views on the stages of change and the impact thereof are to found in literature. The different theories all have three steps or phases in common – the initial phase, the change phase and the end state. The seven capacities of the U-movement of change model of Peter Senge et al., (2004) which is presented in figure 4.6 provides an excellent description of the importance of letting go (suspending, redirecting) into letting come (crystallising, prototyping and ultimately institutionalising). As may be seen in the reference in table 4.1 below to the lesson on change from the New Testament it is clear that these phases of change are archetypal.

Table 4.1   Parallel models of change

Who	Initially		In process				At the end
New Testament	Conviction/confession		Repentance				New birth
Lewin (1951)	Unfreezing		Change				Refreezing
Lifton (1961)	Confrontation		Reordering				Renewal
Hopson and Adams (1976)	Immobilisation	Minimisation	Depression	Accepting/letting go	Testing	Searching for meaning	Internalisation
Merzirow (1978)	Alienation		Re-framing				Contractual solidarity
Kotter & Schlesinger (1979)	Denial	Resistance	Self-doubt	Acceptance	Exploration	Understanding	Integration
Thomas and Harri-Augstein (1985)	Awareness of old learning – robot		Learning trough				New learning level
Janssen (1996)	Denial		Confusion			Renewal	Commitment
Atherton (1999)	Destabilisation		Disorientation				Reorientation
Kets de Vries (2001)	Concern	Confrontation	Clarification			Crystallisation	Change
Senge et al. (2004)	Suspending	Redirecting	Letting go	Letting come	Crystallising	Prototyping	Institutionalising
Viljoen (2015)	New Foundation		Filtering through		Rewiring around the new		Cementing the future

Jim Collins (2001) maintains that perceptions on transitions are sometimes formed from the way the transition appears from the outside, but that it is often experienced in a completely different way from the inside. This is similar to an organic development process. The field of study of transition psychology looks at the deeper psycho-social factors that may impede the natural transition processes and the ways in which individuals will respond to change. The phases and features of the John Hopson and Barrie Adams Adult Transition Cycle are presented in figure 4.4

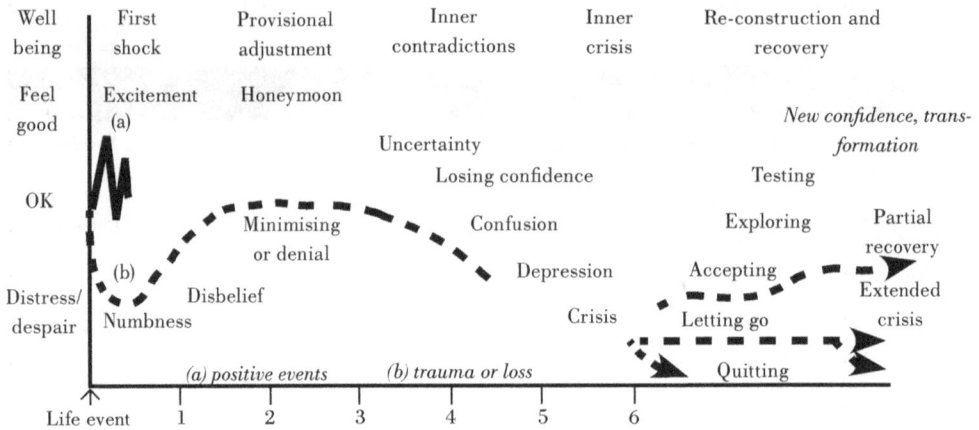

Figure 4.4 *Adult transition cycle, John Hopson and Barrie Adams (1976)*

Elisabeth Kübler-Ross (1973) also contributed to the understanding of emotional experience when she defined the human reaction to change during the process of loss (figure 4.5). These models are still applicable within organisations today as they normalise the emotions related to change and also describe the normal behavioural patterns of both individuals and organisations. By using these phase theory approaches, OCD initiatives like change enablement workshops may help employees and managers to gain insight into human behaviour during change.

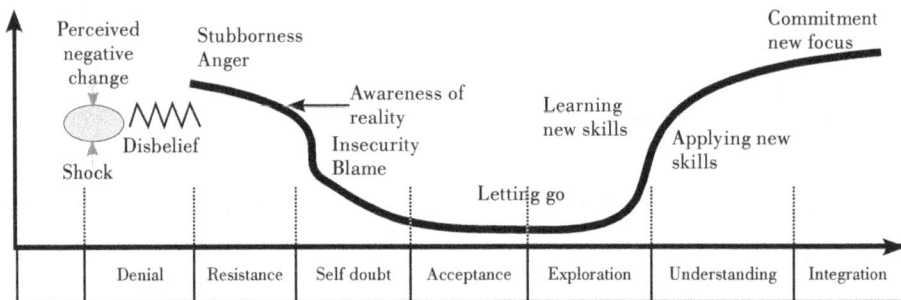

Figure 4.5 *Psychological responses to change, Elisabeth Kübler-Ross (1973)*

It is critical that leaders understand the impact that change has on the functioning of individuals (their own functioning included). In the new world of work, in which change is so prevalent, the challenge is to communicate transition awareness and management skills to all employees so as to optimise human behaviour. A study of the work on the human reaction to change of authors such as Hopson and Adams (1979), Kübler-Ross (1973), Nel (2003) and Senge et al., (2004) has resulted in the emergence of an integrated model that describes the human reaction to change (see Figure 4.6).

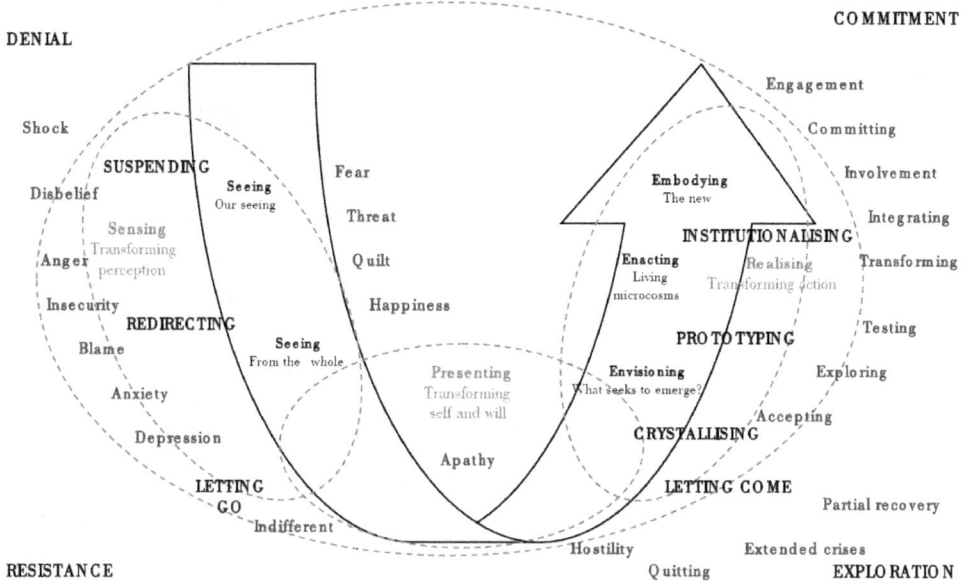

Figure 4.6   Adapted U-movement integrating human reaction to change
Adapted from De Jager, 2003, Kübler-Ross, 1973 Senge et al., (2004) and the author (2009)

Specific emotions are experienced during the different phases. The letting-go phase includes emotions such as denial and resistance which are accompanied by feelings such as shock, disbelief, anger, insecurity, blame, anxiety, happiness, fear, threat, guilt and depression, while the letting-come phase consists of acceptance, the making sense of, the understanding of, and ultimately, the integration of the change, and is accompanied by the relevant emotions of commitment, optimism and engagement. The author of this book is of the opinion that these emotions do not follow a linear pattern. Certain emotions may be experienced in some cases, while others are not. Individuals move forward and backwards during the letting-go phase until the self and the will are transformed and the letting-come phase starts.

4.3   The implications of the human reaction to change on change initiatives

> *"The signals of threat are always abundant and recognised by many. Yet somehow they fail to penetrate the corporate immune system response to reject the unfamiliar"*
> Arie de Geus, 1997

John Kotter et al (1979) identify six change approaches that deal with resistance to change. These approaches include education and communication, participation and involvement, facilitation and support, negotiation and agreement, manipulation and co-operation, and explicit and implicit coercion. OCD methodologies such as appreciative inquiry may assist a system to deal more effectively with the resistance to and the impact of change. These techniques are described in chapter 7.

Al Siebert (2005) describes five techniques that assist in dealing with change, namely, the maintenance of emotional stability, the maintenance of health and well-being, outward focusing by applying good problem-solving skills, inward focusing by working on intra-personal skills, the development of resilience skills, and the development of 'talent for serendipity' – the ability to convert misfortune into good fortune.

Resilience is the ability to experience change and disturbance without catastrophic, qualitative change within the basic, functional organisation. Neil Adger (2000) describes social resilience as the ability of humans to withstand shocks to their infrastructure from the external environment. Resilient people may derive meaning from failure, and use this information to transcend their current reality (Coetzee, 2013). Leo Strümpfer (2003) builds on this view, and adds that, in the case of humans, resilience refers not only to recuperation, but also includes constructive opportunities for growth. Today we speak about having grit.

The concept of emotional intelligence, as defined by Reuven Bar-On (2005a:2) is the accepted definition of emotional intelligence in this book, namely, *"the array of non-cognitive capabilities that enables us to deal with environmental demands"*. Manfred Kets de Vries (2001) views emotional intelligence as the understanding of the forces that motivate the self and others, and states that, given the importance of an individual's internal theatre on cognition, affect and behaviour, emotional intelligence plays a vital role in the leadership equation.

Emotional intelligence theory suggests that there is a direct correlation between adaptability to change and effective functioning, and effective leadership behaviour, Bar-On (2005b) says. The adaptability to change in this model is approached as the interplay of three psychological constructs, namely, reality testing (the alignment of the objective truth and the subjective experience), flexibility (the alignment of emotional reaction to the reality), and problem-solving (the ability to generate possible solutions to deal with a problem, to choose between them and to implement a solution). OCD practitioners can design interventions by focusing on enhancing reality testing, flexibility and problem-solving.

The arguments of Senge et al., (2004) and Kets de Vries (2001) on the importance of seeing reality for what it is, were presented earlier in this chapter. Techniques such as dialoguing and world-café activities could ensure that people receive ample opportunity to assimilate new data in order to adapt their mental models. Story-telling may improve emotional intelligence as it is able to enhance awareness. OCD consultants can facilitate group sessions by using these techniques. More emphasis is placed on it in chapter 7.

Different personality types react differently to radical transformation. OCD consultants should clearly understand how personality, intelligences and diversity of thought impact on planned change initiatives in organisations. Personality type analysis and emotional intelligence tests, feedback and journeys may improve self-awareness, resilience and the ability to deal with environmental demands. Carl Jung (1954) warns that behaviour is far too complex to be reduced to a set of simple questions in a questionnaire. Results from assessments should be viewed as indicators, and not absolutes.

Clare Graves (1974) describes different ways in which individuals adapt to changing life conditions. Beck and Cowan (1996) used the term spiral dynamics to describe the different ways in which individuals and societies determine worth. As different individuals ask different questions of existence, different worldviews emerge.

Laubscher (2013) refers to these worldviews as human niches. However, the author (2014) moves back to the original Gravesian thinking, and interprets the different niches as adaptive intelligence. Chapters 5 and 6 are dedicated to an understanding of the concept of human niches. Transition between different niches has a major traumatic implication on individual and collective psyches. Individuals with different human niches will also react differently to organisational change. OCD consultants should possess an in-depth understanding of how these human niches and adaptive intelligence manifest at work.

An OCD practitioner could assist leadership by explaining ways in which the manager could modify employee behaviour. To a certain extent, the author disagrees with this view. It is the task of individual leadership to take responsibility for its own behaviour and be open to feedback. Rather than rendering assistance to managers to increase their ability to "direct" the actions of those around them, executive coaching could assist leaders to become aware of their own unconscious behaviours and needs, and thus, through enhanced emotional intelligence, come to manifest the personal authority that will ensure followership. Coaching will not be discussed as a methodology here as it belongs in the field of coaching psychology.

It is often the human resources department, and in particular OCD practitioners, who are held responsible for cultural change efforts. Hopefully, if transformation within the field of human resources is successful the human resource (HR) practitioner will be able to take up the role of strategic line partner rather than that of HR officer, and be in a position to consult to line management on the assumption of authority for the culture and climate within the organisation, says Dave Ulrich (1997). In this case the HR practitioner will become the change agent.

Bonnie Erikson (1964) found that typically organisations with strong, coherent and clear identities deal substantially better with radical change in comparison with those organisations that may be described as identity deficient. Chris van Tonder (2004b) elaborated on the work of Erikson and made a significant contribution to the field of change resilience with his explanation that personal and organisational identity exert a positive influence on resilience, and may ultimately result in organisational sustainability. OCD interventions can assist individuals to crystallise their identity and understand their human reactions to change.

The challenge of leadership in the new world of work is to guide the change and transformation of individuals and groups/teams effectively through the change cycle without disrupting job and organisational performance. Change triggers fear, and fear triggers resistance. Resistance is a natural part of the change process and is to be expected.

The fear that the advertised benefits of a particular change intervention will not outweigh the costs involved will offset unconscious defence mechanisms according to Manfred Kets de Vries (2001). Defence mechanisms activate when the individual feels anxious or threatened. These emotions occur readily during transformation. It is the task of leadership to assist employees in not avoiding the issue of change. Instead, they should help their employees to actively engage in dealing with it, even while they themselves are affected. OCD consultants should consult to unconscious defence mechanisms to assist leadership in making their dynamics more aware. Processes such as psycho-analytical events facilitated in a Tavistock fashion can assist with making sense out of non-sense.

4.4 A positive reaction to change

For a seed to achieve its greatest expression, it must come completely undone. The shell cracks, its insides came out and everything changes. To someone who does not understand growth, it must look like a complete destruction.

Cynthia Occelli, 2012

Relatively little research has examined the impact that positive employees may exert on organisational change. Reuven Bar-On (2005a) held the opinion that the ability of a person to deal with environmental demands relies heavily on optimism and happiness. The author (2009) found that positivity on the part of employees would have an impact on change attitudes and behaviours.

It could be argued that the vast majority of organisational change in companies is managed from a technical point of view without recognising or understanding how the human element influences the outcome of the effort. The failure of many large-scale, organisational, transformational strategies may be traced directly to employee resistance. According to Kathleen O'Connor (1993) the management of employee resistance outweighs any other aspect of the change process.

If employees find that their input into changing the current processes requested from them has been ignored, this will lead to disillusionment. Most employees expect that that their views will be taken into consideration and treated with respect. However, instead, some change initiators resort to questionable techniques, such as manipulation and coercion, in order to overcome resistance. Such practices will result in mistrust and resentment, thus making change more difficult to implement. In order to achieve sustainable results by means of transformational strategies, the human resistance to change must be addressed efficiently and the human potential unleashed for the benefit of the individual, group and organisation.

4.5 Overcoming resistance to change

In order to reach agreement on how different people will work together it is essential that they discuss the issue. Conversation, says David Bohm (1998) is a profound action that helps to expand awareness, and connect parts and people that are separated. The '*Who?*' '*What?*', '*Where?*', '*When?*' and '*Why?*' should be discussed. What matters most is how these ideas play out in the workplace and in the lives of real leaders and followers. The OCD practitioner within or outside the organisation can facilitate these conversations,

By tapping into the differences that separate organisations, OCD consultants will be able to challenge unnamed assumptions and thus become more effective and gain access to a wider range of available resources. This principle applies both within and outside of the organisation. The techniques and methodologies used to create a safe space for crucial conversations, which are described in chapter 7, are neither brand new nor mind-boggling.

However, they are often not practised as they are perceived to be very time-consuming. The African saying: "If you want to walk fast, walk alone. If you want to walk far, walk together," comes to mind.

There is an unavoidable risk that changes in only one element of a complex organisation will be subverted by the other elements. An integral approach to transformation is critical, and should permeate all the systems and structures of an organisation. Obstacles to change are often deeply embedded in the formal way the organisation is organised – system and human resource management practices and the culture of the organisation. For any transformation to be successful, all aspects of the organisational culture should be conducive to the projected outcome.

OCD practitioners must assist leaders in organisations to understand the whole system. Story-telling and dialoguing, as discussed in chapter 5, may be very helpful in sharing organisational stories. In order for transformation to be successful, shared understanding of the reason why change is taking place, significance into the change process, good leadership and strategic direction, and learning from previous experiences and from industry best practices, are important.

Although emergent theory suggests that it is possible for strategy and structure to evolve simultaneously, the leadership in organisations often still believes that structure should follow strategy. In order to ensure the sustainability of transformation efforts companies often appoint support structures. Organisational design, however, falls outside the scope of this book.

The author is left with a sense that change policies, such as diversity policies and practices, are often implemented in order to avoid complaints of unlawful discrimination and possible high levels of compensation being awarded against them, rather than from a pure perspective and intent to do the ethical thing. It is essential that it is not only policies that change. New behaviours must be adapted. Behavioural change will lead to a difference in climate, and, ultimately, to a transformation in culture.

Jim Collins (2001) found that often a more successful approach to transformation is to decide quietly and deliberately what to do and then do it, rather than to push the organisation in one direction, to jump in and stop, change direction and, then, to repeat the process. Companies need to build up sustained momentum to deal with change. Core values and purpose sustain successful companies, while strategy and operating practices adapt to the changing external environment.

Stephen Covey (2004) compares values and principles with the anchor of a ship that creates internal stability during an external storm. Another paradox facing leadership in the new world of work is the challenge that the organisation must be flexible, while it should, simultaneously, align around organisational strategy and values.

4.6 Conclusion

The organisation must become the "living" embodiment of that which it wishes to achieve, with all organisational components streamlined to make it possible for the organisation to move in the intended direction Mario Denton and Ernst Bouwer (2003) claim. All organisational components must, therefore, communicate the same message to the employees, customers, business partners and the community. During change efforts focus should be directed onto the systemic understanding of the impact of the change on all the sub-systems within the larger system.

The process of organisational change may be optimised by applying those insights derived from individual change within the domain of organisational transformation. OCD intervention strategies are, therefore, necessary to assist the individual in identifying and interpreting his or her own perceptions of change, thus creating greater personal awareness and understanding of the self. Personal growth strategies and OCD interventions are likely to alter the individual's perceptions of organisational change, thereby reducing the level of resistance and anxiety significantly.

In order to manage any radical change effort effectively business leaders must understand how individuals, teams and organisations operate and function. The author will focus on addressing the dynamics of these different thinking systems in the next chapter as people with different worldviews view change differently.

PART 2
EMERGING DIVERSITY OF THOUGHT

5

HUMAN NICHES – SEEING IN COLOURS

SECTION 1: The first tier – worldviews of subsistence

"And how do you know that you're mad?"
"To begin with," said the Cat, "a dog's not mad. You grant that?"
"I suppose so," said Alice.
"Well then," the Cat went on, "you see a dog growls when it's angry, and wags its tail when it's pleased. Now I growl when I'm pleased, and wag my tail when I'm angry. Therefore I'm mad."

Lewis Carroll in Alice's Adventures in Wonderland

5.1 Introduction

Professor Clare Graves asked his students, in the 1960s and '70s, to conduct research on the following research questions:

- What constitutes mature adult functioning?

- What constitutes a good life and good leadership?

- How do different people adjust to power relations?

Basically, he explored the essence of human nature as it pertains to different distinct ways of thinking or structure of thought. The different structures of thought form the foundations on which underlying beliefs or worldviews are constructed. Eight different ways of thinking can be identified in Gravesian thinking.

Further, Graves (1970) realised that basically there are two ways of responding to authority in power relations. Roughly two-thirds of people will sacrifice the self in order not to disagree with their elders, chiefs, parents or leaders, or upset them. They save 'face'. This sacrificial system was later described as collectivism.

The remainder expresses the self. They do not adjust to authority figures, but may accept inputs from their peers. This expressive system was later referred to as individualism. The eight different ways of thinking oscillate between individualism and collectivism. These systems can be seen in figure 5.1 below.

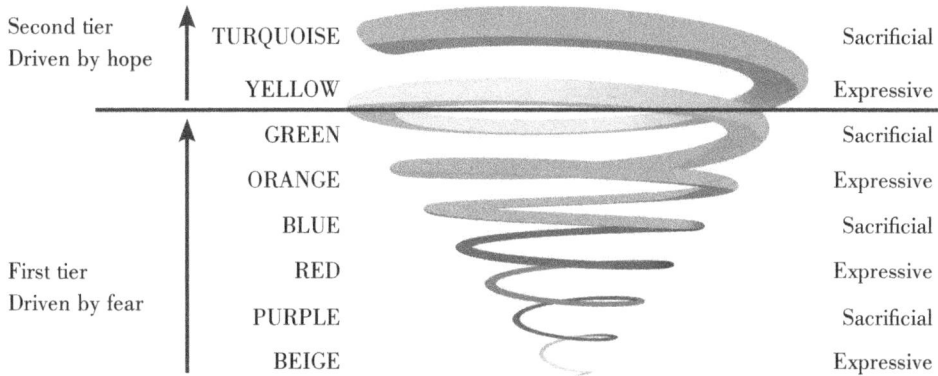

Second tier Driven by hope	TURQUOISE	Sacrificial
	YELLOW	Expressive
	GREEN	Sacrificial
	ORANGE	Expressive
	BLUE	Sacrificial
First tier Driven by fear	RED	Expressive
	PURPLE	Sacrificial
	BEIGE	Expressive

Figure 5.1   Spiral dynamics, Viljoen (2013, p. 5)

Don Beck assigned a colour scheme to these thinking systems, to which he refers as value systems or memes (see figure 5.1 above). These colours first were published in the book *Spiral Dynamics* by Beck and Cowan (1996). These systems must not be confused with personal values. Rather, his conceptualisation of value systems focuses on how different people create worth, or allocate meaning to events and situations. The name spiral dynamics refers to the oscillating, ever-emerging essence of the different categories. In this chapter the first-tier thinking systems are described. In figure 5.2 below, the double-helix nature of the question of existence and corresponding coping mechanism in the brain is portrayed as psychological DNA.

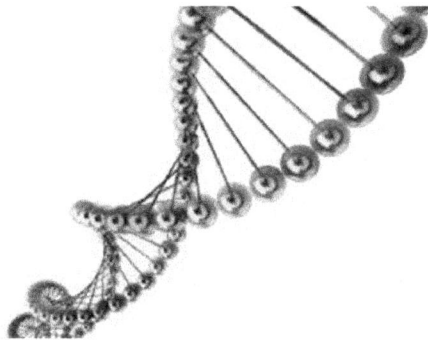

Figure 5.2   Nature of the spiral, Viljoen (2013, p.1)

In the book *Integral Polity*, Laubscher and the author (2015) co-authored a chapter on the origins of human niche theory. The author, here, refers to the different categories of thinking systems as fractals or archetypes. A fractal describes a repetitive organising structure. Basically, the different thinking systems create fractals that contain specific questions of existence and a set of problem-solving abilities in the psyche to deal with changing life challenges.

Beck (1996) assigned high colours, namely, BEIGE, RED, ORANGE and YELLOW to the expressive systems. Low colours such as PURPLE, BLUE, GREEN and TURQUOISE were allocated to the sacrificial systems. Although Beck denies that there is anything more to the allocation of colours to specific thinking systems, it manifests as synchronistic in the external world today.

5.2 How spiral dynamics manifest in society

> *Our differences are our strength as a species and as a world community.*
>
> *Nelson Mandela, 2002*

During the 2014 election in South Africa the ANC secured 62.5% of the votes. Later it will be argued that in the a specific thinking system of purple, it is not frowned upon if your leader lives in a big palace nor is it considered corrupt to build a homestead like Nkandla[3] for him. The red overalls of the Economic Freedom Fighters present an external magnification of the red thinking system. The blue T-shirts of the Democratic Alliance correspond with the blue philosophy of this political party. In similar fashion, Agang wore green shirts. In her research Laubscher found that in South Africa the distribution of thinking systems is stratified and divergent.

The barcode in figure 5.3 is a representation of this. Interestingly enough this distribution mirrors the distribution of votes to the different political parties by the South African population during the latest election.

Figure 5.3   Barcode distribution of South African human niches, Viljoen (2013, p. 2)

Roughly 65% voted for the ANC (there are 65% purple in South Africa). Fifteen percent voted for the EFF (15% are red). More or less 10% voted for the DA (and lo and behold, 10% of people in South Africa are blue). Agang (green) received 1% representation. This correlates with the distribution of thinking systems that Loraine Laubscher found in her live history and described in the book *Inclusive Organisational Transformation*.

5.3 Adaptive intelligence

Thinking systems are used, together with intelligences, personality functions, social awareness and wisdom to make sense of the world, or to adapt or respond to changing life conditions. In fact, it may be assumed that, as archetypes for various questions of existence, the different colours are dealing with the concept of how we adapt to our changing life conditions. Typically, an archetype refers to a symbol or image of unconscious nature. As

---

3   At the time of writing, the president of South Africa, Jacob Zuma, was in the middle of a debacle about allocating taxpayers' money to construct an extravagant complex, for Nkandla, and his wives.

new challenges are facing people, new ways of thinking may be activated to help them to adapt to changing life conditions.

Laubscher (2013) builds on Beck, who explained that changing life conditions require new thinking systems to evolve over time. Humans adapt to the new challenges in the changing context. We are thus dealing here with **Adaptive Intelligence.**

5.4 Human niches

Laubscher (2013) explains that these thinking systems result in the acceleration of groups of people in a specific way of being. In her doctoral thesis she constructed the concept of human niches. A niche can be defined as something at which a person or a group of people excels so that it makes them unique. By framing thinking systems as human niches, Laubscher succeeded in doing what other scholars in this field had attempted to do, namely to warn against the seduction of assuming that the different thinking systems are hierarchical in nature. They are merely different.

Paul Colinvaux (1980) defines a niche as a specific set of capabilities for extracting resources, for surviving hazards, and, coupled with a corresponding set of needs, for competing. He continues to explain that our niches are those things that have changed in some places since ancient times. Not everyone is still a hunter or a gatherer: some have become farmers and others industrialists.

Laubscher (2013) defines human niches as "the areas of social, economical, spiritual, physical and personal dynamics of life at which humans excel due to the distinct question of existence that we ask". If we ask questions about how to conquer the material world, we will excel at conquering the financial world. If we ask questions about how to sacrifice the self for the tribe, we will excel at family relations – not at making money.

Following on Beck (2013) and Laubscher (2013), the nature of human niches can be described as follows:

- Chronological, not hierarchical (levels are not skipped)

- Attitudinal, not behavioural

- Thinking systems, not personal values

- Presenting us with gifts to society as a whole

- Heterogeneous in terms of personality and intelligence.

Human niches best describe the essence of the thinking systems that differ from one individual to another, as well as from one society to the next.

5.5 Underlying assumptions to spiral dynamics

Graves (1974:132) explained that a person's behavioural needs could be ascribed to his or her levels of existence. He mentioned the following:

- A person's nature is an open, and not a closed system. It is forever emerging.

- Human nature evolves by quantum-like jumps from one steady state to another.

- Different value systems exist in each state of existence.

Human niches tell us more about the following according to Laubscher (2013):

- How do we view the world?

- What do we see as the permanent parts of being us?

- How do we see the future?

- What information do we select or receive to see our world?

- What do we do daily (spend time on or pay attention to)?

Answering these questions will help us understand the following life conditions:

- How self-concept is defined

- The sense of time

- The way of perceiving and energy orientation of a thinking niche.

5.6 Human niches, personality and intelligences

Different personalities as described by instruments such as the Myers-Briggs Type Indicator (MBTI), can be found in each of the human niches. One finds people with high emotional intelligence and low emotional intelligence in every niche. So far, no correlation could be detected between complexity-handling ability as measured by the Career Path Appreciation (CPA) and human niches. One can be highly intelligent in purple and general intelligence can be low in orange. Laubscher (2014) reminds us that personality and intelligences are behavioural, but human niches are attitudinal. Don Beck and Graham Linscott explain in The Crucible (2011:157) that every human niche has its own smartness and that all the different systems are essential if the spiral is to retain its strength and integrity.

5.7 Metaphor: The Game of Life

Another way of looking at the different human niches is that it can be compared to playing Monopoly. Some people don't have the capacity to play at all. Others play to be with the family. They take from one child to redistribute to another one to keep them in the game. Another plays the game of life to win. Another group play only if the rules are followed, and they keep to the instruction sheet. Another group of people will play to go past start where money is collected only if there is a chance to have hotels on the most expensive stand so that they can make the most money. Yet, another group of people play life to give back, and because it creates a learning opportunity for all. The ways of thinking described in this metaphor describe beige, purple, red, blue, orange and green human niches.

Alternatively, one can compare the thinking systems or human niches to different states of a computer game. Certain superpowers can be obtained at every stage. If the player doesn't complete one stage successfully, he or she will really struggle at the next stage. Each stage has its own special power. Table 5.1 summarises the superpowers to be gained:

Table 5.1 Superpowers of thinking systems

Thinking system	Super power
BEIGE	Ability to survive
PURPLE	Ability to build communities and families – to play house
RED	Ability to win and to have power
BLUE	Ability to follow rules and to be just
ORANGE	Ability to make money and to be successful
GREEN	Ability to give back and create inclusivity
YELLOW	Ability to understand all other systems and become these
TURQUOISE	Ability to connect globally and even interplanetarily

The following principles apply:

- The thinking systems are stratified – they build on each other. It is not healthy to reject the superpower of the previous stage or thinking system.

- It is a developmental theory – therefore there is a low and a high form of each thinking system.

- Thinking systems only change if the current thinking cannot cope with changing life conditions.

- It can then shift to a different thinking system – it can go in any direction

- Individuals, teams, organisations and societies have barcodes of human niches. These are arrays of human niches that can manifest in the individual or collective psyche.

- Individuals display transparent predominant human niches – like a default mode. There may also be an aspirational human niche – a striving towards something else. Often people also display a latent human niche – something that they fall back on when in a crisis.

- Graves warned – "you cannot be before you are". Until you ask the questions of existence of the subsequent niche, your current worldview will be the dominant one.

- This is not personality or intelligence. All personalities are present in all the human niches. For example, one can be very clever (generic intelligence) in purple and not so intelligent in orange.

- Human niches are attitudinal and not behavioural. Human niches describe the thinking system that contains different personalities and intelligences.

- The human niches all have adaptive benefits. However, if it is taken too far new problems appear.

- Not one of the human niches is bad. Low is not so niche, but the high form is delightful and contains gifts and superpowers.

5.8 Spiral dynamics and motivational theory

Clare Graves was a contemporary of Albert Maslow. Although they initially disagreed in theory, a conclusion was reached on Maslow's death bed that Maslow's hierarchy of needs manifested in each thinking system.

Laubscher (2014) explains that by implication in the different human niches self-actualisation appears differently. In purple to be a good mother or leader in the community is self-actualisation. In blue it can be to be a good citizen, to life ethically and to progress on the corporate ladder. Self-actualisation in orange is visible materialistic success. Investment goals are reached. Human niches drive our behaviours, our decisions, our relationships and how we organise. Understanding these dynamics can assist in understanding self and others. Keith Rice offers valuable insights regarding spiral dynamics and other relevant theories such as Maslow's self-actualisation theory, and interprets this concept differently. For more information the reader is advised to study his work on the website http://www. integratedsociopsychology.net/vmemes.htm.

The different human niches will be discussed in further detail below.

5.9 The different human niches

BEIGE

The dynamics of beige

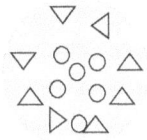

In beige people only need food, water and shelter. A clan of people may gather together to survive. There is no real capacity to engage in long-term relationships. Beige thinking causes behaviour that acts in their interest with the purpose of survival. The organising structure is directly focused on obtaining food, water and shelter. Therefore people form a herd. Here, people can gather together for the purpose of obtaining food, but they will disperse when the threat of surreptitious theft is experienced.

The organising archetype as displayed in the figure above is an indication of this dynamic. An archetype of how beige is organising their world is displayed. 'Bergies' – beggars who are members of the homeless coloured community in South Africa, and who live at the foot of mountains, or people who live in the slums in India have beige human niches. Laubscher (2013) estimated that internationally about 9% of people can be classified as beige.

Although beige people often do not operate well in corporate systems, it is generally assumed that this thinking system is not displayed at work. The author, however, found more and more evidence that beige can be found in spaces where individuals with this thinking system find themselves.

In my work within the health industry, it became increasingly clear that especially in theatre settings often the necessity for gentleness and kindness appears. We do know that when a patient is very ill, beige appears. Also that people with mental diseases also often display this thinking system. It is also visible in the elderly, especially with patients with dementia and Alzheimer's. It was interesting to see how many theatre nurses displayed this thinking system. The ability to build relations drained out, and only survival is at stake.

The reader is reminded of the low and the high version of each human niche. Low beige cannot operate in society. Noises may be too loud, bright lights may make them scramble. High beige has a cunning sense of time. Bushmen who attended a master's degree class in Botswana, explained that they could sense in the space in time where an animal was. Even when there were no hoof marks, droppings or crushed grass in the vicinity they sensed the presence of the animal – often hours before – in the atmosphere. This is a gift – the gift of the 26 senses that traditional Bushmen had – that gets forgotten in other human niches. They have a knowing.

This is the gift of high beige. Beige can function in systems on their condition. They withdraw from social settings, you cannot apply logic to their behaviour, nor can you manage it with typical organisational strategies. The minute that conflicts present, the fight or flight defence mechanism overwrites the typical behaviour.

Crises may also lead to a closing down of other thinking systems, and beige may become the prominent human niche. An almost irrational behaviour may manifest when money, food or safety is considered to be under threat. Disaster relief teams must often deal with this thinking system in its low form.

Every human niche has a bottom line. This is the question that organises everything else in an organising structure or archetype.

The question of existence in beige is: how can I sacrifice in order to survive?

Initially Clare Graves assigned the letter A to this question of existence, and started in the middle of the alphabet to assign letters for the corresponding ways of coping with the specific question of existence. He assigned N to this human niche. Beige (or AN) use N ways to solve A problems. We cannot have red, blue and orange ways to solve beige or N problems. We must use beige or N ways to solve beige or A problems. Congruence is important.

Example of beige

A corporate business woman bought a fridge for her beige mother, who complained that she never had food to eat. Within a week the mother gave the fridge away in exchange for old shoes. The daughter was very upset. The mother became very anxious when the daughter confronted her. The mother explained that motor of the fridge was making too much and that it hurt her ears.

A month later she bought her a TV with a big flat screen. The same thing happened. The mother this time explained that the TV was hurting her eyes. The daughter then tried to buy an electronic foot spa for the mother. This time the mother accused the daughter of trying to electrocute her with water and electricity.

After learning about human niches the daughter realised that her financial solutions did and would not solve the problem of existence of her beige mother. Now she meets the mother in beige. She takes food for the day, provides clothes that can be bartered and does not attempt to change the needs of her mother. Solutions must be congruent with the thinking systems that are challenged by the changing life conditions.

Implications of BEIGE for OCD practitioners

Organisational consultants must be aware that although employees are seldom beige, there may be a component in the organisation that displays this thinking system. Communities in emerging economies often have a small beige component. Employees with drug-addicted children or elderly parents may be confronted with this thinking system. Employees with personality disorders and pathologies may sometimes regress, and display beige. Employee assistance programmes often deal with beige dynamics. Product development departments and marketing departments must understand the dynamics of this market segment.

PURPLE

The dynamics of purple

Purple appears when the question of the existence of beige has been answered and the coping mechanism of purple is activated. The capacity to build a community or a family or a tribe emerges. People in purple are extremely concerned about safety and security.

In purple identity is defined differently from what we find in traditional textbooks. The self is defined in terms of others. The elder, chief or father plays a prominent role in the community.

The elders provide wisdom and experience to the community members who acknowledge an audience with the senior by making them gifts of money and spirits. What for other worldviews may appear to be a bribe, for purple it is good manners. When those who do not have take from those who have, it is definitely not considered to be corruption.

The individual does not express his or her own needs in purple. This fact has a major impact for OCD-identity work. A deep mythology ties the community together. A family or tribe can act as a unit under stress. The social structure often overwrites the corporate structure in organisational life. There is however a residue of danger in purple. When tribal forces are unleashed, exceptional cruelty and brutality may manifest. This may appear like a fight for survival or to the death. One must know the mere fact of organising in a tribe implies that others outside the tribe are excluded.

The organising scheme of purple is circular, as can be seen in the figure above. In sociology we use a triangle to indicate a male and a circle to indicate a female. Typically in purple the community is organised in circles around the elder or chief, and the needs of this chief are served. It might even be the mother and children who serve every need of the father. In South Africa today, in Indian communities, the mother and father are honoured. Even today, in a traditional Zulu family, a highly-qualified daughter will keep her eyes lower than that of her mother and father. She will sit lower than her parents and not leave the room before she is dismissed.

Purple can smell intent. In Ghana, at the international airport in Accra, a big placard states that if you are a paedophile you should please go away, as children should be protected. If you come with bad intent, purple becomes non-responsive. A person who comes with a good heart will be lovingly accepted, and may even be treated as an angel (just maybe the stranger was sent by God and therefore we must be hospitable).

There are self-organising rhythms in purple, but everything does not necessarily happen according to a clock or a calendar. A great deal of consultation has to take place before a collective decision can be made. This self-organising is visible in observing the traffic in India, Brazil, Tanzania or Egypt. With relatively few accidents, and almost no control from authorities, the system works for itself, and patterns emerge out of chaos.

The question of existence in purple is: how can we sacrifice the self for the tribe?

The reader should note that in contrast with the beige question that was posed in the form of "How can I achieve?" the question now becomes a sacrificial one.

Example of purple

A Sotho executive woman stops daily at the local garage to change into either corporate wear to go the boardroom or into traditional wear to take up her role as submissive wife and daughter in her social setting.

Implications of purple for OCD practitioners

Rites of passage are an important part of purple. Initiations mark the various life stages. OCD consultants can use this innate need of purple for ritual and apply it to significant events like promotions, new strategies and achievements.

Laubscher and the author (2015) conceptualised Africa as being purple in the book *Indigenous Knowledge Systems at Work*. They explain that purple has a copying analogue thinking system. This means that in order to enable purple to be productive, examples must be given repetitively in the form of stories, or metaphors. In this system relationships come first.

Purple learns visually, kinaesthetically and through repetition. This nature of Purple has significant implications for OCD practitioners. Learning and development should consider this in designing organisational training interventions. Organisational strategists should take this into account when translating strategy. Communication strategies should design internal branding messages and communication by taking these dynamics into account. It has implications for how we reward, how we motivate and how we lead. Ultimately it has implications for key organisational focus areas such as customer-centricity, patient care or safe behaviour.

Applying the demographic distribution of South Africa to organisational life, it may be assumed that at least 60% of the average organisation consists of people with this thinking system. OCD consultants and business leaders should translate strategies in purple through visible leadership, speaking in metaphors and remembering the collective nature of their people.

RED

 In order to break away from the family, the traditional way of doing things, red needs a high level of energy. In the book *Inclusive Organisational Transformation*, The author (2014) argued that red was needed for the process of individuation. Red emerges when people begin exploring who they are if they are not defined by their culture.

Laubscher (2013) explains that as an expressive, individual system red is self-driven with an expressive energy and a fast rhythm. Decisions are made without considering the unintended consequences or evaluation of the risks. Instant gratification is the order of the day. The Arab Spring is an example of red social uprising, This red energy is a pre-requisite for breaking free from the collective unconscious that is characteristic of purple, the author (2014) stated.

Red has a gang-like archetype. The person with the most power is the boss. The strongest survive. It is as if red can smell fear, and power dynamics are constellated at an unconscious level. The person with the most power is the big boss. He or she takes the decisions. In its low form, it can be described as bullying behaviour. The only way to deal with a bully is to shift the power dynamics – to draw your line and then not run away.

Communication is from the top down only. Big bosses work through other bosses who drive the masses. Red displays visible power, has a need for attention (whether good or bad) and wants to be noticed. These aspects have real implications on manifested behaviour. Bling is worn to differentiate the individual from the group, for example, cheap bling, fake-branded goods, shiny alloy wheels on cars, and rhinestones on pants and jackets.

The question of existence for red is: how can I get power?

Example of red

The organisation launches an incentive scheme that chooses the employee of the month. This only works for red. Purple does not want to stand out from the group. Red however enjoys the attention. Performance must be managed against contract.

The red manifestation in the South African Parliament in 2015 where the Economic Freedom Front (EFF) challenged current leadership's authority is an example of this thinking system. A loss is experienced when red rejects its purple roots, and views it as being backwards. Splits occur, since purple people want to their children to remain unspoiled by the world, and to return to the traditional ways of living.

In the case of a South African organisation where Laubscher worked in the 1990s, the management decided to fire the red people as they were identified as troublemakers. Productivity declined significantly. Red energy is needed to self-start daily to achieve short-term goals.

Implications of red for OCD practitioners

About 15% of employees in organisations are red. This may appear to be self-centred, demanding and entitled. If low red can evolve into high red, warrior-like, strong behaviour can emerge.

Differentiated, stratified remuneration and reward strategies may be designed to include all the different niches. For red, it is important to paint a situation where the individual can feel a sense of power and achievement – in a short time spent. Daily and weekly goals work very well in red.

Purple people are organised around the leader (as can be seen in the purple archetype above). Often a red person is this leader. If purple does not trust management, they revert back to red unions to negotiate on their behalf. Building trust relations in organisations can lead to a situation where management is trusted so much that the functionality of the unions may be compromised.

However, unions can play a valuable role in collective societies. By shifting the role of unions away from being the voice of the people to forming an integrated part of business decisions through a process of co-determination, the pure intent of employee representation and unionism can emerge, and find its rightful place around decision-making tables.

Interstate Bus Lines in Bloemfontein is an example where workers trusted their leadership to such an extent that they did not join a national strike. A process of co-determination was facilitated, and three different unions were involved in co-creating strategy going forward. Different organisational structures and forums were designed to facilitate shared decision-making. Currently a post-doctoral study is being compiled on the topic of co-determination in co-operation with the senior human resource practitioner of Interstate Bus Lines, Henk van Zyl. The legal expert is Marthie Bloem and Mandala Consulting provides a matrix for determining the spiral dynamics distribution and facilitating the OCD interventions to build trust. In this way red power is minimised in the form of strikes or stay-away claims, but is rather wired around organisational strategies. Co-determination may just provide an evolution in how organised labour interacts with business.

BLUE

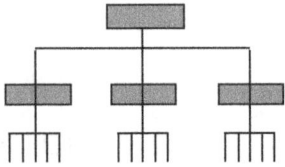

Sometimes, when crises present themselves, individuals adapt a new thinking system, which is blue. A move away from the perceived arrogance of red results in a need for blue rules and regulations and the emergence of another collective system. For about 10% of the people in South Africa and other emerging economies, doing the right ethical things becomes important. In first-world countries this percentage is higher.

For blue, organisational structures make sense. Rigid rules apply. Power is assigned not in the individual but in the formal role. A tight ship is managed through delegation and control. Expectations are documented in appointment letters and job descriptions and managed according to key performance areas in formal performance conversations.

Long-term strategies are contracted that are translated into policies and procedures. Compliance is important. Ethical standards are non-negotiable. It is not proper to jump organisational hierarchical boundaries. Life happens in a controlled rhythm. Blue has a conservative risk profile. Communication goes up and down according to the organisational structure. Emphasis on the collective is visible. Energy is subdued.

The reader can overlay the structured blue archetype over the self-organising circular structure of purple to understand one slice of the problem that different thinking systems present to leadership in organisations.

By summarising purple and red together (about 80% of the people), and realising that in the lower ranks of organisations we often find this distribution in our organisations, the universal leadership dilemma becomes clear. Blue management must get purple and red in organisations to execute organisational strategies, behaviour-based safety initiatives and quality control systems, and to achieve production efficiencies. This is indeed a daunting task.

Blue dislikes red's ego-centricity, and wants to "fix" purple-perceived unproductivity. OCD practitioners can be of great assistance here. Business leaders in emerging economies must learn how to translate blue strategies into purple and red to achieve shared understanding and facilitate buy-in into organisational strategies.

Question of existence of blue: how can we sacrifice self for the future?

Examples of blue

An advertisement on a South African television-broadcast announced that if you wanted to visit a place where everything worked, you had to go to Zurich. A young Swiss-German boy was asked how it felt to live in a place where everything worked. His response was: "If you do what they want, all goes well."

A learning and development expert emigrated to Australia. She changed a light bulb that went out during a training session, and was given a disciplinary hearing for intervening with the electrician's job. In blue we need to follow the rules.

In a mining case study on a sustainable transformational attempt in Ghana, published in the book *Inclusive Organisational Transformation*, the author (2014) shares how a purple workforce can be wired around blue strategies, in this case behaviour-based safety, with long-term sustainable effect. The use of story-telling, industrial theatre and the co-creation of strategy have been successful in achieving increasing levels of productivity, higher levels of employee engagement and better safety indicators.

When sharing the above line of thought with purple executives in Ghana, the response was: "You brunies (westerners with white skins who come over the water), you make things so difficult. If you want to have guests, you make your houses warm." Blue does not do 'warm' spontaneously. In fact it creates a cold culture that one can feel when walking in the streets of Paris, Zurich or Munich. How sad it is that when blue efficiencies occur, spirit or soul seem to be suppressed.

Implications of blue for OCD practitioners

Typically, organisations have blue strategies, structures and policies. OCD practitioners should assist blue leaders to translate in beige, purple and red. Stratified systems thinking can assist strategic consultants through the alignment of business plans and actions. Different time frames of discretion are considered. For example, by ensuring that there are daily goals, weekly and monthly targets, quarterly and yearly goals and two- to five-year modelling, space is created for various thinking systems in which to function.

It is critically important to understand the human-niche distribution in the organisation, as it should inform the culmination and positioning of all organisational strategies and initiatives. The facilitation of diversity of thought interventions, based on spiral dynamics and other diversity factors can assist greatly in understanding that people who think and organise differently from us, are not necessarily malicious, deliberate or unintelligent.

Most organisations in South Africa, Africa and other emerging countries have a large component of purple people. They have a customer-stakeholder perspective or community perspective in their strategies. The gift that purple brings is relationships and a deep wisdom of human relatedness. How one-sided we are by thinking that we can drive our customer satisfaction indexes by focusing on the number of customers' complaints and variance reporting. In fact, under our very blue plans, we are sitting on purple gifts of good relationships and caring. What might happen when OCD can focus energy on unleashing the gifts of purple in line with blue strategies for the benefit of the whole?

Blue systems will, however, unconsciously continue to try and change purple into blue versions of themselves. The fact that purple people think differently from blue people, does not mean that they are not thinking.

ORANGE

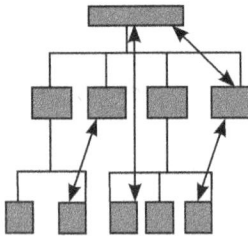

Sometimes the blue constraints become claustrophobic to some individuals. An I-system emerges. This is different from red in the sense that it has a long-term vision, and takes calculated risks that are not visible risk. It wants to achieve success, which is often defined in materialistic terms. Orange has an individualistic rhythm that is on the lookout for opportunities and events that can contribute to its status.

Orange has an organising archetype that is enterprising. Orange individuals will contract with their organisation. They will negotiate. They will give their all if there is an upside in it for them. They will trade their time at the organisation to get something (often financial) back.

Orange people enjoy the finer things in life. They find the conservative blue reasoning process stuffy, and will negotiate and reject conditions that do not serve them. Companies need orange thinking to make money for the stakeholders. It is important that blue and orange components in organisations are aware of the diversity of thought in terms of collectivistic blue and individualistic orange. Orange without blue can be very opportunistic. Blue without orange will make efforts to save now to get later. They do not diversify or innovate.

Only a small percentage of employees in organisations are orange. However, Laubscher and the author (2014) found that 85% of top managers in South Africa are blue and orange, while 90% of workers are beige, purple and red. The international leadership challenge becomes even clearer. We have no choice but to work more inclusively and to translate very deliberately. Leaders must be fluent in spiral-dynamics language and understand the dynamics of different thinking systems to speak in colour.

Question of existence: how can I conquer the material word and be successful?

Example of orange

An orange leader in the South African mining sector recently acquired a mine that was managed by a blue CEO. The CEO disinvested because the perceived risks were too high. The gold price was at an all-time low and the South African labour culture seemed too risky. Furthermore, the assumption was made that purple people in South Africa could not be as productive and compliant as employees in First World countries.

But the new orange CEO achieved exponential growth with the same assets and the same employees in a difficult economic and labour environment. This was done by understanding the various thinking systems in the organisation and by designing an organisational structure and processes that were congruent with the internal DNA.

During his reign as a president of South Africa, Thabo Mbeki showed a lovely orange thinking system, and a highly-developed orange international philosophy was created. However, the thinking was too far removed from the purple majority. The populace wanted their leader to be closer to them and to be more relational. Business leaders in South Africa and emerging economies run the same risk today. If orange is not aware of the impact of not translating their thoughts to the rest of the system, they run the risk of being viewed in the same way as Mbeki.

Implications of orange for OCD practitioners

A clear understanding of orange dynamics may assist OCD practitioners in presenting the return on investment (ROI) of OCD interventions in an orange manner. In orange, the leader speaks about how to optimise the business, how to make money and how to sweat the assets. They easily will say what is dysfunctional and what can be re-engineered – sometimes to the determined of organisational culture. Orange messages should be buffered, as they appear hard, opportunistic and arrogant to the more conservative and polite blue thinking system.

Lifestyle choices are important to orange. There is a very different thinking system about working to have time off, especially in purple. Purple people work to live in purple. OCD consultants should consider this when conducting traditional engagement studies that are not validated in multi-cultural settings. Other aspects such as trust are also differently viewed in different niches. Often, purple will say they cannot put trust in man, they trust Allah or the Lord. By being oblivious towards how different thinking systems construct meaning of individual and organisational psychological constructs, blatant generalisations can be made. Engagement and climate studies can present skewed data and one-sided information, thereby creating more dysfunctional dynamics than they attempted to solve in the first place.

OCD consultants have a very specific task in multi-cultural settings: to decode the complexity of diversity of thought. Orange asks: how do we make money? Blue asks: what processes and systems can we implement to minimise risks? Red asks: what can I get out of it? Purple asks: what can we get for our families? (For example, overtime as purple must take care of an extended family network.) Beige only has the capacity to ask: what do I need to survive today? A niche is etched out for OCD practitioners with a psychological background, namely that of excelling through inclusivity at synthesising different worldviews around organisational strategies.

5.5 CONCLUSION

This chapter dealt with human niches that are driven by fear. Beige is fearful that it will not survive. Red is fearful that it will lose power, blue is fearful that there will not be enough for the future and orange is fearful that it will lose material wealth. Although theoretically green can also fit into the first tier, and therefore may have the question of existence driven by fear – namely the fear to be excluded; it also is the first thinking system that is concerned with inclusivity, and allows the different thinking systems in an effort for all to be equal. For the purpose of this book and the specific focus on inclusivity, green is presented in the next chapter.

6

HUMAN NICHES – SEEING IN COLOURS

SECTION 2: The second tier – worldviews of being

We learn nothing, really, except what marks the wax, which is soft and warm but cold enough for the tracing to endure, adaptive to the point of death but stopping short of it: to write, I read from my flayed skin rather than copying parchments from the library. These days I trust this memory more than data banks, an author speaks for himself. I write on my skin and not on that of others who would answer for me, as Bonnard paints on and exhibits it without shame. I decipher my wrinkles, the engravings of time, written with a stylus; my soul hants this inscription-covered hide.

Michel Serres, 2012

6.1 Introduction

In the previous chapter, human niche dynamics were introduced. Here the remaining systems are discussed. These systems are i) green, a system where humanity strives for peace and inclusivity; ii) yellow, a system that is chaotic, yet where underlying order asks for functionality and iii) turquoise, a system that is carefully balanced with a focus on transpersonal living, collective consciousness and energy field-awareness.

The human niches as described in this chapter correlate with Lawrence Kohlberg's (1973) social contract (green), principled conscience (green/yellow) and transcendence morality (turquoise), says Keith E Rice.

Typically, green is typically not presented with yellow and turquoise as it belongs to the first tier of the spiral, and not the second tier. However, as this book focuses on inclusivity and the thinking system of green focuses on this specific aspect, it is discussed here.

GREEN

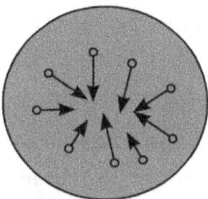

Some individuals may sometimes feel that orange people are too materialistic and self-absorbed. A more philanthropic thinking system emerges. Green wants to give back. It organises for mutual benefit. All are perceived as being equal.

The green archetype does not have one leader in the middle. Leaderless groups emerge with a humanistic growth purpose. The people take decisions in a group. In green there is frequent communication at all levels. The emphasis is placed on reaching consensus. There is sensitivity for the feelings of all participants and the human needs of employees.

Green has little concern for status or privilege. In fact, they often reject orange. Blue is too rigid for green, whereas red is viewed as totally too aggressive. Green and purple have similar circular organising structures. Yet, in the green archetype there is no leader in the middle, and the question of existence shifts from the tribe to the world. Green has a lower, yet accommodating rhythm. It is slower, as it needs to reach inclusivity by way of consultation.

Questions of existence of green: how can we sacrifice self for the world?

Example of green

Angelina Jolie, Microsoft's Bill Gates and Bono of U2 show evidence of a green philanthropic nature – one of giving back. Sometimes, however, individuals are green but they have not solved orange, and no longer have any commercial intent.

In a big international mining company one leader displayed a green thinking system. He was so popular in the local community that they honoured him by making him a chief. However, the orange people found him indecisive and scared. Every time he received additional information he adopted a different viewpoint. He understood where everyone came from. This made him seem fickle to his orange subordinates. His blue subordinates viewed him as not giving enough structure and too relational. The purple people loved him.

Laubscher and Beck were instrumental to the facilitation of the South African Constitution at a green level (Laubscher 2013). Internationally, this constitution is viewed as one of the best there can be. However, it may be too vague for people whose heads calculate more digitally.

Implications of green for OCD practitioners

OCD consultants often have green hearts. For them the question of existence is often how to make thinking people grow, and how to involve everyone. It is important that OCD consultants actively engage in continuous self-development, that they attend international conferences, develop their theoretical understanding and deepen their psychological understanding. The need to incorporate all may, however, lead to a lack of judgement on what is good for the whole.

Often green leaders want to become involved in corporate social investment initiatives. They don't do this for triple bottom-line purposes, but because they want to give back. A philanthropic intent evolves.

Growth groups and humanistic facilitation have green roots. The same applies to Rogerian facilitative processes and process work. It may be too soft, open-ended and idealistic for orange and blue business leaders. Psycho-analytical facilitation works very well in red and Skinner-Watson or NLP processes in blue. Jungian psychology has a stratified application, so it works well in purple as it remembers the basic roots. For red and orange people it facilitates the individuation process. Its archetypal nature also makes sense in green.

Green becomes accepting of different approaches, different religions and different cultures. Diversity work can be facilitated from a purple view where cultures are shared, a red object-psychological way, a blue legislative-orientated way where we must do the right thing to comply, an orange way where the business imperative is stressed or a green way, where differences are appreciated and accepted. A yellow way can also be followed, as described in the next section.

YELLOW

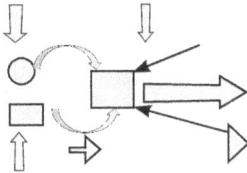

Green has an egoless architecture. However if green thinking can no longer make sense of changing life conditions, yellow may emerge. Here, the individual is attempting to find his or her voice again. Laubscher (2013) remembers how Graves explained to her that yellow was beige to the square. It is a way of saying that it is a survival system again, yet this time on a much more complex level of how the world can survive.

Green has a need to include everyone (maybe not the red people who are viewed as egocentric, nor the orange people who are seen as materialistic). They will, however, attempt to include all, and become very saddened and disillusioned if not everyone buys into the idealistic view of equality. Yellow thinking is different in this regard. It truly can celebrate the gifts of beige, purple, red, blue, orange and green. It can celebrate the gifts of all thinking systems, yet at the same time become aware of its own viewpoints. This unique ability may also paralyse yellow thinkers to the degree where they want to shout out loudly for help!

Yellow may become very angry if others do not see the patterns. They are outcome-orientated, and have functional thinking. They communicate only when needed. They adapt their structuring of a situation according to the external environment. They see cause and effect and consult on the leverage point, long before others see the dilemma at hand.

Question of existence of yellow: how can you and I survive?

Example of yellow

I had the wonderful opportunity of meeting and journeying with a political leader last year. I have no political agenda, as my field of study is multi-cultural psychology, and is inclusive of different political and even religious viewpoints. However, I travelled closely with Dr Mamphela Ramphele during the last election from a leadership perspective.

Dr Ramphele had a self-organising stance during the 2014 elections in South Africa. She became very aware of what was happening in South Africa, and could see the gifts of the various thinking systems. She was so moved by the disconnection between worldviews that she felt obliged to form Agang, a political party that focused on providing alternative solutions and minimising the side-effects created by the ANC, the EFF and the DA.

Dr Ramphele had never before been involved with party politics, but was moved enough to invest her pension fund in forming Agang, and at age 67 took on the challenge of saving South Africa. Around her she appointed blue, orange and green advisors, all with different opinions on how Agang could achieve its philosophy.

One of her closest advisors was an elderly white Afrikaans male. He asked very difficult ethical questions, and she responded very patiently to these. She also visited various rural towns. When she was speaking to purple people, she unconsciously took on the role of an elder. Her eyes went down, she connected and spoke purple. She always left a sense of magic behind.

In her meetings with red people, Dr Ramphele changed her posture. Then she strictly dictated how things would be done. However, she displayed huge compassion for the red youth. Here she would challenge them to take up their power and assist in sorting out South African problems. She very comfortably spoke blue to the Afrikaner Vryheidsbeweging (blue) and to other more traditionalist groups. In dealing with business leaders she put on her orange power suit and challenged them cognitively. Her green heart did not miss an opportunity to teach and support selflessly and to invest time and management in educating our youth, liberating our women and motivating the populace.

Her yellowness became very clear the day after the election. The polls predicted a 6% vote for Agang. The results showed a disappointing 1%. Everyone was scared to call her: the red people were angry, the blue people felt they lost, the orange people started to ask questions about money. I called her the morning after the election, with the intent of doing some trauma counselling, and I was utterly surprised by her response.

Very calmly and maturely she explained to me that this was the democracy for which she had given her youth, and that we all should accept the results as coming from the people. She did say, however, that she knew she was not a politician but an activist in her heart.

A few months later, she was a speaker at the Society for Industrial & Organisational Psychology South Africa (SIOPSA) conference. She opened the large group conversation by saying: "I am a failed politician, but an active lover of my country." She went on to explain that she was in love with South Africans, who were her people, but that now that the blinkers had fallen off, she was no longer a naïve teenager, but a mature lover of her country. She left the session's audience in awe of the greatness of true yellow leadership, and everyone there was touched.

Nelson Mandela, our beloved Madiba, had a similar impact on people. He truly could connect with everyone on the spiral, everyone in our diverse rainbow nation.

Implications of yellow for OCD practitioners

Beck (2011) passionately argues that we need YELLOW leadership to weave together new questions that will result in different societal, political and economic structures. These must be leaders who can deal with the complexity of synthesising the different thinking systems together and leaders who can apply functional thinking to systemic problems. He continues on every single opportunity to say that only in South Africa the various thinking systems are presented naturally, and if the world is looking for new solutions, answers will come from our beloved country.

OCD practitioners and business leaders alike should strategise from yellow and speak in colours. By somehow removing oneself from the internal dilemmas, one can see the systemic interplay and leverage points in the system. Inclusivity as a radical organisational philosophy discussed in chapter 2, can provide a methodology to interweave the gifts of the different value systems into a beautiful multi-coloured tapestry.

All strategies should be translated to ensure shared understanding in organisational systems. This may bring about differentiated, stratified approaches to all practices in organisations. Congruence also becomes increasingly important.

TURQUOISE

The global soul: a small, deep place, not far from the region of the emotions. The local, storm-prone, surface soul: a viscous lake, ready to flare up, on which the multiple, rainbow-colored, slowly changing light plays...

Michel Serres, 2012

According to Laubscher (2013) turquoise is purple to the square. Every experience is reflected on and is viewed as a personal message to learn from. A deep sense of empathy is felt and turquoise senses a connection with all forms of life – even interplanetary life. Therefore turquoise has a deep sense of intuition. This intuition often is interpreted by purple as being psychic. Turquoise is concerned with energy flow in themselves and others and do their work on this domain. Often the need for using words and talking disappears.

Question of existence for turquoise: how can we collectively sacrifice for the cosmos?

Example of turquoise

During a conference on studying spiral dynamics at the Adizes Business School where Beck lectures, a delegate did not speak for a week. On approaching her to inquire why she was so quiet, someone touched her hand. She reacted by saying that words were not needed, as she could feel it in the body. It later became known that this lady was the head of integrated health in a state in America. In this state, clinical medical physicians formed communities of practice. Reiki, kinesiology, iridology and other forms of alternative medicine were integrated with scientific methods in an effort to move away from chronic medicine in favour of natural alternatives.

The dynamics in the movie Avatar can be studied to obtain a sense of the turquoise thinking system. We will meet each other in the collective unconscious, where words have lost their functionality, and where collectively we are concerned about our cosmos.

Implications of turquoise for OCD practitioners

It is highly unlikely that turquoise will find its space into the corporate sphere. However, in individual leaders there may be some turquoise residue. Here and there leaders may declare that they manifest what they need, and where indigenous knowledge and Western logic are integrated, the results are an exponentially more complex sense of self, others and the galaxy.

This chapter of the book touches on alternative modalities to incorporate intervention attempts in OCD to show how turquoise solutions can find their way into blue organisations.

Clare Graves (1974) explained that leadership was contextual. The best leader is the congruent one. The author (2014) documented an integral approach to determining congruence. In chapter 11 a discussion is presented on how to determine congruence of diversity of thought and the systemic problem at hand.

6.2 Shadow niches

The author (2014) integrated Jungian psychology with spiral dynamics and the human niches theory. Carl Jung's construct of the shadow was comprised of the denied aspects of the self (1954). An antonym within itself, it defines the wisdom not only to understand the origin and potential for inner conflict, but the very solution to preventing their emergence in the first place.

In the opposites lies an inherently incompatible binary relationship. Every niche has an opposite archetypal niche. Laubscher (2013) describes the opposite archetypal states for each human niche. On the positive side, each niche or thinking system results in gifts. By demonstrating the gifts that the specific thinking systems present in an inclusive manner that shares personal metaphors, narratives and stories, the imbalances in what is viewed as being less evolved or more so, are marginalised.

However, there are also side-effects to every niche. Beige people may exclude themselves from society. Purple may harbour superstitions and be non-responsive. Even in 2015, witch-hunts are going on – the recent killings of women in Tanzania are evidence of this.

Laubscher (2013) describes red as egocentric, aggressive, domineering and exploitive on the one side, but hero-like and warrior-like on the other. Boko Haram's terror reign is an example of this. The dysfunctional side to red is described as low red in human niche terminology. The lovely energy that red radiates is referred to as high red. The same principle applies to all the different human niches.

Low blue implements rules and forms, resulting in an organogram as an organising structure (refer chapter 5). Strategies are implemented for the sake of implementation. Checklists become the focus rather than the philosophy behind it. Blue manifests in organisations where performance management is reduced to yearly KPA meetings only. Organisations are driven by customer complaints, rather than by understanding how customer satisfaction and delight are maximised.

The side-effect of low orange is that it is viewed as materialistic and overly concerned with what it can conditionally get from a situation. This is done with almost fatalistic risk taking (where blue compliance and sureties are ignored). The credit crunch at the end of the last decade in America was an example of this.

In the low form green is indecisive and non-committal. It focuses on having some calling or other one in life – often not systemically understanding all the causal implications – leading to a narrow attention to a course, to the exclusion of others. The reductionalistic nature of this thinking system strips away the green gift of inclusivity and its philanthropic nature.

The shadow side of yellow is that it can become irritated with other systems for not seeing the systemic patterns. Further, it can be so self-organising that there is no structure. Low yellow can disappear into their own world, without manifesting the ability to use the super powers in themselves and others of beige, purple, red, blue, orange and green. It may be very confusing to others. An example is the lady who never ate curry. On a trip to India with her husband, however, she ate curry every day – much to his dismay. Yellow thinkers do things contextually.

Lastly, the shadow manifestation of turquoise is esoteric. It loses the need to use words. An alternative reality is experienced.

6.3 Spiral and integral theory

In the book *Inclusive Organisational Transformation* (2014), the author synthesises integral theory as described by Ronnie Lessem and Alexander Schieffer, with spiral dynamics. It is important to note that in this interpretation the unit of study is ontological, not pragmatic. The integral approach is indicated in figure 6.1 below.

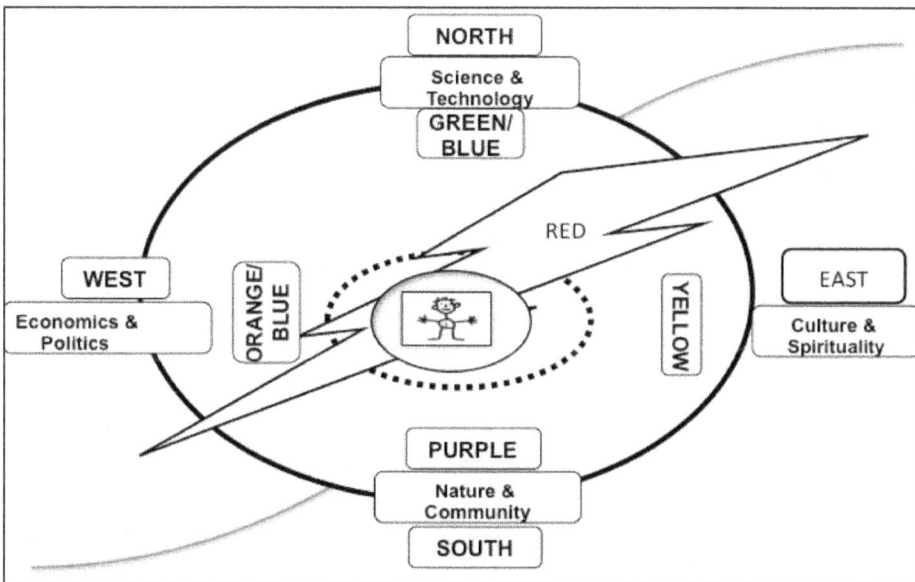

Figure 6.1 Integration – human niches with integral theory, Viljoen (2015, p. 124)

Ronnie Lessem and Alexander Schieffer (2010) write in *Integral Research* that a person must depart from the south in a research or reflective leadership journey. Here, an individual grounds themself in their story. The author (2014) added purple to the functionality of the south. Here people remember their roots.

Red energy is needed to break away from the tribe. The thunder in the middle of the figure is indicative of this transformation. As with all the shadow niches, low red has the power to be a destructive force – both individually and collectively. However, if red matures, it becomes individualised.

In the integral approach, a person must then go east, where an ethnographic experience of culture and spirituality is explored. It becomes important to understand the containing system in which the individual finds themself. In systems thinking analysis Russell Ackoff also supports the social understanding of the containing system. Eastern philosophy is yellow in essence.

Going north equips an individual with theoretical applications, models and methodology. Here, scientific assumptions and lessons learned from nature can ground the transformational journey by triangulating it. Blue and green thinking are prevalent here.

Last, the lessons learned from the south, east and north must be applied in the west. The impact here is pragmatic and focused on the *doing*. The thinking is orange in nature. Economics and politics are applied here.

Carl Jung (1953) decades ago stressed the importance of integration and assigned the mandala as a symbol thereof. The Lessem-Schieffer integral approach can assist an individual to incorporate other worldviews even if he or she is currently displaying a particular thinking system. The next part of the chapter underlines the importance of designing OCD initiatives from an integral approach.

6.4 Designing from yellow

Beck has a wonderful way of metaphorically explaining the dilemma that presents itself, by having his groups recite the following rhyme:

> *Humpty Dumpty sat on a wall,*
> *Humpty Dumpty had a great fall.*
> *All the king's horses and all the king's men*
> *Couldn't put Humpty together again.*

Beck (2013) looks towards the rainbow nation of South Africa, where all the different human niches are present, to come up with the solution for mankind. It is clear that purple tribalism, red dictatorship, blue authoritarian political structures and democracy, orange capitalism and green socialism all have serious side effects, and do not provide the stratified solutions the world need. Every one of these human niches solves specific problems of certain life conditions. However, new problems are also created as a new niche emerges.

The author (2014) proposes that the international leadership challenge is that orange and blue leaders must reach orange and blue business strategies through red and purple people.

In societies – as in organisations – the challenge for leadership is to find ways to wire together the different thinking systems that exist, around a common goal. Together we must put Humpty Dumpty together again. In proofreading the script of this book, Dr Marthie de Kock commented, tongue-in-cheek, that we should rather build a new Humpty Dumpty: she may just be right. By co-creating a future world that is integral and inclusive, we may just construct the future that we all want.

We need to design from yellow – from a space where the gifts of the different thinking systems can be woven together in an inclusive manner to create the best possible condition for all. OCD consultants have a very important role to play here.

First, in the strategic design phase, consultation is needed about the function and reasoning of the different thinking systems. In the translation of strategy through the systems, leaders must be enabled to speak in colours. Lastly OCD interventions should not focus on attempting to make a shift, for example, for purple people to become blue, but rather on how we can get purple to play blue. Learning and development practitioners can incorporate insight into spiral dynamics in constructing strategic learning architecture, and should focus on how the high version of each human niche can be developed, for example, how low red can be developed into high red. For this question, Laubscher (2013) offers a potential solution – go back to the basics. Teach traditional supervisory skills or planning, organising, leading and control theory.

6.5 Conclusion

It is critical to understand the different thinking systems or human niches in organisations. By consciously designing OCD interventions from an inclusive stance, OCD practitioners can ensure inclusivity that will lead to significance into the task at hand, that will result in an increase in positive business indicators. To determine the distribution of human niches in organisations or societies the instruments described in chapter 11 can be applied. Alternatively, the individual business leader or OCD practitioner can simply connect with their workforce by asking the question: "What is the biggest concern to you?"

The bio-psycho-socio nature of human niches stresses the importance for multi-disciplinary links between various theoretical fields. These include neuro-science, neuro-leadership, sociology, wellness, positive psychology, quantum-physics, behavioural sciences and consulting, IO psychology, consulting psychology and international psychology.

PART 3
NAVIGATING OCD – APPLIED

7

INCLUSIVE OCD METHODOLOGIES

Economists view talk as cheap and culture as insignificant. Yet human beings are talking animals ...
The talk probably matters. Why else would the human animals bother doing it?

Arjo McCloskey and Deidre Klamer, 1995:unknown

7.1 Introduction

In the previous chapter, the business case was presented in terms of the concept of inclusivity. This was a process during which the gifts and value-adding contributions of the individual, group and organisation in the context of both the relevant industry and society were systemically interwoven to enable the unleashing of inherent human potential. Specific methodologies can be applied to create an environment that is conducive to inclusivity, and these can be used during OCD interventions.

There is a specific ethos or underlying philosophy to all the methodologies that are discussed here. This ethos allows for different voices, and respects and values every person and every opinion. Different views are encouraged and sufficient time is allowed for group members to voice what they need to voice in a natural, spontaneous and authentic way.

The safe space created by these methodologies allows people the opportunity to become vulnerable, to expose development areas and to explore their defence mechanisms. An interplay of these methodologies can be used for weaving together an integrated inclusive OCD intervention, and this has the potential of contributing to sustainable organisational transformation through the creation of Inclusivity.

The methodologies of appreciative inquiry, dialoguing, storytelling and world café are discussed with the aim of providing an explanation of how inclusivity can be created. As the essence of these interventions is centred on crucial conversations and actual organisational dilemmas, it may contribute significantly to both organisational understanding and awareness. It may also enhance the probability that OCD interventions will be sustainable.

More than ever before, employees are stretched out, exposed and tired of participating in yet another strategic planning session, problem-solving process or team-building exercise. Therefore, great care must be taken not to implement change initiatives unnecessarily or mechanistically with a one-size-fits-all approach. A clear OCD strategy should encompass all initiatives and interventions. As discussed before, organisational transformation is always accompanied by cultural change. The question of how inclusivity can be created thus arises.

7.2 Appreciative inquiry (AI)

Appreciative inquiry refers to the ability of seeing what others cannot see, encouraging the sharing of different vantage points and focusing on the use of positive language in order to facilitate or unleash the positive energy of thought. It involves the heightening of the awareness of the value, strength and potential of both the self and others, and overcoming the limits that are imposed, often unconsciously, on one's own capabilities by the choice of language used to define the scenarios that are being described.

To a large extent, the fundamental methodology underlying appreciative inquiry was developed by Richard Barrett (2000). Gervase Bushe (1990) contributed significantly by refining the methodological process of appreciative inquiry that forms part of the OCD methodology. This is referred to as action research. Action research projects can be directed towards diverse goals, and therefore different variations of the technique are found. Appreciative inquiry represents a viable complement of the conventional forms of action research in that it does not attempt to deny the existence of problems and concerns, but prefers to seek a constructive solution by taking past successes into account and encouraging a feeling of accomplishment in members.

Appreciative inquiry is thus able to find effective solutions to current problems. A more empowered, open-minded attitude is encouraged. The mind is not permitted to be bogged down by allowing downward-spiralling, problem-focused and depressing discussions. This, in turn, energises a discussion-focused and action-planning session rather than deflating it, say Wendell French and Cecil Bell in their book on organisational development first published in 1999. During organisational change efforts, appreciative inquiry can be used for focusing on what is right rather than what is wrong in terms of the situation. As all members within the organisation typically engage in the appreciative inquiry process, it will obviously result in a sense of being included.

What is appreciative inquiry?

Appreciative inquiry is a vehicle for social innovation that aims at advancing the theoretical knowledge of consequence, say French and Bell (1999). It represents an alternative approach to problem-solving. Instead of identifying, analysing and solving problems, appreciative inquiry treats organisations as positive forces that are able to generate leverage beyond problem-centred focus points by directing the focus onto the strengths of the organisation.

By means of careful questioning, appreciative inquiry uncovers the strengths of the team or organisation, and these strengths are then used for changing the present scenario or planning the future more successfully. This approach focuses on solving real problems by focusing on strengths and future positivity. It avoids becoming bogged down by a negative, downward spiral. This negative spiral often leads to the identification of imagined or unrealistic problems by the group, owing to anxiety that is caused by fear of the negative. Appreciative inquiry deliberately focuses attention on what works, what is possible and what imbues an experience with vitality, Juanita Brown and David Isaacs (2005) suggest.

It assists in uncovering hidden assets, and, by focusing on aspects of the desirable future, it involves living in the now. Appreciative inquiry is an applicable methodology to be used during the feedback phase of organisational research, for example, in climate studies.

Core assumptions and principles

French and Bell (1999) summarise appreciative inquiry as qualitative, diagnostic research that focuses on the strengths within organisations, and which assists in co-creating shared understanding and meaning. The following four principles apply:

- Research of topics must begin with appreciation.

- Questions and foci must be applicable.

- Enquiry into scenarios must be provocative.

- Inputs generated must be collaborative and focused positively.

The interventions that are used in respect of the technique and methodology of appreciative inquiry consist of either small group discussions or organisational meetings. When applying appreciative inquiry, a researcher, in collaboration with the organisation, aims at identifying the most significant growth possibilities latent in the system that could be leveraged. For example, the inquiry might centre on one of the following:

- When did people attain the highest motivational levels in the life of the organisation?

- When did people feel the most fulfilled?

- What do staff members do to make themselves, their tasks, their team and the organisation successful?

Criteria for appreciative inquiry

The research enquiry must be a shared effort on the part of both the leadership and the stakeholders of the organisation. The problems and solutions must be relevant so that focus on learning and forward growth can take place. The focus must be client-centric and not expert-centric. In other words, the organisation must be the central focus, and this focus must not be on problems only, but also on strengths.

It is important that the right people are in the room. People who are directly impacted on, and those who have a mandate to do something about the task at hand, should participate.

The process of appreciative inquiry

According to Richard Barrett (2000), the steps of appreciative inquiry consist of data collection, reporting back on data to the target population, implications of the data studied and highlighted during the appreciative inquiry session, joint action planning to cater for interventions at all levels, third-party interventions and the re-measurement of data in order to ascertain growth and subsequent steps.

It is now widely accepted that the 4-D Cycle, as described by David Cooperrider, Margaret Wheatly and Jacqueline Stravros (2003), conceptualises the process of appreciative inquiry effectively. In Figure 7.1 below this process is visually explained.

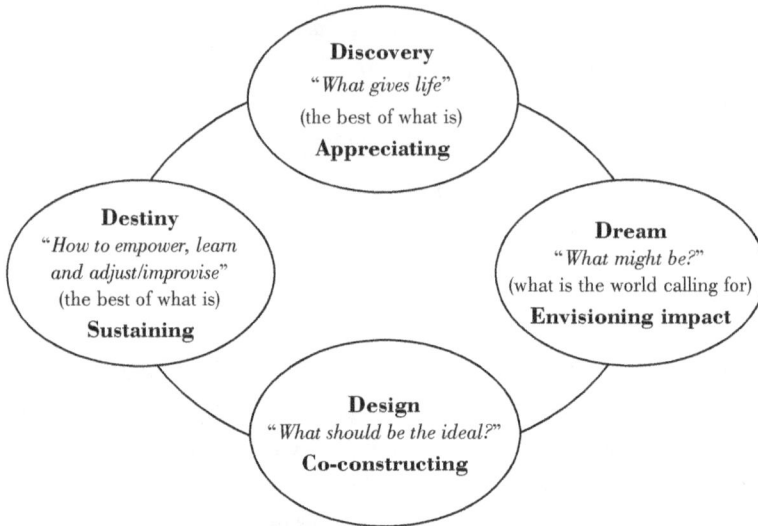

Figure 7.1   4D-process of appreciative inquiry, David Cooperrider, et al (2003:5)

During the discovery phase participants are requested to share past strengths and successes with one another. Effective questions to ask during this phase are the following:

- Why did you join this company in the first place?

- What made you successful so far on your journey?

- Why do you spend your precious life energy here?

- What made us successful in the past?

This type of question may lead to a sense of building on things that worked in the past and remembering innate goodwill that is often just skin deep.

During the next phase, the group dream together on what the future may hold. This could be compared to visioning. Creative tools may be used, such as working with clay, drawing, sculpting or vision boards. A shared picture of the future dream is co-constructed. Here, questions can include the following:

- Where do you see yourself in 10 years' time?

- What will be the best future vision of what you can be?

- What is the future that you would like to co-create?

- If you wake up 10 years from now, how should life manifest?

The next phase, the design phase, focuses on the part of the dream that the group as a whole want to make happen. Other methodologies could be incorporated here for co-creating a design or for continuing the inquiry at this stage. Balanced scorecard principles can be incorporated and strategy maps can be co-created. In this case, the following questions could be asked:

- What resources must you invest in today to ensure that you build your dream?

- At what internal processes must you excel to reach your dream?

- What must you do to satisfy your customer?

- How must you appear to your stakeholders?

- What do you need to enable your systems to reach your ideal future?

The final part is the delivery phase. Here different work-streams are allocated to different people. Project plans are co-created, and sponsors and project leaders are identified. Typical balance scorecards and/or performance measures may be used during this phase.

Appreciative inquiry versus typical organisational research approaches

The differences between appreciative inquiry and typical organisational research approaches are summarised in table 7.1.

Table 7.1 Appreciative inquiry versus organisational research
Adapted from Wendell French and Cecil Bell (1999)

Phase	Typical research	Appreciative Inquiry
Data collected	Management, small sample	All employees
Data reported to	Management, small sample	Everybody who participated Management
Implications of data	Consultant to advise management	Everybody works on implications

Phase	Typical research	Appreciative Inquiry
Third party Interventions	Consultant to facilitate interventions	Solutions co-created by client and consultant and implemented/ facilitated
Positive extent of change	Low	High

In view of the fact that appreciative inquiry is usually used as a qualitative research methodology it is compared to other types of research.

Critique regarding appreciative inquiry

As a result of its open, positive focus, appreciative inquiry is able to create a platform from which group flight behaviour can occur. However, as the intervention focus is primarily on strengths, and as the methodology is usually combined with other OCD interventions, this technique may add immense value.

It is extremely important to view appreciative inquiry as a research methodology that encourages other OCD interventions by means of which this initiative can be supported. If the problems that are identified within an organisation are not relevant, then using this methodology could be pointless.

Appreciative inquiry generates energy and anticipation within a system, and, if this energy is leveraged towards the shared future outcome, it may contribute significantly to alignment, enablement and transformation. Appreciative inquiry is a much-needed tool in the diverse South African environment.

7.3 Dialoguing

> *We are all connected and operate within living fields of thought and perception. The world is not fixed but in constant flux; accordingly, the future is not fixed, and so can be shaped. Humans possess significant tacit knowledge – we know more than we can say. The question to be resolved: how to remove the blocks and tap into that knowledge in order to create the kind of future we all want?*
>
> David Bohm, 1998: unknown

Peter Senge (1990) emphasises the importance of dialogue for generating collective learning. Shared meaning and commitment for the implementation of new routines can be established through dialoguing. David Bohm (1998) viewed thought as a tacit process, and was of the opinion that what was verbalised actually constituted a very small part of a person's wisdom or insight.

In the knowledge area it may be a competitive advantage if the tacit knowledge within the organisation is released. Dialoguing may assist in translating this tacit knowledge in originations, and this may lead to inclusion. In particular, dialoguing may be used during a change effort in order to create shared understanding and buy-in in terms of the new directions to be followed.

What is dialoguing?

Dialogue is the process that underpins the principles of systems thinking, explain Susan Mohrman, David Finegold and Janice Klein (2002). Bohm (1998) describes dialoguing as a form of free association for a group who have no predefined purpose in mind other than mutual understanding and the exploration of human thought. It allows for preconceptions, prejudices and patterns of thought to surface and become conscious.

According to Mohrman and colleagues (2002:11), dialogue refers to a conversation that connects multiple perspectives in order to enable the unit to "transcend deeply held individual and collective views and create new meaning that goes beyond any individual's previous understanding".

Bohm (1998) defines the process of dialoguing as "aimed at the understanding of consciousness per se, as well as exploring the problematic nature of day-to-day relationships and communication". The purpose of dialoguing is to transcend existing assumptions, to suspend own perceptions and to explore a phenomenon from various angles, therefore arriving at a more holistic, inclusive understanding of the issue at hand.

Core assumptions and principles

Connected awareness, a willingness to set aside agendas and judgements and a positive desire to examine a given topic from every possible perspective are all fundamental to dialoguing, according to Michelle LeBarOn (2005). The nature of dialoguing is illustrated in Figure 7.2. According to Bohm (1998), it is critical for dialoguing to have a crisis of meaning. Relationships between comments must be made visible. The group must be challenged to inquire into statements rather than to react from a judgemental stance.

The spirit of dialoguing is critical for it to be effective. According to LeBarOn (2005) there has to be a spirit of inquiry, release, witness, engagement, creative action, perspective and acknowledgement. It is important that participants adopt an ethnographic mind-set with openness to explore different viewpoints.

Dialoguing builds on the process of inquiry to explore the mental models of individuals and team members. The process may aid both learning and understanding on the part of the individual and of others, and may lead to communal agreement and potentially creative solutions. This approach develops personal and collective insights into the thinking processes, particularly when responses are conditioned and biased by needs, fears and desires, and are distorted by culture, race or gender.

Figure 7.2   The principles of dialoguing, adapted from David Bohm (1998)

Criteria for dialoguing

According to Bohm (1998), tremendous power would be generated if people were to think together in a coherent way. The object of dialoguing in teams would not be to analyse, win an argument or exchange opinions, but rather to suspend one's own opinions, to consider the opinions of others, to listen to them and to suspend them, and, finally, to understand what is entailed, explains Willem de Jager (2003). Sensitivity is crucial during dialoguing. The atmosphere created by the facilitator must ensure that members feel safe and that their opinions are validated.

Shared meaning is created through collective thought. The emphasis should be on awareness. The focus should be on the micro-cultural context, undirected inquiry and impersonal fellowship. The paradox of "the observer and the observed" presents itself during dialoguing, Bohm (1998) reminds us. Dialoguing must be applied when shared understanding is the projected outcome, and may be applied in order to enhance inclusivity.

The process of dialoguing

Groups sit in a circle, as this is conducive to dialoguing. The whole group becomes a mirror for everybody – the effect each person has on the others is the mirror. The purpose is to communicate coherently and truthfully. Bohm (1998) points out that the way a dialogue group usually commences is by talking about dialogue, discussing why it is taking place, and what it means.

The leadership role is shared, and all members assume responsibility for the time, process and contents boundaries. In dialoguing nobody is trying to win. Everybody wins if anybody wins.

Michelle LeBarOn (2005) summarises the following steps for dialogue engagement, namely, to attend and assess, to suspend judgments, to engage with the other side, to reflect, to integrate and to inquire. A rain stick can be used to indicate how voice can be allocated to ensure equal participation. In an organisation the following questions may be effective for the purpose of dialoguing:

- Who are you?

- Where are you now?

- Where must you be?

- What can we do to make a difference?

In processes that focus on transformation, the following questions may shift consciousness:

- What if we replaced your exco team with the exco team of a successful firm in another industry?

- If an international shareholder took over your company, why should they keep you?

Alternatively, a thought-provoking statement may be made that rings close to home, such as: "This process is just more of the same and will not work."

It is important that leadership rotates and that the facilitator does not direct participants. Participants must attempt to build on viewpoints, and must try to understand hidden assumptions and worldviews.

Time, space and content boundaries provide psychological safety. The facilitator must contract these boundaries. The time boundary will bring the session to a close somewhere in the near future, and the discussions must be linked to the space where they were shared. The facilitator and group members should keep to the topic at hand.

Difference between dialoguing and other approaches

As a rule people find it difficult to communicate in a group. An opinion is an assumption, according to Bohm (1998), and people usually defend their opinions. People coming together from different cultures and sub-cultures, as in teams and organisations, will have different assumptions and different opinions, and this could lead to conflict and power games. During a dialoguing session members are challenged to stick to their assumptions, and not to suppress them but to carry them out. The leadership role is shared within the group, and everybody is treated equally.

The differences between dialoguing and discussion or debate are summarised in table 7.2. David Bohm (1998) explains that during dialoguing one is verbally dancing with other members of the group or one engages in fighting with style.

Table 7.2   Dialogue versus discussion and debate, De Jager, 2003

Dialogue	Discussion/debate
Build the whole among the parts	Break issues into parts
Seek connections between parts	Seek distinctions between parts
Inquire into assumptions	Justify/defend assumptions
Learn through enquiry and disclosure	Persuading, selling, and telling
Creation of shared meaning	Agreement on one meaning

Critique regarding dialoguing

It is sometimes difficult for a group to start dialoguing. The introverted members of the group will be challenged most, as introverts do not think aloud as extroverts do. However, there is a primate rhythm to a good dialoguing session, and group members will possess an inherent knowledge of the rules of the game.

Wolf-Michael Roth, Daniel Lawless and Kenneth Tobin (2000), stated that the application of dialoguing usually differed from what was anticipated. They applied dialoguing with great success and energy within a learning environment, and provided feedback on the positive outcome of personal development.

There is limited academic literature on the effectiveness of dialoguing. Mogobe Ramose (2000) criticised the technique of dialoguing, and labelled it as pretentious rather than enlightening. He was of the opinion that it did not achieve any real purpose. The researcher cannot help but wonder whether Ramose understood that the process of dialoguing is more important than the content, and that, subsequent to the dialoguing, the benefits of the shared understanding may often manifest at a later date when the altered paradigms influence the decision-making process within the organisation.

There is little academic evidence to prove the statement of David Bohm (1998) that "... it is proposed that a form of free dialogue may well be one of the most effective ways of investigating the crisis which faces society". Moreover, it may turn out that such a form of free exchange of ideas and information is of fundamental relevance to transforming culture and freeing it of destructive misinformation, so that creativity can be liberated.

The benefits of dialoguing are to be found in the shared understanding of a topic or strategy, enhanced empathy for different viewpoints and the innovative and creative solutions and insights that would have remained unconscious without the dialoguing effort. Future research may attempt to contribute to this field of study by documenting case studies (especially South African case studies), and by providing qualitative and quantitative evidence of the effectiveness of dialoguing.

7.4 Storytelling

Without the continuity of storytelling and the messages they contain from the leadership
of the group, the people of any tribe or corporation will forget who they are.

Max de Pree, 1989: unknown

Narratives can be used as a valuable lens for both understanding and managing organisations in the 21st century. They are often perceived as either ephemeral and relevant mainly to entertainment, or as something that only children enjoy and primitive societies engage in.

There is, however, a valuable application for storytelling in the new world of work. It often happens that the top executives in large corporations are hardly ever seen by their employees, say Juanita Brown and David Isaacs (2005), and stories about them could create confidence in the organisation. Every organisation seems to create stories (narratives) as a way of making sense of organisational life. The story related to new employees, the informal discussions during a break and the speech of the CEO during a video conference are all part of organisational storytelling. Narratives and storytelling constitute an obvious and central aspect of every functioning organisation. Cultural messages, Michelle LeBarOn (2005) reminds us, are passed down in stories.

What is storytelling?

Stories are the carriers of behavioural norms, and provide information on how to behave. According to Brown et al., (2005), people display remarkably stable behaviour over time and, although there are subtle changes, the continuity and endurance of behavioural norms owe much to stories.

Stories help to explain the social fabric of the organisation. Any discussion about an organisation that does not place narrative and storytelling at the centre is bound to be misleading and incomplete. Stories become embedded in legends and myths.

Stories about the past constrain behaviour in organisations. These stories may wield so much power that economists refer to this occurrence as path-dependency, implying that the road you take will determine where you go.

Stereotypes are created because human beings relate to stories about other human beings, according to Juanita Brown et al., (2005). Stories are one of the ways in which knowledge, such as social knowledge, is transmitted and therefore stories are critical in knowledge management strategies.

Storytelling may be applied with great success during the translation of strategy, or else archetypal stories may be used in growth processes. Storytelling can take many forms – it may be the managing director who addresses people with passion, someone with a life lesson could translate learning by means of his or her story, or the storytelling could form part of the creation of strategy or the translation of values. Employees can be taught how to write their own stories, or stories could be told dramatically through theatre, Henk du Plessis (2004) says.

Core assumptions and principles

People are able to recall something easily when it is told by way of a story. Karl Weick (1995) identifies the need to make sense of the organisation and the environment as the strongest impulse in many organisations. Just as a story needs context, say Brown et al., (2005), organisational stories refer to the organisation as it used to be at a specific time and place. Storytelling is one of the ways in which norms and values are transferred. Stories endure, and although the names referred to may change, the behavioural lessons remain the same.

Stories are salient. Purposeful storytelling can reach large numbers of people within a short space of time and is relatively cheap. Narratives communicate naturally as human nature reacts to authenticity and universal truths. Storytelling communicates collaboratively, persuasively, holistically, contextually, intuitively, entertainingly, interactively, emotively and kinetically in order to invoke action. Brown et al. (2005) state that storytelling spurs double-loop learning; reaching speedily into the deeper recesses of the psyche and changing values and attitudes. This methodology enables human beings to unlearn what they have been taught.

During transformational efforts storytelling can be used to create shared understanding so that listeners comprehend the reason for the change, to relate to the transition and to describe behaviour that is suitable to the new reality.

Criteria for storytelling

Juanita Brown et al. (2005) indicate that stories can be used for entertainment, conveying information, nurturing, promoting innovation, preserving organisations and also for changing organisations. Carl Jung (1954) described archetypal stories as stories that are not subject to the laws of time and space. So a person is able to experience a good story as if he or she has lived that story himself or herself.

Brown et al., (2005) maintain that the conventional view of communication is to ignore the internal dialogue within every individual. They state clearly that it is not the story that has the impact – it is the process of storytelling. A good story may be funny, clever or moving. A story has to be true to one's own sense of how things work. Storytelling can be used to translate tacit knowledge into consciousness. Stories must be understandable, told from the perspective of a single protagonist (a person who is in a situation typical of the organisation) and must convey a degree of strangeness, but must still be plausible and embody the change idea as fully as possible. The story should be as topical as possible to convey a sense of urgency.

Arvid Huss (2004) stresses the importance of authenticity during storytelling. Brown et al., (2005) state that the best story is true, is told in a minimalist way, and has a happy ending. They maintain that the storyteller must be passionate as he or she translates an emotive message with the story. A story must be true to one's own sense of how things work. When carried out correctly, storytelling is invisible to the listener. Storytelling can be used to translate tacit knowledge into conscious awareness and shared insight.

The process of storytelling

There are no definite steps in storytelling. It is, however, critical that shared experiences be created by the storytelling. It is valuable if the story is analysed after it has been related.

Within organisations stories can be told with great effect to translate norms, share visions and promote change initiatives. If a leader shares passionately from the self the audience will relate to the authenticity and respond emotively, suggest Brown et al., (2005). A good story is funny, clever or moving. It may be used to communicate complex ideas, motivate people to change, persuade people to work together, share knowledge, deal with rumours, transmit values and lead people to a shared outcome.

Storytelling can happen at individual level. Participants can be asked to tell their own story beginning with:

- Once upon a time...
- Then...
- Ever since that day...

Organisational storytelling can focus on the organisational strategy and values. Industrial theatre is a form of organisational storytelling.

For example, leaders in the organisation who share their own stories about how they managed to be ethical, or how they overcame serious challenges, can be viewed as inspirational. By sharing the organisational strategy in story format, shared understanding is created. The use of metaphor and stories that translate business principles into archetypal insights can be an excellent way of breaching cultural divides in multi-cultural systems.

Differences between storytelling and other approaches

Storytelling is how human beings share the expertise, reliability and trustworthiness of other people. Owing to the fact that organisational operations are increasingly becoming global, this perceived outcome becomes increasingly important.

Brown et al., (2005) state that there are no alternatives to telling stories – no other system or human resources department is able to take its place. Storytelling in person is intensely interactive, whereas other forms of communication are passive. Storytelling can assist people in perceiving reality in a new way.

Every person has a different way in which he or she hears a story, a different way of being engaged and of experiencing what is being told. Archetypal storytelling allows for the listener to interpret the story in his or her own way.

Tacit knowledge, which forms part of the intellectual capital of an organisation, can be identified as the most important resource in any organisation. So storytelling can be used with great success in organisations. It can ensure the translation of strategy and the creation of shared meaning, and, thus, significance and buy-in within organisations. The power of a story is unleashed through its application to the lives of the employees.

Critique regarding storytelling

Stories can be perceived as nebulous, ephemeral, subjective and unscientific. Much still needs to be done to convince traditional line managers that storytelling should form an integral aspect of their leadership skill set. Recognition of the importance of storytelling can constitute a challenge to leadership within the new economy of work.

Stories can be subjective, topic-specific or even culture-specific. In the book *Inclusive Organisational Transformation*, the author presents a case study where industrial theatre was the vehicle to sustainable transformation. In this Ghanaian case study, spiral dynamics theory was used to ensure the cultural understanding of the storytelling was congruent with local culture. Another case of industrial theatre in Tanzania failed due to humour used in the play that was not understood. Stories often consist of archetypal wisdom that is applicable across cultural boundaries.

Stories are a very powerful way in which to convey complex, multi-dimensional concepts. While a certain amount of knowledge can be reflected as informative, stories are a fundamental aspect of unlocking vital knowledge which remains beyond the reach of easily codified information. Storytelling can be perceived as a knowledge management tool, as it assists people and organisations in to discovering the hidden values in ideas and intellect. Storytelling communicates collaboratively, persuasively, holistically, intuitively, entertainingly, movingly, freely and interactively.

7.5 World café

> And through our conversations, as we work together, we discover
> a greater wisdom that reveals our path forward.
>
> Margaret Wheatly, 2005: unknown

World café methodology reintroduces the age-old process of good conversation during which discussions take place on vital issues. This is a place, Margaret Wheatly (2005, viii) states "... where we're not separated, classified, or stereotyped; a world that constantly surprises us with the wisdom that exists, not in any one of us, but in all of us. And a world where we learn that the wisdom we need to solve our problems is available when we talk together."

What is world café?

Café conversations are based on the assumption that people possess the innate wisdom and creativity required to confront any difficult challenge, say Juanita Brown and David Isaacs (2005). Wheatly (2005) advises that it is necessary to depend on diversity during a world café process. World café has the ability to bring all people together in terms of issues that matter. It provides freedom from stereotypical classifications such as personality type and EQ categories. World café techniques can be used to ensure that an outcome is co-created. Co-creation and shared understanding lead to significance which, in turn, manifests in commitment.

Core assumptions and principles

World café reawakens two fundamental beliefs, namely, that we are all human beings who wish to discuss those issues that are really significant and that, collectively, we possess greater wisdom than we do individually. Small groups rotate in order to ensure that everybody ultimately participates in all the discussions. A host remains behind to invite the next group and to share the learning of the previous group.

World café conversations enable participants to self-organise naturally, and they create a sense of community in which knowledge is shared and innovation ignited, according to Brown and David Isaacs (2005). World café focuses on intimate exchange, disciplined inquiry, cross-pollination of ideas and possibility thinking.

Criteria for world café

The café approach enables groups to participate in evolving rounds of dialogue with three or four others, while, at the same time, remaining part of a single, larger and connected conversation. Conversations develop, and become intimate while people move between groups, cross-pollinating ideas and discovering new insights. The sense of becoming whole becomes significant, and the collective wisdom of the group becomes more accessible. Possibilities for innovation then emerge.

The process for world café

Juanita Brown and David Isaacs (2005) describe the following steps that are necessary for world café interventions:

- Setting the context, creating a hospitable space.

- Exploring issues that matter.

- Encouraging all participants to contribute.

- Cross-pollinating and connecting diverse perspectives.

- Listening together for patterns, insights and deeper questions.

- Harvesting and sharing collective discoveries.

The facilitator again takes responsibility for the time, space and contents of the session. Different cafés are created in different spaces. Each space deals with a question or statement that is real to the participants. The facilitators rotate the groups when conversations become saturated at the various venues.

Rotation can take place clockwise, or the delegates can choose where they want to go. The first option is more controlled. The second option should only be implemented if the facilitator is able to deal with some chaos. A host remains behind at each table to share the contents of the previous conversations with the new group. Hosts can rotate after they have shared information with the next group, or they can remain for the full session, and a new host can be appointed at the end of the session. Alternatively, the host can stay for the full intervention.

The benefit of the latter design is that the host has in-depth insight into the specific topic. After everyone has been rotated at all the cafés, a last rotation can take the participants back to their original cafés. This also allows time for the host to quickly see what resulted in the other conversations. There is no need for feedback to a big group as everyone has now participated in all the different conversations.

The facilitator must take the following into account:

- Different participants have different rhythms. As a rule of thumb the facilitator should continue until 50% of the participants have become bored. The balance may still be catching on.

- The boundaries between the cafés may become blurred, and it would be sensible to stop the proceedings in the world café when people at all the tables are saying the same thing. Shared understanding may then be assumed.

- Do not be scared to place a controversial statement on the table, or to tackle tacit opinions in the room. As different people co-create the outcomes, the individual voice is protected.

The following typical questions can be asked:

- What actions do we have to stop?

- What must we start doing?

- What must we continue doing?

Another approach can be linked to the inclusivity model described earlier. Questions here include the following:

- How has the world of work changed over the last 10 years? How will it change in the future?

- What is the impact of the new sciences on the world of work?

- What are the implications of the rising levels of consciousness internationally?

World café may also be applied with great effect if there is little time for facilitating a strategic planning session. Different cafés can deal with strengths, weaknesses, opportunities or threats, or the resource process, customer and financial perspectives of the balanced score card can be allocated to different cafés in a process where everyone co-creates organisational strategy.

Afterwards the facilitator may need to clean up the output of the various café sessions if such output is required. If strategy is co-created in this way, the group must understand that the contracting phase of what exactly strategic objectives and initiates represent must still take place.

Difference between world café and other approaches

World café is similar to open-space technology. Instead of facilitating within a large group or working with a representative grouping only, a large group can be accommodated. Everybody co-creates the outcome. This is the only technique in terms of which everybody speaks to everybody else.

The positive, unintentional consequence of employees connecting in terms of important topics with management must not be underestimated. It contributes to a sense of inclusion, and ultimately to participation, ownership and engagement.

Critique regarding world café

There is little literature to be found on the methodology. From a facilitative perspective the outcome is shared understanding. However, the larger the group, the longer the process may take.

7.6 Conclusion

In this chapter various OCD methodologies have been presented. These methodologies have the ability to create shared understanding. Their purpose is to encourage participants to experience a sense of belonging and to feel that they have been consulted. Voices of minority groups are unleashed, and a better future is co-created. All these methodologies can be used to enhance inclusivity.

In the next chapter alternative OCD modalities are discussed. These modalities can be integrated in appropriate OCD interventions with great success.

8

ALTERNATIVE INTERVENTION MODALITIES

Co-authored by Tonja Blom

8.1 Introduction

"In many shamanic societies, if you came to a medicine person complaining of being disheartened, dispirited, or depressed, they would ask one of four questions: When did you stop dancing? When did you stop singing? When did you stop being enchanted by stories? When did you stop finding comfort in the sweet territory of silence?"

Gabrielle Roth (2011)

For organisations and individuals, change occurs on multiple concurrent paths. Human reactions to change were discussed in chapter 4. In this chapter alternative modalities that can assist humans to move through difficult organisational transformation efforts are discussed.

When dealing with workforces with a greater degree of demographic diversity, technological change and increased international competition, Tonja Blom (2015) found (in her thesis), the importance of increased individual awareness and consciousness. The intervention modalities discussed in this chapter allow us to hear different voices and opinions, allowing individuals and groups a safe space where authenticity can grow and flourish. The essence of these intervention modalities revolve around crucial conversations and actual organisational dilemmas; contributing significantly to organisational understanding, awareness and eventual sustainable change.

Paradoxically, these intervention modalities, which can be described as spiritual- and body-based, are the most recent and yet most ancient global methodologies. Traditional business leaders may frown upon introducing these modalities in the workplace. However, these intervention modalities all have the potential to contribute to sustainable organisational change, allowing individuals and leaders to view organisational change from a different perspective.

8.2 Emotional and bodily human reaction to change

Howard Bloom (2010) reminds us that humans do not take kindly to change. New ideas scare us and fill us with anxiety and doubt. Straying from the beaten path makes us fearful and even self-destructive. Human reactions to change may stem from the individual, groups, community, the organisation or a combination. Fear of the unknown, habit, self-interest and economic insecurity, failure to recognise the need for change, general mistrust, social disruption and selective perceptions all contribute to individual resistance.

Ben Swanepoel and his colleagues (2003), found that structural, cultural and group inertia, threats to existing power relationships, threats to expertise and resource allocation and previous unsuccessful change efforts are organisational factors that hamper successful change management interventions.

The body is like a mandala: if you look inside, it is an endless source of revelation. Through improved embodiment, individual consciousness can also increase. James Lake (2001) conceptualised the body as the interaction of subtle energies and matter. These dimensions should be incorporated holistically to ensure optimal contribution, resilience and coping effectiveness (figure 8.1). Unfortunately, when caught up in change or when under stress, individuals tend to forget the role of the body.

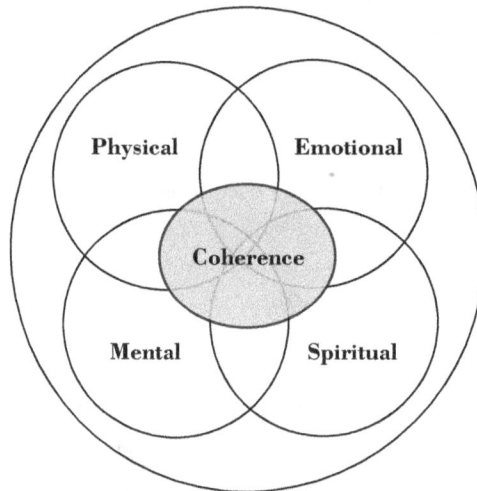

Figure 8.1   Elements of the whole psyche, Tonja Blom (2015 , p.152)

Figure 8.1 displays the basic, significant elements of the whole individual. An individual's mental, spiritual, physical and emotional aspects should all be considered to ensure cohesion, optimal functioning and minimal resistance. This figure represents a very simple mandala. Depicting the importance of the circle in individual life, allows the whole person to be set free to awaken and expand individual consciousness.

8.3   The purpose of alternative intervention modalities

Alternative intervention modalities promise to create higher levels of consciousness or awareness of the self as well as insight into the behaviours of others confronted by organisational change. These intervention modalities may lead to enhanced levels of interpersonal skill and might assist both individuals and leaders to identify and interpret their change perceptions. Personal growth will most probably alter the individual and the leader's perceptions of organisational change, which in turn may result in reduced resistance, Blom (2015) explains. The intended outcome is to enable individuals and leaders to take up their role and/or responsibility in the organisation to ensure successful and sustainable change.

8.4 Alternative intervention modalities

In this part of the chapter different alternative intervention modalities are discussed. Ways of integrating these approaches in OCD processes are shared. The way, the benefits and the proposed outcomes of the following modalities are discussed below: music, meditation, holotropical breathwork, tremoring, chanting and distant healing modalities.

MUSIC

"Music is a higher revelation than all wisdom and philosophy. Music is the electrical soil in which the spirit lives, thinks and invents."

Ludwig von Beethoven (1770 – 1827)

Both eastern and western traditions have recognised the value of music for thousands of years. Plato believed that music helped man to attune to nature's intrinsic harmonies, being a direct bridge into the order of the universe. Barry Sultanoff (2001) found that in listening to music one might find balance and peace within oneself, by coming into harmony with the cosmic order of nature.

Isaacovich Altschuler (1948) realised that music can alter mood. Research done by Jacob Jolij and Maaike Meurs (2011) found that listening to music can change the way we perceive the world. Music has an even more dramatic effect on perception: even if there is nothing to see, people will see happy faces when they listen to happy music and sad faces when they listen to sad music.

John Diamond (2001) said music is therapeutic and transcendental because of its tremendous potential to raise our life energy. And life energy is the body's healing power. This life energy is also called prana or chi in some eastern traditions. In order to overcome any disability or anxiety, be it mental or physical, we have to raise our life energy, and music is a very effective, universal means of doing that.

Sultanoff (2001) found one effect of singing is that breath resonates through the body, resulting in a full-body massage. This vocally generated self-massage activates life energy, aiding in emotional balance. It lifts the mood, reduces stress, allays anxiety and improves focus. It vibrates organs, bones and muscles, improving circulation. Singing therefore reduces feelings of separateness and aloneness.

Using percussion instruments such as bones, castanets and drums is encouraged, as it is impossible to play a wrong note on these. The use of drums will free purple and red from the fear of making mistakes. Singing encourages free and continuous breathing while utilising whole-brain activity, which involves both hemispheres simultaneously.

For organisations there can be a clear rationale for using music as a tool to reduce stress, fatigue, negative emotions and possibly even organisational resistance. Music enhances well-being, positive mood and mental clarity. Given the interrelationship between attitudes, emotions and change, music can be an inexpensive and easy method to facilitate organisational change. In addition, given the traditional organisation, playing repetitive music that lacks complexity can facilitate learning for purple and red.

Different music can be used to achieve different outcomes. Playing music to purple workers on a production line will most likely improve productivity. Playing classical music in a classroom environment will enhance learning. In many offices popular radio stations are heard throughout the entire day. Changing these popular broadcasts to soft, soothing or classical music may improve mood, mental clarity and well-being. Using music and song within an organisational context could elevate mood while reducing anxiety, and simultaneously creating increased affiliation and interrelatedness.

OCD practitioners can use the powerful modality of music during interventions. Each group member can bring a piece of music to a team-building session and share it during a sacred ceremony with each other. Soft background music can create a calm ambience where reflection is stimulated during personal development sessions. Music can also form the base of other interventions such as drumming and bio-dancing – events that can be facilitated separately during team development sessions or as part of a longer process such as a three-day OCD intervention. If facilitated, the learning from interpreting emotional experiences and insights, may lead to rising levels of awareness.

MEDITATION

"Soaking in silence is like being bathed from the inside out. Whatever needs attention, warmth, love, purification, liberation, is invited forth from the shadows to be seen, felt, drawn back into the wholeness that belongs to our Being."

Dorothy Hunt, 2015

Not long ago meditation was relatively unknown and even feared. However, today we know that meditation allows us to live more fully in the present moment. Meditation provides a space in which attention is brought back to the simple reality of being. As Dean Radin (2013) reminds us, we are starting to understand that meditation is about expanding and clarifying awareness, not about contracting it.

Many of the issues we see in our world today stems from a lack of mindfulness and a takeover of egocentric individuality. Seeing beyond our perceived perceptions and gaining a connection to others, could therefore create a more peaceful and joyous reality.

According to Rael Cahn (2006), across meditative traditions, advanced practitioners occasionally report transcendental states of deep absorption. During such experiences, common distinctions – between subject and object, me and you, and past, present, and future – begin to diminish. Zoran Josipovic (2013) claims that with sufficient practice all distinctions dissolve into an undifferentiated state of awareness, sometimes accompanied by an impression of timelessness or a vastly extended present moment.

Meditation, silence, improved self-awareness and mindfulness hold the possibility of minimising negative thinking patterns, allowing more positive thoughts to emerge. During times of organisational change and/or stress, positive thoughts could enhance optimal functioning and mental abilities. Meditation can aid the individual to experience a more unified state of awareness and interconnectedness. This in turn, could lead to reduced anxiety and the ability to life more fully in the present moment.

During meditation our brains stop processing information, which is generally indicated by beta waves. Sara Lazar's (2009) neuro-scientific research suggests that when beta waves decrease, we see a decrease in information processed. Studies done by Eileen Luders and her colleagues (2009), which compared long-term meditators with matched control participants, found that meditators had larger grey matter volumes than non-meditators in brain areas that are associated with emotional regulation and response control. Britta Hölzel and colleagues (2011) compared existing differences between meditators and non-meditators and found the meditating group had increased grey matter in the left hippocampus, a brain area strongly involved in learning and memory.

According to Caroline Leaf (2013), meditation may also result in fewer negative emotions. Meditation enables individuals to stay on a task longer as a result of improved concentration. Switching between tasks becomes more effective, coupled with improved cognitive and emotional functioning. Meditation also improves self-esteem and self-motivation, while reducing emotional volatility. The reduction of emotional volatility alone will improve all aspects of organisational change.

Meditation skills must be learnt. However, once an individual comprehends the method, these skills can be applied in the office, at your desk. Observing breath, repeating a mantra or even just smiling can increase mindfulness. Meditation may lower individual stress levels with obvious benefits to the organisation. These benefits might relate to increased emotional stability, improved cognitive performance, increased interconnectedness and improved individual coping. Within an organisational change context negative thoughts and emotions were shown as prevalent. Few organisations do not require a shift from negative to positive.

OCD interventions such as personal purpose sessions, career mastery interventions, vision quests and authentic leadership development courses can incorporate daily meditation sessions. Attempts should benefit through an individual willingness to move from chaos, distraction and confusion to focus and improved ability to distinguish between true reality and perceptions. Sacred silence can be introduced as a way to facilitate thoughtfulness and mindfulness. Sitting in each other's space without speaking also increases levels of trust and a shared sense of community. Meditation leads to enhanced self-awareness, and incorporating sessions that practise mindfulness in OCD interventions, may not only enhance the effectiveness of the intervention, but can also teach valuable modalities that the individual can continue practising in their private capacity later.

HOLOTROPICAL BREATHWORK

Holotropic literately means moving towards wholeness. During a facilitated session, accelerated breathing and evocative music are used in a sacred setting. While lying on a mat, with closed eyes, each person creates an alternative state of consciousness though the use of their own breath and the music that is played. A set of internal experiences is activated, that can be described as a natural inner healing process of the individual's psyche. A very unique individual experience is activated, and each session differs from another.

After the breathing session, the practitioner should provide a safe space. Pastels and paper can be provided and the participant can use art to work through his or her experiences. This process integrates insights of different fields of study that include anthropology, transpersonal psychology, eastern spiritual practice and modern consciousness research.

The OCD practitioner should either be accredited to conduct the breathwork themself, or commission a trained practitioner. It is very important to ensure a safe environment and to contain the emotional experience of the participants. As part of a personal purpose process, a well-facilitated and contained breathwork session can lead to increased levels of consciousness and awareness.

TRAUMA RELEASE EXERCISE – TREMORING

Dr Peter Levine (1997:16) stated that "trauma is a fact of life. However, trauma is not, will not, and can never be fully healed until we also address the essential role played by the body". Some cathartic methods encourage intense emotional reliving of trauma. Equally, talk therapy often requires the reliving of traumatic events. According to Levine (1997), talking about trauma often causes more uncontained emotion. He believes body sensation (our physiology) to be the key to healing trauma.

Traumatic symptoms are often not caused by the triggering event. They stem from the frozen residue of energy that remains unresolved. Levine (2010) reminds us that such residue remains trapped in the nervous system, causing havoc in our bodies and spirits.

In trauma, the mind becomes profoundly altered. Remarkable mechanisms such as dissociation and denial, freezing, fight or flight allow us to navigate through these critical periods. Psychology approaches trauma through its effects on the mind, which is wholly inadequate. The body and mind, primitive instincts, emotions, intellect and spirituality must be considered together as a unit to understand and heal trauma. These reactions are a normal outcome of organisational change and transformation.

When the brain perceives something as threatening, muscles respond through the flexor muscles, which are located in the anterior of the body. When these contract, they inhibit the extensor muscles located in the posterior of the body, resulting in flexor withdrawal. This creates a foetal-like enclosure that causes us to feel safer by protecting our vulnerable soft parts – our genitals, vital organs, and the head with its eyes, ears, nose and mouth.

Two of the primary flexor muscles that contract to protect the underbelly of the human animal are the psoas muscles. David Bercelli (2007, 2012) found that this protective procedure, stored deep in the brain, automatically springs into action to contract these muscles when we are threatened, spontaneously taking us through the steps required to contract the body for our safety.

The primitive world is still alive in all humans. When humans roamed the hills and valleys, gathering berries and hunting wild animals while living in caves, our existence was linked to the natural world. We were constantly on alert to defend ourselves and our families.

The life-threatening events prehistoric people routinely faced moulded our modern nervous systems to respond powerfully whenever we perceived our survival to be threatened. Modern life offers few opportunities to use this powerful capacity. Consequently, most of us have become separated from our natural, instinctual selves; without easy access to the resources of this primitive, instinctual self, humans alienate their bodies from their souls.

Dr David Bercelli (2007), whose thesis was developed as a result of trauma work throughout the world, developed a method to deal with trauma, Trauma Release Process™ or TRE, to assist individuals to reconnect body, mind and soul.

It is vital to be able to turn off the muscular response to stress. Various stress reduction techniques attempt to interrupt this conditioning activity of the Hypothalamic-Pituitary-Adrenal (HPA)-axis. One of the most promising is physical exercise; however, the individual performing aerobic exercises is only capable of performing the exercises and relaxing to the degree that their cortex allows.

Neurogenic tremors, however, are generated from within the limbic system of the brain. Since this system is not under conscious control, the individual is able to affect changes in the limbic system that they could not do otherwise. Neurogenic tremors, as developed by David Bercelli (2012), give the individual unconscious access to the limbic system which automatically reduces their stress response without their conscious control or awareness.

Tremors in humans are the natural response of a shocked or disrupted nervous system attempting to restore body and mind to homeostasis. Tremors can aid recovery because they don't cause us to relive the traumatic experience, yet they turn off our fight, flight, or freeze mechanism. Tremors discharge the excess energy from an aborted fight-or-flight response, quieting the HPA-axis: this is referred to as neurogenic tremors.

Through continued tremoring, we gain greater clarity about our true self, and a more obvious connectedness to others, coupled with a significant drop in anxiety. According to David Bercelli (2012), experiences of tremoring have been paradoxical: people experience feeling more like themselves, but at the same time completely connected to the universe.

Tremors are introduced through participating in a range of specifically identified exercises during the TRE™-process. The vibrations created during the exercises present us with an opportunity to access the place where matter interfaces with pure energy. The tremors help dissolve our sensation of separateness, birthing in us a new sense of oneness. Tremoring helps us to reconnect with our essential being in the present moment. This process can shift consciousness into a bodily awareness.

Lorraine Laubscher (2013) indicated that stress results in a downshift of human niches. The reduction of individual stress and trauma could thus first inhibit a downshift of human niches. Second, the reduction of individual stress and trauma could potentially allow individuals to upshift through their current human niches. An individual who is able to upshift to another human niche will perceive organisational change differently while most likely being in a better position to cope with the related change and uncertainty.

Applying the TRE™-process within an organisational change context could allow for a shift and unfolding of individual consciousness while dissolving feelings of separateness. This in turn, could result in the emergence of a new paradigm which is so deeply required during times of organisational change. All that is required to apply the TRE™–process in an organisational setting is leadership open-mindedness, a safe setting, a qualified TRE™-practitioner and a couple of yoga mats.

OCD practitioners can introduce a TRE™-process as part of a change resilience initiative. The underlying theory can be shared in a session. Over a period of three days the group can engage in a tremoring session every day.

A Rogerian facilitated group process can provide the emotional containment needed to intervene in organisational settings. Individual group members can continue TRE™ after the session. The use of personal journals is highly recommended. Individual sessions can also be facilitated by a TRE™-practitioner.

In environments where trauma is the order of the day like emergency environments, TREM can be facilitated in large group events, by involving more TRE™-practitioners. A typical tremor session lasts between 20 and 30 minutes. Another 30 to 60 minutes should be allocated to debrief the event.

CHANTING

Barry Sultanoff (2001:209) claimed chanting is a near universal way of engaging a meditative experience: the rhythmic speaking or singing of words or sounds, often primarily on one or two main pitches, called reciting tones. The practice of chanting is broadly called *akshara laksham*, literally translated to mean as many hundreds of thousands of chants as there are syllables in the mantra.

In Hindu tradition "Om" is the simplest and arguably the most powerful and profound mantra. The mantra, Om or Aum, harmonises the physical, emotional and intellectual forces. Om is the primordial sound, the sound that is said to have its origins at the time of the creation of the cosmos; also referred to as the Big Bang. According to Gyan Rajhans (2013), Om is an affirmation of the divine presence that is the universe.

Zoran Josipovic (2013) found that repeating mantras on a regular basis will cause profound changes in mind-body physiology and psychology. Chanting mantras is a holistic method of stilling and opening the mind. Mantra sounds can lift the believer towards the higher self. Different sounds have different effects on human psyche. The soft sound of wind rustling through leaves soothes our nerves, the musical note of a running stream enchants our heart, and the sound of thunder may cause awe and fear.

The chanting of Om in Transcendental Meditation is now widely recognised. Om is a universal healing sound; when you chant Om you adjust your own vibrational frequency to resonate with this primordial sound of creation. Sultanoff (2001) argues that chanting facilitates the integration of the various parts of an individual's life into a more coherent whole. However, chanting words such peace, release or harmony, similarly raise individual awareness and consciousness.

Rhythm, humming and repetitive chanting come naturally to purple and speak strongly to purple's spirit. Chanting sounds can assist both purple and red to integrate their higher selves through enhanced consciousness. This in turn could reduce organisational resistance, negativity and distrust. Chanting is a simple and easy method with large potential for heightened individual empowerment, compassion and individual interconnectedness.

In a facilitated event OCD practitioners can lead a group in a chanting activity. It can form part of a three-day OCD process, where group members can engage over the period in six rituals of increasing length. A group could start with 10 minutes. On the last day, the session could last 30 to 40 minutes. A circle is formed, and a note that resonates deeply with each individual is chanted. Sometimes, laughter is used to start off the process; in as little as 10 minutes the laughter often deepens into soulful chanting. The group is left with a sense of connectedness and individuals report that they feel recharged. As Dante said centuries earlier, "The more souls who resonate together, the greater the intensity of their love, and mirror-like, each soul reflects the other."

JUGGLING

Juggling is a complex activity, requiring accurate arm and hand movements, grasping of fast-moving objects and the ability to track objects in the periphery of one's vision. Research by Heidi Johansen-Berg (2009) showed improved connectivity in parts of the brain involved in making movements necessary to catch the juggling balls. Changes in grey matter have been shown following a new experience and learning. Teaching adults to do something entirely new increased white matter in the brain as well as increased periphery of vision. White matter is the nerve strands that help different parts of the brain to communicate with each other.

Research proves that adult brains are not static or even starting to degenerate. According to Heidi Johansen-Berg (2009) it is possible for the brain to condition its own wiring system to operate more efficiently. Organisational change requires rewiring of individual thinking systems. A relatively simple activity such as juggling could be used effectively to rewire the brain towards improved functioning with related benefits to the organisation.

The benefits of humour and laughter date to early observations by Sigmund Freud (1964). The clowning around while juggling could thus have further therapeutic value to the individual. A physical activity such as juggling could particularly benefit red, while simultaneously improving brain functioning. Adding a competitive flavour to the activity will further enhance red's learning experience. Starting an OCD session with juggling as an ice-breaker could enhance relatedness while improving brain functioning.

Organisational change is stressful and results in uncertainty, stress, anxiety and mistrust. Therefore, John Darling and Victor Heller (2011) believe that leaders should help individuals to identify a purpose in every major life event or issue that arises as well as around the organisation.

Whether prayer should be conceptualised as an alternative medical intervention is open to discussion. From certain vantage points, prayer is central to the value and philosophic systems of many individuals across various faiths and cultures. Implicit within the discussion of prayer is the concept of prayer in coping with negative or stressful life events. Dean Radin (2013) argues that praying for oneself may be thought of as a reasonable coping mechanism in the face of uncertainty and dire need.

Understanding that human intentions may directly affect others in ways that are not entirely understood may profoundly change how organisations engage with their employees. The purple human niche already knows this. Purple is very aware of this interconnectedness with each other. This interconnectedness might refer to the concept of *ubuntu*[4]. This is important from a leadership perspective. Acknowledging this interconnectedness and working within a concept of relatedness, will improve trust, understanding and general wellbeing within the organisation; especially for purple. The spirit of purple needs this interconnectedness to flourish. Through simple acts of goodwill, the spirit of purple might again be engaged within the organisation.

8.4 The brain and alternative healing modalities at work

When two brains interact, very peculiar effects are observed that resemble those observed in elementary particles. Interaction correlates objects, and a measurement on one component of a correlated state collapses the other component as well. Jacobo Grinberg-Zylberbaum and his co-workers (1994) found this to be the case, even at a distance. Their research also indicated that human brains are capable of establishing close relationships with other brains and may sustain such an interaction at a distance. Dean Radin (2004) further found correlations between brain electrical activities of distant human brains.

Little intentional acts such as sending mentally good wishes for recovery, to keep one's fingers crossed, or mentally cultivating a positive image of a beloved person while being separated are examples of a wider group of behaviours related to what is often expressed as distant intentions. According to Stefan Schmidt (2012) these behaviours can be seen as the basic underlying procedures of more formal practices of distant healing.

Robert Charman (2006) argues that our brains are connected with each other. Marco Iacoboni and Roger McHaney (2013) explain an understanding of empathy, being able to share, sympathise, understand and experience another person's emotional state through the concept of mirror neurons. They reason that people in the workplace are connected with roots hard-wired in the brain. However, a further implication of the above is that a leader's thoughts have a frequency, are magnetic and determine the nature of communications that are emitted.

Times of change require meaningful responses, quality and versatile leadership, sensitivity and creativity, as well as thoughts and feelings to address the adjustments needed

---

4   The concept of 'ubuntu' comes from the saying 'Ubuntu ngumntu ngabantu' [isiXhosa], which appears in different forms in different indigenous languages of South Africa. It means 'A person is a person because of other people' and relates to the interconnectedness of human beings.

by individuals affected by organisational change. Understanding empathy, being able to share, sympathise, understand and experience another person's emotional states requires more humanistic approaches. Tapping into the possibilities of physiological correlations at a distance can improve our interconnectedness, which in turn may alter negative perceptions, aiding the development of trustful relationships. Altered perceptions, trust and meaningful relationships need to form the foundation during times of organisational change.

Max Planck (1931) reasoned that consciousness is fundamental; matter is derivative from consciousness. Everything we talk about, everything we regard as existing, postulates consciousness. Carl Jung (1954) confirmed this, finding unconscious processes a major mental reality, and the history of an individual alongside the history of humankind as the main determinants of human behaviour.

Contemporary science typically considers consciousness an implicit function of brain physiology. This area of research offers a unique window into the nature of consciousness by proposing direct manifestations of consciousness in the physical world. Evidence of such effects has been gathered under controlled conditions and the evidence raises puzzling questions. Therefore Dean Radin and his colleague Roger Nelson (1989) found it difficult to avoid the conclusion that under certain circumstances, consciousness interacts with random physical systems.

David Hawkins (2005) documented the non-linear, spiritual realm on a level of consciousness (LOC) map using a muscle-testing technique called Applied Kinesiology (AK). Each LOC coincides with determinable human behaviours and life perceptions representing a corresponding attractor field of varying strength that exists beyond our three-dimensional reality. The numbers on the scale represent logarithmic calibrations (measurable vibratory frequencies on a scale that increases to the 10th power) of the levels of human consciousness and their corresponding levels of reality. The numbers are arbitrary; the significance lies in the relationship of one level to another.

AK uncovers what is going on in the body while determining whether or not a specific remedy would be beneficial. By testing the instantaneous response of a particular muscle, AK practitioners are able to clearly navigate the complexities of the human body; if a tested muscle stayed strong, a substance was good for the body, and if it went weak, it was not.

According to this map the two greatest spiritual growth barriers are at level 200 (the level of courage, represents a profound shift from destructive and harmful behaviour to life-promoting and integrated lifestyles) and 500. Currently, approximately 78% of the world's population is below the significant 200 level. According to Hawkins (2005), the destructive capacity of this majority drags down all of mankind without the counterbalancing effect of the 22% above 200.

Thereafter, Hawkins (2005) informs the second great barrier is level 500 (love); a way of being in the world. The 500s represent a very difficult hurdle with only 4% of the world's population calibrating in this region. This level denotes a shift from the linear, provable domain (classic physics or Newtonian physics) to the non-linear, formless, spiritual realm.

Hawkins (2005) claims that a person's LOC remains rather steady throughout their lifetime. However, through awareness, a person's LOC can jump dramatically. Table 8.1 displays the LOC which determine the reason why people behave the way they do. Research on human reactions during periods of organisational change predominantly indicated levels of falsehood. Feelings of indifference, fright, hopelessness, guilt, grief, anger, anxiety and enslavement were prominent. These feelings range from 30 (guilt), to 50 (hopeless), to 75 and 100 respectively for grief and fear. This clearly indicates that levels of falsehood are dominant during times of organisational change.

Further, in times of organisational change, no emotions related to levels of truth were mentioned. Researched indicated extremely low levels of trust. Little or no understanding was reported. Nobody felt optimistic or inspired. Not feeling meaningful also featured. No emotions within the levels of truth range were even mentioned. It seems clear that optimal change and optimal organisational performance will remain elusive until such time as we are able to elevate consciousness to higher levels.

Table 8.1 divides these levels into positive and negative energy-taking levels. The negative levels from the lowest to the highest are: shame, guilt, apathy, grief, fear, desire, anger, pride. The positive levels are: courage, neutrality, willingness, acceptance, reason, love, joy, peace, enlightenment.

Table 8.1 Map of consciousness, David Hawkins (2005), adapted from Wendell French and Cecil

God-View	Self-View	Level	Log	Emotion	Process
Self	Is	Enlightenment	700-1000	Ineffable	Pure Consciousness
All-being	Perfect	Peace	600	Bliss	Illumination
One	Complete	Joy	540	Serenity	Transfiguration
Loving	Benign	Love	500	Reverence	Revelation
Wise	Meaningful	Reason	400	Understanding	Abstraction
Merciful	Harmonious	Acceptance	350	Forgiveness	Transcendence
Inspiring	Hopeful	Willingness	310	Optimism	Intention
Enabling	Satisfactory	Neutrality	250	Trust	Release
Permitting	Feasible	Courage	200	Affirmation	Empowerment

↑ Levels of truth

↓ Levels of falsehood

God-View	Self-View	Level	Log	Emotion	Process
Indifferent	Demanding	Pride	175	Scorn	Inflation
Vengeful	Antagonistic	Anger	150	Hate	Aggression
Denying	Disappointing	Desire	125	Craving	Enslavement
Punitive	Frightening	Fear	100	Anxiety	Withdrawal
Uncaring	Tragic	Grief	75	Regret	Despondency
Condemning	Hopeless	Apathy	50	Despair	Abdication
Vindictive	Evil	Guilt	30	Blame	Destruction
Despising	Hateful	Shame	20	Humiliation	Elimination

Everything around us can affect our LOC: the music we listen to, the people we interact with, even the books we read. Consciousness is like a lens through which we view reality. While the object you are viewing can remain the same, a different consciousness level can result in those outputs being widely different.

Chua Celes (2009) maintained that first world societies are deeply entrenched in fear (100), desire (125) and pride (175). Fear includes fear of rejection, failure, loss and uncertainty. Desire encompasses the quest for material possessions, status, power and belongingness. Pride takes root from dualistic views such as elitism, competition and attachment to status, wealth and goods.

Roland Fischer (1971) created a symmetrical model of altered states of consciousness where meaning is meaningful at the level of experienced arousal. During the self-state of the highest levels of hyper- or hypo-arousal, this meaning can no longer be expressed in dualistic terms, since the experience of unity is born from the integration of interpretive and interpreted structures.

Since this intense meaning is devoid of specificities, the only way to communicate its intensity is the metaphor; only through the transformation of objective sign into subjective symbol in art, literature and religion can the increasing integration of cortical and sub-cortical activity be communicated.

This model of Roland Fischer incorporates ergotropic (sympathetic nerve system) and trophotropic (parasympathetic nervous system) arousal. Ergotropic arousal includes creative, psychotic, and ecstatic experiences denoted by behavioural patterns preparatory to positive action. Trophotropic arousal results from an integration of the parasympathetic nervous system with somatomotor activities to produce behavioural patterns that conserve and restore energy and decreased sensitivity to external stimuli and sedation.

As per this model, figure 8.2 brings the ecstatic and mystical experiences together in a model where hyper-aroused states are characterised by increased muscle tone, decreased skin resistance, increased body temperature, increased heart rate as well as the extreme dilation of pupils. Consciousness extends either between states of drunkenness or sobriety with complete amnesia between the two discontinuous states of sobriety and drunkenness.

As we depart along either continuum from the I toward the self, the separateness of object and subject gradually disappears and their interaction becomes the principal content of the experience. The interaction is a reflection of the gradually increasing integration of cortical and subcortical activity. In this state of unity, the separateness of subject and object that is implicit in dualistic, Aristotelian logic and language becomes meaningless; only a symbolic logic and language can convey the experience of intense meaning.

NORMAL

DAILY ROUTINE · RELAXATION · SENSITIVITY · CREATIVITY (REM state) · AROUSED · TRANQUIL · ZAZEN (slow wave) · DHĀRNĀ

AROUSAL

PERCEPTION

HALLUCINATION ← PERCEPTION → MEDITATION

ANXIETY · ACUTE HYPERPHRENIC STATES · CATALEPSY · ERGOTROPIC · TROPHOTROPIC · DHYĀN · SAVICHĀR SAMĀDHI

HYPERAROUSED · HYPOAROUSED

MYSTICAL RAPTURE · NIRVICHĀR SAMĀDHI

ECSTATIC · 'SELF'

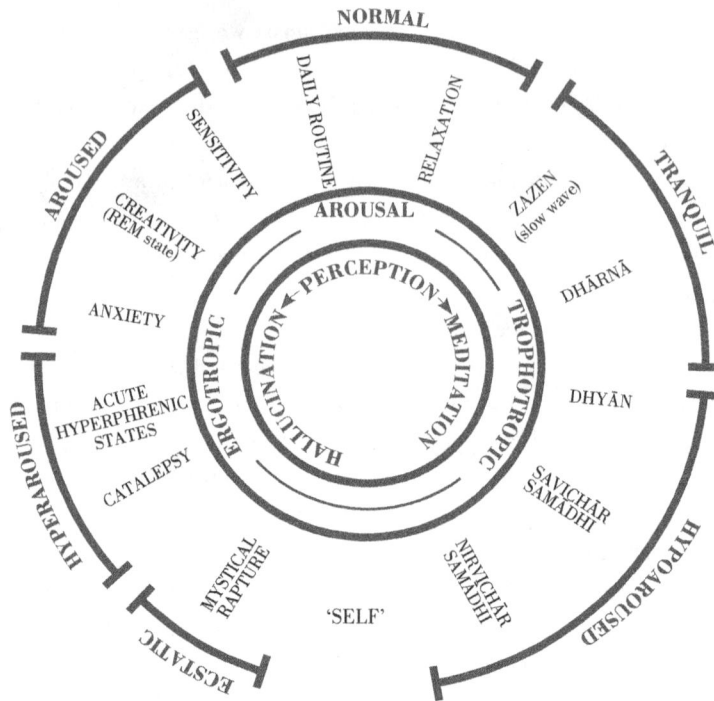

Figure 8.2 Variety of conscious states, Roland Fischer's (1971)

Figure 8.2 displays the separateness of subject and object during the daily routine levels of arousal. This is a reflection of the relative independence of cortical interpretation from subcortical activity and is of survival value in the I-state. Ecstasy is a state of emotion so intense that one is carried beyond rational thought and self-control. In contrast, Samadhi is generally accepted to be the highest stage in meditation, in which a person experiences oneness with the universe. The loop connecting ecstasy and Samadhi represents the rebound from ecstasy to Samadhi.

Gaining a deeper understanding of consciousness will play an exceedingly important role the future of organisational and individual change. Dean Radin (2013) explains that if the evolution of knowledge in this century exceeds that of the last, we can look forward to a future that is likely to redefine our concepts of reality far beyond any of the strangest concepts we have encountered so far. From an organisational change perspective, gaining a deeper understanding of consciousness allows for the expansion of individual awareness and mindfulness. This in turn might negate the negative impact of stress and even trauma that the individual experiences during organisational change.

The author, in an experiment that lasted 24 months, incorporated AK in a traditional OCD process. What was found through psychometric testing, and specifically by measuring how an individual coped with environmental demands as described by Reuven Bar-On, was mirrored in the individual kinesiology sessions, where the accredited practitioner, without words, dealt with the bodily truths of the participant. Through these interventions the average EQ-i of the participants increased from 98 to 112 (from average to almost enhanced emotional functioning)

8.8 Conclusion

This chapter touched upon alternative intervention modalities which could be applied to affect the human reaction to organisational change. These modalities promise to create higher levels of consciousness or awareness of the self as well as insight into the behaviours of others confronted and/or influenced by organisational change. These intervention modalities may also lead to enhanced levels of interpersonal skill.

"Emotion is the language of spirit; body is the language of mind" (Jerry Wyker, 2001: 288). If we can change our thoughts and perceptions, we can alter our output. Alternative intervention techniques can heal human relationships through the transformation of our perceptions of others, whilst improving our self-talk and self-belief.

Change is an art. Subtle skills are at times so evanescent that they could perhaps even be intuitive in nature. The arts have become the victim of our materialistic business landscape. However, balance can be restored, meaning recreated and self-imposed limits eradicated. Individually and collectively, individuals and organisations have the ability to bring about transformation.

9

OCD INTERVENTIONS FOR INCLUSIVITY

"Rather, you have to get them to experience it in a way that evokes its power and possibility. Instead of pouring knowledge into people's heads, you need to help them grind a new set of eyeglasses so they can see the world in a new way."

David Brown, 1991: unknown

9.1 Introduction

In the previous chapter methodologies were described that can be applied during interventions to create inclusivity. The focus now shifts to different interventions that promise to create higher levels of consciousness or awareness of the self, and insight into the behaviour of others who are confronted by organisational transformation.

Second, these interventions may lead to enhanced levels of interpersonal skill. Intervention strategies are needed to help the individual in identifying and interpreting his or her perception of change. This, in turn, will create greater personal awareness and understanding of the self.

This personal growth and development is likely to alter the individual's perceptions of organisational change, and, thus, reduce the level of resistance. The intended outcome is the enablement of leadership to take up its role within the organisation in creating a climate that is conducive to diversity of thought, and thus to inclusivity.

9.2 Experiential learning

Experiential learning is one of the best ways in which to facilitate adult learning. Experiential education (or 'learning by doing') is the process of actively engaging delegates in an authentic experience that results in both benefits and consequences. Discoveries are made, and ample space is created for experimentation with knowledge instead of merely hearing or reading about the experiences of others. Reflection is used in order to enhance awareness and new ways of thinking, says Christa Rudd (2013).

Experiential education is related to constructivism learning theory, according to which people learn effectively through *making* things. A learning experience should be facilitated if integration of learning and, thus, sustainability is the required outcome. Adventure training can form an integral part of experiential learning. However, if not facilitated well, it may have negative effects.

Practical application

A team-building session can rely on experiential learning. The facilitator must delay the urge to pre-empt answers and solutions and create a learning experience for the participants and facilitate it afterwards. Different group dynamic activities can be introduced to create building blocks in a facilitated process that enhances understanding of a specific dynamic in a team or individual.

Time span

Experiential learning could be used in a few hours. Alternatively, two- or three-day sessions where a variety of experiences are interwoven to create deep insight into own behaviour and that of others may be facilitated.

Participants

A natural team of eight to 14 people can attend. Alternatively leadership dynamics can be explored in mixed teams. The sample size is capped at 14 to ensure in-depth facilitation. Larger groups can participate if more than one facilitator is introduced.

Theory to incorporate

Some relevant theories that can be used during the design phase or during the actual OCD intervention are:

- Group formation theory

- Personality type theory – typology of Carl Jung

- Roles in team – Belbin

- Human niche theory – Laubscher and the author

- Theory on trust, values, high-performance teams

Type of facilitation

The following schools of facilitation can be used:

- Group dynamic facilitation

- Humanistic/Rogerian facilitation

- Accredited adventure training instructors

Typically sessions are facilitated by group reflection on the following questions:

- What happened here?

- What worked, and what could be done differently?

- How can we apply these insights in our workplace?

Pre-requisites for success

The following aspects should be considered:

- Optimal venue away from the work

- A private venue

- Potential accommodation if the budget allows for it

- The creation of a safe space by the facilitators

- Challenge by choice – facilitators to minimise unhealthy group pressure.

- If a natural team is present all members should attend.

- Participants must commit to issues that are discussed in the context of the intervention.

9.3 Industrial Theatre

Industrial theatre provides emotive solutions based on dramatic media comprising various forms of live theatre, video and corporate events. If drama is combined with the disciplines of psychology and OCD, as well as comprehensive strategic business knowledge, unique dramatic solutions may be created.

Industrial theatre influences assumptions, attitudes, beliefs, mind-sets and frames of reference, and creates an understanding of all these elements, as well as how these elements impact on the learning, behaviour and personal growth of the individual. In this way industrial theatre brings about an understanding of complex (business) issues and is a very effective way of educating, mobilising and motivating people. If effectively facilitated, effective leadership behaviours can be derived through appreciative inquiry and/ or story-telling. The shared archetypal metaphor created by industrial theatre could lead to sustainable transformation.

Practical application

A theatre play is written, based on organisational behaviour theory and multi-cultural theory that visually enacts organisational dramas. Professional actors may be cast. Alternatively people from within the organisation may be used as actors.

Industrial theatre may be used with great success if the problem at hand has to do with deep underlying mental models or thinking systems. Typically, music is used and a meaningful song is created to ensure the cementing of the message even further.

Different types of industrial theatre interventions may be presented. A fixed script may be written and enacted (for example an HIV/Aids play). Improvised theatre is very effective (for example in customer-centricity, behaviour-based safety or values translation). The play should be clearly linked with organisational strategy or values.

From a sustainability point of view, it makes sense to present short skits, and facilitate the learning afterwards.

Time span

Over a short period of time all the employees who are available at the organisation are invited to participate in the industrial theatre. Typically a show lasts from one hour in the case of a scripted play to three hours for improvised theatre.

Participants

All the employees at the organisation must be allowed to attend. Top management must attend all the sessions.

Theory to incorporate

Some relevant theories that can be used during the design phase or during the actual OCD intervention are:

- Human niche theory as described by Laubscher and the author is presented in chapter 5 and 6 in this book. This is important to ensure that different worldviews of the audience are stimulated and the message is accessible to all.

- Inclusivity theory by the author in 2009 and 2014 and described in chapter 2 in this book.

- Theory that supports the specific focus of the intervention – such as behaviour-based safety theory.

Type of facilitation

The following facilitation types can be used:

- Large-group facilitation
- Small-group debriefing

Typical questions that may be asked include the following:

- What happened in the skit?

- What could the character have done differently?

- How can we apply this learning in the workplace?

Pre-requisites for success

Pre-requisites for success include:

- Support of top-management team

- Ideal venue must be cool and comfortable

- Overtime must be paid if needed

- Excellent sound is essential

- Deep theoretical understanding of the culture

- Professional script-writing is needed. It is important that the humour of the specific environment is incorporated, and the local language must be used.

- Visibility of top management

- Linking the intervention to organisational strategy

9.4 Action Learning

Although Action Learning (AL) was developed in 1945 it has only recently received the recognition it deserves. According to Michael Marquardt (1997) AL is an approach to leadership, team and OCD that utilises action research as introduced by Kurt Lewin (1951) on the part of cross-functional teams composed of high-potential middle managers.

AL capitalises on the need to deal with real-life organisational issues that are anchored in real time and are responsive to time pressure. By paying attention to their unfolding experiences and learning from them, the individual members of action-learning teams develop their leadership capacities, identify and solve real problems, and enable their organisations to learn how individual teams and systems develop the skills needed to build high-performance teams. At the same time, Rachel Carson and Charles Lowman (2003) explain, the individual members of the action-learning teams gain self-awareness and self-esteem through their earning of recognition, appreciation and respect.

In the event of inclusivity being chosen as the organisational strategy a special effort should be made to ensure that individuals understand themselves and others. They must also understand how they relate to others in normal circumstances and under pressure (for example, pressure caused by uncertainty generated by change).

Practical application

A group is asked to identify a workplace challenge. Through focused sessions and complex problem-solving techniques such as systems thinking principles and design thinking, the group co-creates a solution that may have significant business implications. Typically a senior line manager poses a few questions and the workplace challenge is linked to one of these questions. The solution that is proposed is presented to the top management or exco team for approval.

Time span

Typically, an action learning experience will run over a period of six to nine months.

Participants

Participants from various departments are selected to engage in the action learning experience.

Theory to incorporate

The following theories can be considered:

- Decision-making techniques
- Systems-thinking (Johan Strümpfer, Peter Senge, Russell Ackoff)
- Cynefin methodology (Dave Snowden)
- Value Circles (People mandalas of Laubscher)

Type of facilitation

The interventions can consist of:

- Lecturing
- Group process facilitation
- Adult learning

Typical questions include the following:

- What are the systemic causes of this problem?
- Why, why, why, why, why?
- What are the unintended consequences of this solution?

Pre-requisites for success

It is critical to ensure the following:

- Support from top-management team
- Openness to different answers for current organisational problems
- Continuous efforts of all participants
- Healthy organisational politics

9.5 Large-group interventions

A large-group event is a way of ensuring that a message is passed on to a large number of employees at the same time. In smaller organisations, or provisional or regionally structured organisations, an attempt can be made to gather the whole system in one room. A different way of facilitation ensures that all participants feel that they have a voice. Groupware and other software can assist facilitators.

More planning is required for this than is the case in other events. A team of facilitators is deployed. Typically a dress rehearsal is run to minimise hitches in the process. The principles of inclusivity apply here. An agenda is prepared that interplays presentations of small-group work with open-space technology or world-café methodology as described in the previous chapter.

Practical application

During translation of strategy in a big corporate, leaders from a province can meet to translate strategy constructed by top management. During the process a message is shared to the whole province at once. The group can then plan how this strategy can have an impact on the province and co-create plans for provincial implementation.

Another example could be when a bank wants to create a culture of customer-centricity. Theory about the topic can be introduced. By means of a large-group facilitated event, shared understanding can be created, significance into the strategy is stimulated and alignment is an outcome. A case study where large group events were facilitated with sustainable impact is shared in chapter 12.

Time span

Typically, a one-, two- or three-day session is facilitated.

Participants

From 100 to 300 participants meet in a large room. The layout of the room creates various stations for participants to engage in group conversations or repair to break-away rooms.

Theory to incorporate

- Theory on strategy
- Customer-centricity theory
- Theory on the task at hand

Type of facilitation

Typically the following facilitation types are important:

- Large-group facilitation
- Hosting
- Small-group facilitation

There is usually a lead facilitator with supporting facilitators and/or translators. Typically roaming microphones are provided and the lead facilitator solicits feedback from the other facilitators throughout the session so that shared understanding can be reached in the collective. Scribes often type the output of the various working stations in real time so that the output can be used as input during consecutive sessions.

Typical questions that can be asked include the following:

- What did you hear during the presentation?
- What can you do in your space to support this initiative?
- What are the implications for us as a province?
- How can you get the rest of the people in your area aligned?

Pre-requisites for success

The following are pre-requisites for success:

- Support from top management team
- A skilled team of facilitators that have shared understanding of the process

- A lead facilitator who can deal with large-group dynamics

- A well-designed process that interplays theory, activities and group work

- Visibility and support of top leadership

9.6 OCD interventions

During the implementation of an organisational transformational strategy, the unintended consequences of the chosen approach and the risks of implementing the specific approach will be identified. A planned, systemic and integrated approach in the form of an OCD strategy should be complied with, to ensure that the behavioural stretch that is needed is fast-tracked.

Such a journey often manifests as an interplay of different methodologies such as dialoguing, world café and story-telling. These are used in a combination of interventions at individual, team and organisational level. Carefully designed, custom-made and culturally sensitive OCD interventions may contribute significantly to sustainable transformational efforts. In Figure 9.1 below a typical OCD strategy that incorporates various interventions over a specific period of time with a focus on various domains is displayed.

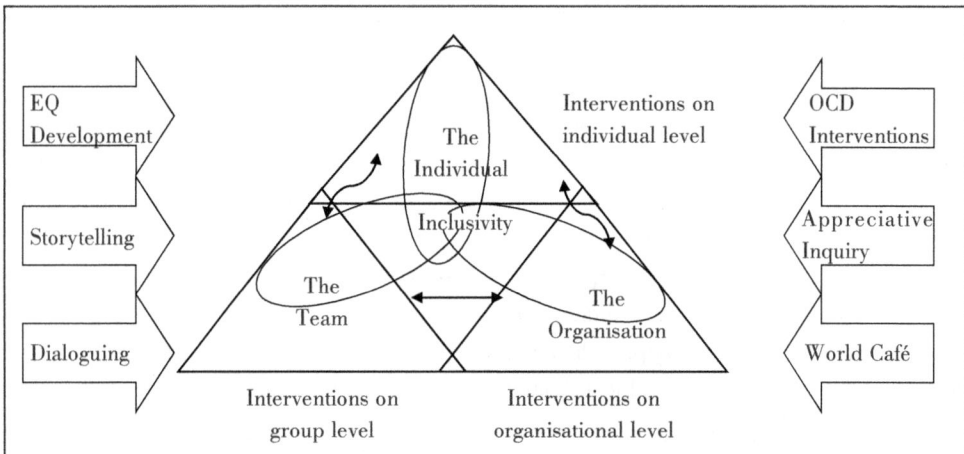

Figure 9.1   A typical OCD strategy, adapted from Viljoen (2015, p. 284)

These interventions can manifest in the form of strategy translation, group processes, large-group events, executive coaching, team-building and others that are focused on the individual, group and organisational level. The ultimate aim of these methodologies is to create an environment of inclusivity in which engagement is optimised to the benefit of the individual, the group and the organisation. The next section of this chapter focuses on specific OCD interventions that can enhance individual functioning.

Diversity interventions

Diversity interventions are critical in multi-cultural contexts. Diversity training encompasses far more than merely awareness training. If positioned optimally, diversity training will constitute an integral part of a transformational strategy.

Diversity interventions typically focus on an awareness of differences and the enhancement of interpersonal skills and empathy – all aspects of emotional intelligence as described by Reuven Bar-On (2005a). Diversity of thought is prevalent due to different personality types, different intelligences and different thinking systems (human niches), to list a few diversity factors. It is important to business to optimise business decision-making.

A diversity intervention can be facilitated from a psycho-analytical stance, with a humanistic approach or with a technique or theory that stimulates understanding of diversity of thought. These different approaches are discussed below.

Psycho-analytical events

In practice, a significant number of diversity efforts are devoted to information-based training sessions. Frans Cilliers (2000) postulates that it is only possible to study and understand diversity and its behavioural dynamics in its unconscious depth from a systems psycho-dynamic stance, which, in turn, includes the implementation of an intensive and lengthy experiential learning input.

Pieter Koortzen and Frans Cilliers (2002) describe different approaches to group processes. A facilitative approach may add value should there be a lack of interpersonal sensitivity, acceptance, realness and empathy within the group. The Tavistock-model, however, may be applied with great success if, for example, the team is presented with conscious or unconscious conflict, unhealthy splits and problems with authority. Both processes may be used in the facilitating of diverse groups.

The psycho-analytical approach incorporates systemic interrelations, the exploration of power dynamics, and the object-relations theory. This approach therefore underlines the relationship between individuals, based on what they represent, Manfred Kets de Vries (2001) explains.

When using the Tavistock approach, sense is made out of non-sense, verbal and non-verbal behaviours are interpreted, and occurrences take place in the here and now. The basic hypothesis to this approach is that the worker approaches the work situation with family needs which are unfulfilled and unconscious. He or she wants to fulfil these needs in the work situation. Because these cannot be realised in the work environment, the individual unconsciously experiences conflict. The need also includes the need for power over colleagues and even the father or mother figure. Anxiety is experienced because inherent needs do not fit the reality of the work situation. Splits in the team are explored. Diversity dynamics materialise as defence mechanisms such as pairing, fight and flight, and projections become conscious.

Practical application

During a psycho-analytical event a business case is presented to the participants. The group is confronted with a situation in which role and title fall away, and the individual is left to his or her own devices to make sense of the non-sense. Over time, as all attempts fail to deal with the task at hand, unconscious defence mechanisms manifest.

Deep and honest conversations may often occur after initial resistance, barriers are bridged, and sustainable shifts in consciousness may occur – in both the individual and the group domain.

An event is designed with very strict boundaries in terms of time, content and space. Consultants physically leave the space when the time scheduled for a session is over. Consultants do not make eye contact, do not consult to the space between people, and do not make working hypotheses on unconscious group dynamics. Different types of sessions are incorporated in the programme of the event. These may include large-group events, small-group events, review and application groups, lectures and institutional events. This approach is congruent with change resilience and diversity work.

Time span

An event that is presented in an organisational setting typically would last three days. The Robben Island Diversity experience, where diversity is explored annually, stretches over six days. This event is organised by Marius Pretorius of South Africa's department of trade and industry (DTI). The Leicester Conference presented by the Tavistock Institute is spread over 14 days.

Participants

This approach can easily deal with groups from eight up to 60. More designated consultants are employed if the number of delegates increases.

Participants from a natural or mixed team may attend.

Theory to incorporate

The following can be incorporated in the facilitation of psycho-analytical events:

- Defence mechanism

- The unconscious at work

- Power dynamics

- Taking up personal authority

Type of facilitation

Different events require different types of consultation. Typically psycho-analytical consultation is provided to unconscious group behaviour by designated consultants. Different hypotheses are made during different parts of the process. At the end the participant may ask himself or herself the following questions:

- What part of the process caused conflict in me?

- How did I respond to that?

- What can I do to manage my reaction in future?

Pre-requisites for success

The following aspects are critical pre-requisites for success:

- Psycho-analytically accredited consultants.

- External consultants often have a better impact, as they are not already well-known or trusted by the participants.

- Understanding by the line partners that learning does not necessarily happen during the event, but often months later.

- Strong leadership that buys into OCD processes as the lack of content may be seen as a shortfall.

- The additional benefit of exploring interdepartmental co-operation may present itself when delegates from different departments attend the event.

Rogerian or humanistic interventions

Facilitation from a humanistic perspective or a Rogerian approach may be viewed as a person-centred approach. In terms of this approach, a climate that is both open and trusting, as well as the opportunity for learning, is created. The above is conducive to respect, realness and empathy. Carl Rogers (1973) is the father of this approach, which is applicable for diversity interventions and personal growth groups. The application of this process could result in the significant enhancement of psychological optimal-functioning and relationship-building skills. Here, all views are accepted as equally important, and the facilitator may weave a safe culture where groups can explore group dynamics at different stages of group formation.

Practical application

In the case of a diversity intervention, the facilitator creates a space where total acceptance of differences is fostered. Individuals are invited to share their voices in a safe container. Differences that are celebrated as sameness are discovered. This can be a pure process without real content, or some tools may be incorporated.

The Diversity board game is an excellent tool in creating understanding for different cultures. This game tests the basic understanding of different cultural practices, rituals and religious practices. A video like *American History X* can be shown and facilitated. By exploring the impact of prejudice and discrimination caused by ignorance or a judgemental worldview in other countries, parallels can be drawn to what is happening in the country where this intervention is presented.

The Myers-Briggs Type indicator is an excellent indication of personality preferences. Personality differences lead to conflict, irritation, splits in groups and perceived group dynamics such as pairing and unconscious differences in thinking systems. Insight into different thinking systems, worldviews or human niches lead to enhanced self-awareness, empathy and interpersonal relationships.

Time span

A three-day session allows enough time for the different group-formation phases to develop. Due to budget constraints and lost time on the job, organisations may request a one-day or two-day intervention. Although this is not ideal from a behavioural change perspective, shorter interventions may be carefully designed and facilitated from this stance.

Participants

Ideally groups from eight to 14 can be accommodated. Individual attention is given and there must be ample time to allow for individual growth processes to take their course and for trust to develop. Participants from a natural or mixed team may attend.

Theory to incorporate

Amongst others, the following can be incorporated as theoretical framework in a Rogerian facilitated session:

- Personality types
- Emotional intelligence
- Videos on diversity
- Human niches

Type of facilitation

Rogerian or humanistic facilitation places the facilitator as a member in the group. He or she also shares from the self and ask questions such as:

- Where does that statement leave you?

- What does that statement do to you?

Delegates are challenged to speak from the self, not to interrupt others, and to share the impact on the self with others.

Pre-requisites for success

The following are pre-requisites for successful interventions:

- Well-trained Rogerian or humanistic facilitators

- Facilitators who are not scared, and can hold the emotion of others in a safe space

- Enough time

- Effective boundary management

Comparison of the psycho-analytical and Rogerian approaches to facilitation

In table 9.1 below the differences between this approach and a psycho-analytical approach is discussed.

Table 9.1   Differences between Rogerian and psycho-analytical facilitation

Phase	Rogerian / humanistic approach – the facilitator	Tavistock / psycho-analytical approach – the consultant
Forming	Two facilitators (equal)	Three designated consultants – one "in charge" and one observing.
All phases	Facilitators do not give structure. They engage with individual members.	Consultants give structure. They keep to time limits. Don't mix with members, and eat and drink alone.
All phases	Share of self and speak of the "I".	"It seems that certain members..." is a typical statement that can be made. Hypotheses are group-orientated.

Phase	Rogerian / humanistic approach – the facilitator	Tavistock / psycho-analytical approach – the consultant
Forming	Facilitator speaks of "us as team members".	Consultants are distant, representing authority – Exco.
All phases	Facilitators are real persons Form relationships with members.	Consultants are almost not human.
All phases	Facilitators make eye contact.	Eyes are kept down.
Storming	Facilitation focused on building relationships.	Consultant focused on splits in the group.
Storming to performing	Facilitator may open sessions by asking: "Where do you find yourself now?".	Due to the spiral, the interaction stated already on another level.
Storming to performing	Facilitators are on an emotional level.	Consultants don't share emotions. They almost ignore individual feelings.
Norming to performing	The facilitator can backtrack.	Aggression is towards consultant/object. Consultants never make a wrong interpretation – just project it back if they experience resistance by saying " Oh, you are resisting ..."
All phases	Democracy	Authority
All phases	Facilitator is relaxed and laid-back.	Consultants respond to backstabbing, male vs. female split, leadership and other authority issues.
Norming to performing	The facilitator checks with individuals, small groups, big groups by asking: "Are you all right? "Is this facilitative for you?"	The consultants only focus on the group and address issues indirectly "It may seem that a member has a problem with ..."
Norming to performing	The facilitator provides a context or learning opportunities.	The facilitator provides space to test issues to authority, study-group relations, and understand how they act under uncertainty. Insight is created into individual defence mechanisms.

Self-mastery, personal-purpose and change-resilience processes

Self-mastery, personal-purpose and change-resilience interventions focus on assisting the individual to find his or her authentic self and own his or her voice. These OCD processes rely heavily on different facilitation approaches described above such as psycho-analytical and or humanistic approaches. Different methodologies such as appreciative inquiry, world-café methodology and other methods described in the previous chapter may be interwoven to create life-changing interventions.

9.7 Conclusion

In this chapter different OCD interventions were discussed. The optimal time-span needed, the number of participants, the underlying theory that can be presented, the type of facilitation, and the pre-requisites for success were introduced. The master OCD consultant will be able to facilitate any of these sessions. Exposure to the different approaches to facilitation should be incorporated in the development plan of an OCD consultant. This chapter emphasised the *being* side of participants or leaders. The next chapter will address the *doing* side and will deal with business decision-making, strategy formulation and translation.

10

VALUE CIRCLES – PEOPLE MANDALAS

Co-authored by Dr Loraine Laubscher

"The only thing that guarantees an open-ended collaboration among human beings is a willingness to have our beliefs and behaviours modified by the power of conversation."

Sam Harris (2004, np)

10.1 Introduction

Value management became an essential part of operational processes in organisations in the 1980s as part of Continuous Improvement or Kaizen (1986).[5] This is an ongoing effort to improve products, services or processes. In Japan, W Edwards Deming (1950) taught top management representatives how to improve design and therefore service delivery. Quality circles formed an integral part of these processes, David Hutchins (2008) postulates. Various versions of this process are still found today in manufacturing businesses such as Green Circles in Interstate Bus Lines and Quality Circles in Toyota South Africa.

Keith van Heerden (1985) writes that Japanese high-quality products have resulted in an increase in exports with subsequent friction with other countries. They describe the basic philosophy of quality-circle activities as follows:

- Contributing to the improvement of the organic structure of the company, as well as to the company growth.

- Making the job site an enjoyable and yet challengeable place by paying respect to human personality.

- Demonstrating full capacity of human beings so that potential human capability can be used unlimitedly.

A quality circle, Hutchins (1995) explains, is a volunteer group composed of workers together with their supervisor (or team leader), who are trained to identify, analyse and solve work-related problems). The solutions on how to improve the performance of the

---

5   Masaaki (1986)

organisation are shared with management. During the process, employees are motivated. He continues (1995:23) that: "… quality circles are an alternative to the dehumanising concept of the division of labour, where workers or individuals are treated like robots".

Different problem-solving techniques are taught to team members. These include fishbone diagrams, Pareto charts, process-mapping, graphic tools such as histograms and the pie chart, run charts, control charts, scatter plots and correlation analysis flowcharts.

In the 1980s companies in South Africa tried desperately to implement these Japanese philosophies. For many of these companies this initiative was like most other fads: it soon faded. One of the reasons identified by Van Heerden (1985) was that, unlike in Japan, 50% of South Africa's adult labour force in any given factory was illiterate. The statistical methods followed in the Japanese quality circles thus presented problems.

However, it became clear to Laubscher (2013) that in Japan very different thinking systems from those in South Africa were at play. Blue optimisation initiatives did not impact on purple systems[6]. A different approach was needed to ensure that different thinking systems would connect across the boundaries of diversity of thought.

Laubscher began to integrate the spiral dynamics philosophy and theory when conducting a Quality Circle. The workers at Litemaster developed the name Value Circles and created a logo. After being part of a circle, and experiencing its value they were asked: "What should we call this circle?" They then drew three intersecting circles, and explained that one circle was for Quality, another circle was Quantity and the last was Cost. According to them the three together would give you Value. The concept 'value circles' was born. In the facilitating of a value circle, the emphasis is on finding a balance between quality, quantity and cost through the inclusivity of all. In this chapter the approach of value circles is positioned, a typical process is discussed and five case studies are shared.

Mandala (Sanskrit for 'circle 'or 'completion') is a term used for referring to a circular fractal. It is a circular pattern that has a symbolic or metaphysical meaning. Laubscher therefore uses the term, 'people mandalas' for a grouping of humans who try to bring their voices to the organisation's table to provide an in-depth examination of 'the work' in which they are involved, and through a process, develop implementable actions. These actions, together with management, will improve all aspects of their combined world of work.

10.2 The process of people mandalas

"Most mandalas have an intuitive, irrational character and, through their symbolical content, exert a retroactive influence on the unconscious. They therefore possess a 'magical' significance…"

Carl Jung, (1954)

Stakeholders such as customers, shareholders, unions and management have specific expectations from systems. Through a systemic process of input, transformation and output, a final output is delivered that can lead to stakeholder satisfaction. During the transformation

---

6   Detail about spiral dynamics or human niches is presented in chapters 5 and 6.

phase of the process, support is provided by service functions such as Human Resources and Finances. The process improvements are co-created through a process of inclusivity as defined by the author (2009) and through understanding human niches as positioned by Laubscher (2013). Inclusivity is discussed in chapter 2 and human niches in chapters 5 and 6.

Basically, People Mandalas stimulate personal growth in individuals. They also facilitate an enabling shift from right-brained people to using their left brains and vice versa. In that way, they are good for harvesting latent brainpower.

Van Heerden described Value Circles as a programme that allowed participation and stimulated implementation of solutions. Laubscher adapted this concept to integrate different thinking systems in a holistic whole, a people mandala. The people mandala process is described in figure 10.1 below.

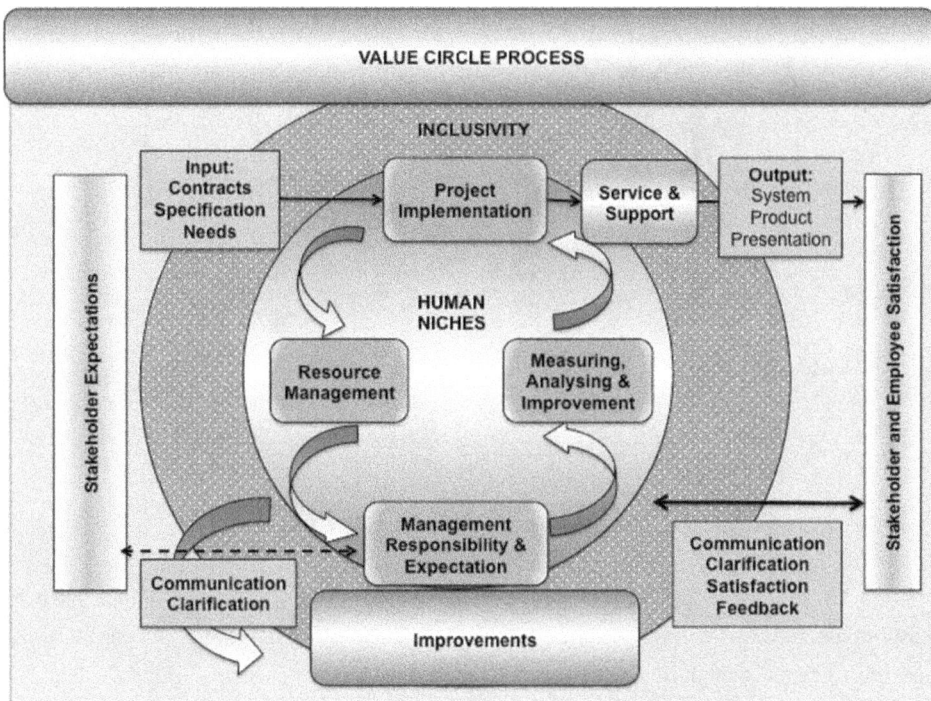

Figure 10.1 People mandala process, adapted from Loraine Laubscher (2013, p.163)

During this process the consultant alternates analogue and digital thinking activities. In such a process the consultant draws heavily on human niche understanding, especially that of purple and red as described by Laubscher (2013) and documented in chapters 5 and 6. Mostly, consultants ignore how these thinking systems differ from blue and orange worldviews. This results in confusion when carefully planned strategies seemingly have no impact whatsoever.

Laubscher (2013) applied the metaphor of the three-legged pot to a people mandala. An organisation identifies an area (a system, a mechanical or a human-resources problem) that is causing dissatisfaction. Employees appointed to solve the dilemma must be those who noticed the difficulty or who complained about it. This may be referred to as 'fitness for purpose'. Observations about the attitude and behaviour of people are integrated with the study of various psychological theories, management theories, the writings on thinking and an understanding of industry. In figure 10.2 the metaphor of the pot is presented.

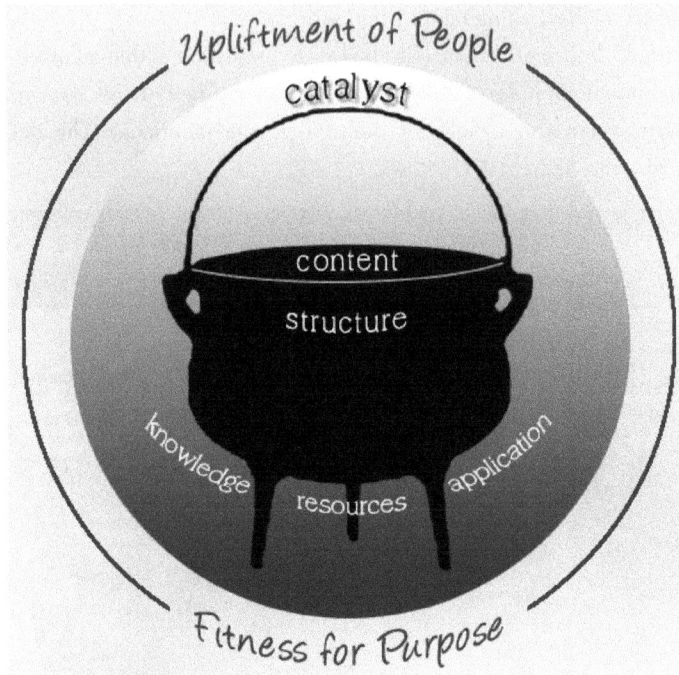

Figure 10.2   Three-legged Pot Metaphor, Loraine Laubscher (2013, p.23)

In figure 10.2 the concept of a catalyst is highlighted. An OCD practitioner should have the nature of a catalyst. A catalyst maintains its own dimensions although it is inserted into and removed from the system in which it enables change.

10.3 Value Engineering

African cultural insights should be integrated into the practice of value engineering. Value engineering principles are implemented in a way that incorporates human niche insights. The structure of the people mandalas methodology and the structure of the thinking of the people who are tasked with solving the situation, will provide an answer that is suitable for the workplace at that time. The contents of the intervention are provided by the company with a specific need, and the people they delegate to address that need. When the need has been satisfied, the people who solved the difficulty will be uplifted.

10.4 A typical people mandala process

The "squaring of the circle" is one of the many archetypal motifs which form the basic patterns of our dreams and fantasies. But it is distinguished by the fact that it is one of the most important of them from the functional point of view. Indeed, it could even be called the archetype of wholeness.

Carl Jung (1962)

In table 10.1 below a typical process flow of a people mandala is discussed. The outcome of this process becomes the input for reportback meetings.

Table 10.1 People mandala process, Loraine Laubscher (2015)

Method	Questions
Objective	What is your problem? What do we need to discuss?
Information/Function	What is happening at the moment?
Evaluate	Which function is the most important?
PERATO principle	Concentrate on the top 20%
Creativity	What else can we do? (No judgement must be allowed at this point.)
Evaluation/Development	Which of these ideas can we join together to make a good plan? What will it cost?
Five-star rating	Which of these ideas can receive a five-star rating? Which ideas receive 1,2,3,4 or 5 stars?
Report/Plan	Star ratings
Feedback/Adjustment	Solution proposed Rejected Reason for the decision Responsibility Report back (stipulate the deadline) Inform action taken

In the *next part of* the chapter different case studies are presented to illustrate how the use of people mandalas and insights of human niches successfully impacted on people and organisations.

10.5 People mandalas case studies

Quindiem Consulting (Pty) Ltd

Quindiem Consulting was established after a group of qualified actuaries who were working in different companies and firms decided to pool their resources and set up a consulting firm. One of the new partners had served as a university lecturer to the others, and he brought everyone together. Some of them were still interns, and only completed their internship after joining the newly-established consulting firm.

They were all highly-qualified professionals who thought that they did not need any rigid structure in their team, and that they would only come together to work. However, later on clashes began to occur between personalities. In November 2002 the company called in the assistance of consultants when they realised that certain difficulties within their consultancy firm needed professional attention.

The participants in the workshop wanted to know where they were going. They understood that they needed to focus on a goal, and they sensed that they needed structures, but there were different opinions within the group of what those structures should be. So they needed guidance on what their future destination should be, and what resources they required for achieving that destination.

It was also evident that some members were individualistic, and others were quite happy playing as members of a team. The consultant, Laubscher, pointed out that they needed to blend individual and company needs and interests. They needed a framework to assess what they should do and should not do, and had to clarify the issues that needed to be sorted out, as well as identify wrong actions that were being taken. The skills and personalities of the individuals needed to be identified and balanced.

To elicit this information, different collective discussions were initiated. Some of the interesting and surprising items that were discussed were a lack of desks, a completely inefficient decision-making process and a lack of future thinking. They had opted to be reactive, instead of being pro-active, hence their income was not regular, but see-sawed according to work availability. This caused a lack of balance between incomes, and hampered the further development of the group.

All of this pointed to a lack of direction in terms of the stakeholders. They were in agreement that a capital injection would solve all their difficulties. Some of the older members of the group were concerned about retaining their equity within the company. There was a continuous tug-of-war, and everyone was battling for the resources that were available. Naturally, at times this led to conflict.

The members all wanted market-related salaries. However, at that stage costs were growing at a faster rate than income, and the firm was relying heavily on one big client. The general feeling was that better use had to be made of students and staff resources. It was clear that there was not a proper understanding of each other's personalities.

Furthermore, there were issues about the day-to-day management, as well as the functioning of the office. Questions were asked about how individual performance had to be measured, and how accountability had to be established. In addition, the manner in which roles, functions and responsibilities were to be established, had to be cleared up.

The members were good at mapping out action plans, but they were not able to follow through with them. Their internal time management and efficiency were lacking. Ad hoc decisions were made, and no decision structure or role clarity was in place. The participants identified a need to be able to measure and evaluate the suitability of a project, a product and a process in terms of its contribution to wealth creation and the skills available in the organisation.

It was obvious that they needed to know and understand more about each other at a psychological level than simply as a 'hail-fellow-well-met-at-a-pub' relation. This meant normal social integration.

The following assessments were administrated: a Change State Indicator, a Psychological Map, a CPA, and MBTI[7] with each individual of the group. Every individual was profiled and given feedback, both individually and in the group.

Although this was done anonymously, the different profiles were displayed for everyone to see. This made the participants aware of how different their thinking patterns and worldviews were. At that time the Cricket World Cup cricket was being played in South Africa, and since most members of the team were cricket supporters, they could all understand the rules of the game. From this wealth of information that was gathered, and by using the analogy of a cricket team, the consultants and the group together could identify the position in a cricket team in which each profile would be best suited.

The team manager needed to be blue, as he would be precise and more digitally orientated. He had to draw up a list of the equipment that the team would need. More than likely, he would have to do the bookings ahead of time. So he had to have a time-line view of what would be needed over the following six months.

The umpire needed to be red so that he could have more energy, because he would be on the playing field all day. Even more important was that he had to be strong-minded enough to risk the displeasure of the other team members by settling disputes. The umpire was also the timekeeper and needed to interpret the rules correctly.

The bowler had to be red-blue. The main attribute of a bowler is that he needs to have high energy and be aggressive, because he has to bowl physically for a long time. However, he still has to follow the rules.

The batsman had to be blue-orange as he too had to follow the rules, but he had to be able to take a calculated risk on when to try and make runs.

The captain had to be high orange, moving into green. The reason being that the high orange had to take calculated risks on where he placed and moved the players on the field. He had to have a touch of green to do this in such a manner as not to upset the players.

---

7   Detail about the assessments described here can be found in Chapter 10.

The selector needed to be yellow since he had to select those players at every match in every country and on any type of ground that would meet the specific needs in a specific situation.

So by considering the positive aspects of their thinking niches, and applying the analogy of cricket to the business study the group were able to have everybody understand where they fitted into the business. This resulted in a more competent and innovative group of people who felt that they were on the right track to making Quindiem a successful actuarial practice.

Taxi violence in the Greater Pretoria Metropolitan Council (GPMC)

At the beginning of the new millennium there was a huge problem with taxi conflict in Pretoria. The taxi drivers began killing each other and setting one another's vehicles on fire.

Andrew Barker, who had worked closely with Laubscher before, had done previous work for the national transport department. He was approached to facilitate a meeting between the taxi associations, the public and the authorities of the provincial government. He requested her assistance. The objective of the workshop was to develop an implementable plan that would result in a transformed, violence-free taxi industry within one year.

After talking to stakeholders the conclusion was made that the business phrases that were being used were foreign to the thinking of the people in the taxi industry. A mechanism had to be identified to catalyse their understanding of the sophisticated English terminology of business.

Laubscher derived that the most meaningful entertainment in their lives would be soccer. They were soccer addicts. Andrew Barker collected as many balls as he could from different kinds of sport like soccer, rugby, tennis and so on. He collected balls from his children and the neighbours' children, as well as from Laubscher's own collection. The next day the consultants started to toss the balls to the consultants in Greater Pretoria Metropolitan Council (GPMC) boardroom where the workshop was being held. They tossed the balls back. This was a method used to take them out of the threatening conflict situation.

The consultants explained to the stakeholders that the balls represented games that had rules and regulations, as well as punishment for non-compliance. However, ball games were not only all about discipline, and could still be exciting and pleasurable.

Laubscher proposed that the group should look at the conflict situation through the framework of a soccer game. In soccer there are also strict rules and all participants, including spectators, must understand the rules. People are in control, and every participant has a part to play in the game. Every participant also has a specific function to perform in the game. If the taxi industry could be restructured into a first-class soccer team, the violence could be eliminated. The metaphor of soccer was used to create an understanding of the complexity of the taxi industry, since soccer was something that they could associate with.

All stakeholders in the taxi industry were knowledgeable regarding the rules of the soccer game. Everyone knew what the goalkeeper was supposed to do, and the consultants were able to translate the rules of the taxi industry into the understanding of the soccer game. For instance the goalkeeper could be the safety officer. The taxi was the playing field, and the referee was the taxi inspector.

The atmosphere in the room changed drastically when those present realised that because they understood the game of soccer, they also could understand what to them appeared to be the complexity of business. This was magic!

After working strategically through all the identified aspects, and applying these in the proper ratio, the functions needed were identified. Parallels with soccer was drawn, and built a structure for the taxi industry. Table 10.2 below is an extract from the original report to illustrate how the roles and rules of soccer were equated to the taxi industry.

Table 10.2   Roles and rules in the taxi industry form a value circle

Function: no function and recommendations identified			
Game – soccer		Life – taxi industry	Recommendations
	Questions and statements	Concepts and ideas	Concepts and ideas	Actions and activities
1	Identify the ball	Focus	Vehicles are the focus	None
2	What is the game?	To win	The game is survival	None
3	Who are the players?	Teams	Players are taxi owners	None
4	How do you learn the game?	By playing where you want to play	By having a vehicle and using it	None

Table 10.2 describes the concepts and ideas of the game of soccer, and then aligns them with the concepts and ideas of business within the taxi industry. From these, recommendations could be made on the actions and activities that were needed to achieve the goal. With the co-operation of the stakeholders the role that everyone should fulfil, and the date by which it should implemented, could be determined.

The workshop turned out to be very successful, and the consultant submitted a report to the GPMC. Later the department of transport requested a copy of the report, and the entire structure of the taxi industry in Pretoria was structured according to the outcomes of this workshop.

Hostel beds at Western Deep Levels Gold Mine

Another example of the implementation of value circles happened under the sponsorship of Richard (Dick) Solms, the manager of Western Deep Levels Gold Mine. Fourteen mineworkers were selected to attend the workshop to make it as inclusive as possible, with a further understanding that more participants could be chosen from the 3 000 to 4 000 low-level employees on the mine.

This group was granted the opportunity to choose anything in the hostel they would like to improve. There was agreement that all of them would like to improve the beds.

In the hostel all beds were of the double-decker type, and the space underneath the beds had to be shared by the two occupants of the beds. The beds were studied, and it was found that three things were problematic to the users. There was no place to put a Bible (or any other book) when one went to bed. If you were a smoker, there was no place to put an ashtray. The third major difficulty was the space under the bed, because all kinds of things such as wet boots, odds and ends and even left-over food were stuffed into that space. There was also the difficulty of other people touching and interfering with your personal belongings under the bed.

This revealed another difficulty. When the miners came up from underground, their boots had to be washed, and they remained wet for a long time. The hostel manager tried to solve this problem by erecting a structure of wooden poles higher than 75cm. Miners could put their boots upside-down on these poles to dry. This worked well, except at night, because if you had new boots, chances were great that someone would steal them. Therefore the wet boots ended up under the bed. Naturally this practice was totally unacceptable.

The members of the people mandalas group were required to come up with constructive answers to address these identified difficulties. They suggested that by welding a metal ring to the head of the bed into which an ashtray could be inserted as well as a Bible or book holder, this problem could be solved. The first of the two problems was therefore attended to.

The second one remained. Here the most innovative plan was that they wished to have the space under the bed enclosed. Alterations were made to the beds so that wet boots and jackets could be accommodated in a safe and dry space where the draught of air could dry them out.

This proposal was presented to the mine manager who offered to put a boilermaker at the team's disposal for this purpose. However, the boilermaker was not allowed to give them any advice. So they had to build a prototype without the assistance of the boilermaker. Eventually the participants ended up with a prototype bed, and a group of very proud men who had designed a plan, rebuilt the bed and solved the problem.

This was placed on display outside the hostel manager's office where the representative of a company that supplied the mines with various types of equipment saw it. This company asked whether they could borrow the prototype, and make a bed that would be acceptable to the mine. The plan for this bed was based on the one the miners had made. So away went the prototype, and back came a painted bed that looked very smart. Management decided to place an order for these 'new-type' beds to replace beds when they became obsolete.

Normally all orders are delivered to the mine stores, but these new beds were delivered direct to the hostel at 6pm. The sun was just about to set. All the senior management had already gone home. Laubscher was finishing off work with another group. The hostel police were contacted, and were told that the new beds would be stacked on the veranda. The alternative was to send the beds back to Johannesburg, and have them returned the next day. The beds were left on the veranda, and the watchmen were requested to guard them. The hostel manager would distribute them fairly the next morning.

On arrival the next morning only the dilapidated old beds were visible on the veranda. On investigating it was found that during the night senior personnel had claimed the new beds for themselves. Juniors were ordered to take out their old beds and put them on the veranda. The group who were responsible for the newly-designed beds were not resentful, because even though senior personnel had claimed the beds, this was an approval of and accolade to their designing skills.

From then on when a value circle (now referred to as people mandalas) was announced no-one resisted. In fact they were all very keen to be considered to partake in the OCD event.

Oil on the roof

In a different time and place, Laubscher was acting as a consultant at a factory that manufactured electrical fittings. The strategy for the business had been value managed, and an insightful manager suggested that an opportunity be given to every worker to make a contribution in his or her work area. Ten sections or work stations were identified, and a people mandala process was applied.

A particular group, who referred to themselves as Group Itekeng[8], complained that there was always grease on the floor. They were sure that one of the machines was leaking, and they wanted to have it fixed. These men were trained to perform specific functions, and were told to carry on working, and deal with the difficulties that they understood. However, they insisted that the machine was leaking oil. The catalyst, Laubscher, realised that there was a lack of general knowledge and education. These people did not know something that most people learn in primary school. This was that hot air rises. She therefore tried to find a way to help them discover this knowledge for themselves.

The next day Laubscher took a glass teapot and a small container of Condy's crystals (potassium permanganate) to work. She poured water into the teapot and put the crystals in the water. The teapot was placed on the hot plate, and as the water heated the crystals melted, and a purple stream of the heated bubbles rose up from inside the glass teapot. The group was asked why the bubbles were going up. Suddenly one said that it had to be because hot air was going up. He turned to her and asked whether that could be right. It was confirmed. The consultant then asked how this principle could assist them in their problem-solving initiative. Then the magic happened. They all looked up, and felt the oil dripping from the roof. They could actually see the drops of oil dripping onto the floor.

They then discovered that there was a fan directly above this particular machine. There was an outlet, but it was all clogged up, and was of no use. They told Laubscher that the fan had not been working for years. They understood that their dilemma came from the

---

8   A Sotho word that means 'let us try'. Today Sotho is one of the 11 official languages of South Africa.

condensation of steam and oil lubricants from the machine, and that hot air was taking the oil up to the roof.

A solution now had to be put forward to management. It was clear that the roof and the fan had to be cleaned, and that the fan had to be serviced. However, these people went one step further, and said that they would be prepared to come in to do the cleaning on a Saturday morning. Their condition was that the foreman and the consultant also came. Management had to supply brooms and a chemical substance that would remove the oil from the roof, floor and extractor fan. Everybody turned up, and spent the Saturday morning cleaning up the mess. They ended up with the cleanest floor in the factory after everything was cleaned. Management brought in experts to service the fans.

An agreement was made with management that the fans would be checked monthly and serviced when required. The workers agreed to clean it thoroughly every six months. They were happy and production increased.

Buffelsfontein

The general manager of the Buffelsfontein mine came up with a proposal that would improve their safety record, the stoping width, and water and electricity consumption. After investigations in the different departments, the consultant, Laubscher, became aware that to be able to have positive results one would first need to look at the training school and implement strategies that would produce improvement at the bottom of the organisation. The reason for working from the bottom up was because previous top-down strategies had not achieved the desired results.

Laubscher started by examining the methodology that was used in the training centre. At that time it was customary at mines that on returning from leave the worker was required to spend one day at the training school. This was done so that the worker could be updated on new regulations, and could have his previous training reinforced.

After a few years of working on the mine these miners could recite the training programme word-for-word. The trainer required the miners to learn the manual by heart. She spoke to a man who had 17 years' service on the mine, and asked him: "What do you do when you arrive at your work station?" He immediately recited: "When arriving at your work station you must observe the safety rules."

Laubscher then questioned his understanding of 'the safety rules' which he had just recited and found that he had hardly any understanding of them. She decided to retrain the trainers, and change the training room's seating from a school-room setup to horse-shoe style.

In addition she requested that all the trainers have a week's training. During the first week half of the trainers attended the session, and during the next week the other half did. The methodology of action learning was discussed, and a way was sought to get the trainers to ask questions instead of talking at the people. A video camera was used to record the training efforts. Everyone was giving feedback to someone else. They then practised their training methods until they could do them very well. It became a competition between the trainers to become the best in the class.

With Laubscher's help three members of the value circle department designed the programme and its contents for the different job-graded levels. The total workforce from a mine overseer's section was used for a day. It took a month to cover all the sections.

Initially, when the manager gave us the task of improving the safety record, they held the bottom position on the McKleland shield. After being measured at the end of 12 months they were awarded first place, and won the shield. During the same period the stoping was reduced by 7 cm, and the cost of water and electricity was halved.

This proves that an understanding of the thinking, culture and motivation of the workforce is absolutely necessary. This insight must be used at every interface if productivity at the bottom of the organisation is to be improved. Workers must contribute their own ideas to all initiatives that are needed to improve productivity.

Anglo Platinum

An Anglo Platinum mine invited Laubscher to attend their safety-training session. A complete set of safety signs was available, but they were individual examples of all the safety signs that were used in a mine.

Signs of all the different gloves were referred to by the same name. When asked whether there was any difference between the gloves in the signs, nobody had an answer. They could see no difference between the glove that should be worn when acid was being used, and the glove to be worn when working with wood to protect the worker against splinters.

At the close of business for the day the consultant hurried off to town to buy a sheepskin, and managed to obtain some acid. She also bought a dropper. The next morning Laubscher took these articles to the training centre. She put the sheepskin down with the woolly side up, and poured some acid on it with the dropper.

The onlookers were stunned. They thought that some kind of magic had to be involved because the acid was burning holes in the sheepskin. She was then able to show them that the gloves that were used when working with acid were different to those when working with wood or metal for instance. They could now understand this. The results reminded me of the story of the 100th monkey syndrome. Very soon everybody knew that special gloves were to be worn when working with acid.

The place that listens: Western Deep Levels

At Western Deep Levels an enlightened management corps led the mine in the late 1990s. They were aware of the fact that the mine had a semi-literate workforce. The management team were looking for a way to help these people understand all the rules and regulations on the mine.

The manager, Dick Solms, was approached with a proposal to create a comic-book leaflet to explain HR procedures such as grievances to the workforce. When the leaflet was printed, the information centre was overwhelmed by the demand for them, and the reason for this increased demand was investigated. Workers started to collect the whole series, and took them home to places like the Transkei and Lesotho to explain to their children what the mining world was like by means of the pictures. In figure 10.3 is an example of this pamphlet describing the grievance procedure.

Figure 10.3   The place that listens, Laubsher (2013, p. 178)

When Dick Solms commissioned a people mandala to investigate the information needs of the workforce, a building designated by the people was created. He wanted to put a big ear on the building to say that it was 'The place that listens'.

Before the official opening of the information centre, a competition was held to find a suitable name for it. For entries to qualify the name had to convey the function of the centre and, most importantly, it had to be in the mine vernacular. Most of the people who took part had a hard time with this problem, but to the eventual winner it was no sweat. All Joseph Khanyile did was change his own name from a noun to a verb. Hence 'Khanyisela Thina' was born. In Zulu, 'Khanyisela thina' means 'show us the light' or 'enlighten us', and both interpretations are pertinent to the function of the information centre.

This proves that with a little thought and ingenuity much can be accomplished. An answer to any problem is always close at hand if only everyone can keep an open mind and approach it from a different view. The information centre was responsible for issues such as pay queries, procedural queries, and appeals regarding disciplinary hearings, timetables for long-distance bus journeys and education on HIV/Aids. A register was kept of every query that failed to be answered. These unresolved queries were investigated and the lack of information was corrected.

10.6 Benefits of a people mandala

"It became increasingly plain to me that the mandala is the center. It is the exponent of all paths. It is the path to the center, to individuation."

Carl Jung (1954)

The benefits that typically manifest from a people mandala include:

- The creation of an open environment within the company for unrestricted communication at all levels.

- By the participation of workers at all levels the company is able to fully use the abilities and skills of all of its human resources, and owing to their involvement, the staff are far more motivated towards affecting improvement within their areas of responsibility.

- The voice in the organisation is heard and inclusivity is strengthened.

- Decision-making becomes more structured and sustainable. Creative, cost-effective decisions can now be made at all levels.

Tangible benefits to the various companies materialised in the form of production, staff involvement and engagement and ultimately monetary turnover. Simultaneously staff turnover decreased. Participants of these sessions reported a permanent shift of consciousness. This did not only change how they functioned and worked, but also how they fulfilled their roles in their families, communities and society at large.

10.7 Conclusion

In this chapter the process of people mandalas was described. Some case studies were discussed where these mandalas had practical and sustainable results. It is important to incorporate this approach in a book on OCD. Although OCD is concerned with the entire organisation, and should be mandated from the top, its application must be translated throughout the organisation. As an OCD approach, people mandalas, can be facilitated with great effect to ensure engagement, collective decision-making and inclusivity.

Without Laubscher's knowledge, the author of this book concludes this chapter with a reading by Pat Beck[9] during a ceremony at the 2000 International Spiral Wizards Confab held in Dallas:

> "Laubscher is at her most effective as a trouble-shooter. She quickly senses the value system conflicts between emerging black leaders who show evidence of red or orange thinking. She is adept at translating between these elites-in-the-raw and the blue minds which flourish at middle management levels and within manpower functions. She unravels such problems by running three- to five-day workshops or mediating between the conflicting rings on the spiral. Feelings run high, raw nerves

---

9   Don Beck's wife

are exposed, but the disciplined thinking inherent in the value management process, coupled with Laubscher's ability to read and interpret the deep value structures at play, often results in the forging of a new and imaginative solution which none of these groups or parties believed possible. Since this essentially democratic process builds in compliance and support, the solutions agreed on usually work. Whether the issue is the quality of hostel food, inter-group work relationships, or even the question of peace and harmony in the wider community, the technology appears to be highly successful."

Recently one of the participants of a people mandala intervention wrote on the evaluation form to Laubscher: "You are my ancestor." A bigger compliment cannot be imagined.

PART 4
EFFECTING - FUNCTIONAL
INTERRELATEDNESS OF OCD

11

DESCRIBING INDIVIDUAL AND COLLECTIVE BEHAVIOUR

"There is no ideal leadership style. The better leader is the congruent one".

Clare Graves (1974)

11.1 Introduction

Societal culture determines our view of the world, and each culture perceives a different reality. This is because people need to make observations and gather knowledge that makes sense within their particular cultural perspective.

To be able to deal with differences, leaders need to understand the psychological and cognitive processes that characterise the perceptions of ethnically different individuals. Different assessments and psychometric tests can be used to inform OCD processes such as diversity and change resilience interventions. Further, understanding the multi-cultural dynamics in an organisation can assist leadership to translate sensitively and with culturally intelligence.

In this chapter different assessments are presented. Some of the assessments report on relatively constant parts of the psyche. These assessments can be used to increase awareness and enhance interpersonal skill and empathy by explaining different ways of being. They are very helpful in personal and team development interventions.

Other assessments have a variable nature that can be developed. Therefore, it is ideal to administrate them before OCD interventions are facilitated. OCD strategy and intervention design can then be influenced by the specific dynamics indicated by the assessment. A post-test after the transformational journey can provide information about the effectiveness, sustainability and return on investment of the transformational effort.

In this chapter, the different assessments are discussed. Specific emphasis is placed on the Change State Indicator (CSI) and the Benchmark of Engagement (BeQ) because of their particular relevance to the field of OCD.

11.2 Individual differences that contribute to diversity of thought

"Because we are aware of so little of our cultural makeup, we often act automatically, without inserting awareness and choice into the decision-making loop."

Michelle LeBarOn (2005)

Personality

The first aspect of diversity to be explored is that of personality, which provides insight into the preferences of an individual. The metaphor of producing music may be effective in describing the impact on behaviour of the diversity aspects under discussion.

Personality may be viewed in terms of the type of musical instrument that people play. Certain people play the piano, while others play guitar. Certain people play the drums and others the violin. The Myers-Briggs Types Indicator (MBTI) measures personality as a diversity factor. According to Carl Jung (1954) personality preferences are relatively fixed and inborn. The MBTI can be used in personal and team development interventions.

Level of complexity

Different individuals are proficient in playing different types of music in a specific way on the preferred instrument. The aspect of different types of intelligence may explain the level of complexity with which an individual feels comfortable (Bach or a children's tune – both beautiful, but different in terms of complexity), the comfort in terms of the impact of the music on others and the confidence in playing the tunes.

This metaphor for the ability to handle complexity describes the extent to which a person prefers to deal with the ambiguity of the time-span of discretion as described by the Career Path Appreciation instrument and methodology (CPA). According to Elliot Jaques (1997) this aspect is relatively fixed, and will develop over time on a projected curve as described by the Mode Plot.

This interview-based assessment helps the individual to understand whether he or she is in flow, misused or underused. Constructing a graph where different team members' current levels of work are plotted can be very insightful. This can be used for organisational design purposes. In the scope of the book, namely OCD, it can be applied at individual and group level to create understanding of differences in individuals and teams.

Question of existence

Different people join organisations for different reasons. The question of existence determines why a person does what he or she does, Laubscher (2013) teaches. The Psychological Map and Change State Indicator (discussed in the next paragraph) can be used as a framework in diagnosing the diverse and often conflicting world-views of people. These apparent differences begin to make much more sense when analysed through the prisms of this psychological model.

Although the Psychological Map may seem both complex and conceptual, it does lend itself to the formulation of specific managerial behaviours that make sense to each of the stations on the map and establish the type of milieu that each system needs in order to survive and prosper according to Beck (2013). Human niches, as indicated by this instrument, may shift as individuals adapt to changing life conditions.

Insights gained from spiral dynamics theory can be used at individual, group or organisational level during OCD interventions. In the metaphor of music, human niches explain why we play the game of life. The Psychological Maps give an indication of the current human niche of an individual or a collective, and also indicate which human niches are emerging.

Change States

The Change State Indicator (CSI) is administered in conjunction with the Psychological Map. It assesses the change dynamics of an individual, a group and an organisation. Therefore, it is particularly important for OCD consultants.

Clare Graves (1974) identified different states of change that describe the dynamics of change that individuals, groups, organisations and societies display in multi-national settings. These stages are displayed in Figure 11.1 below.

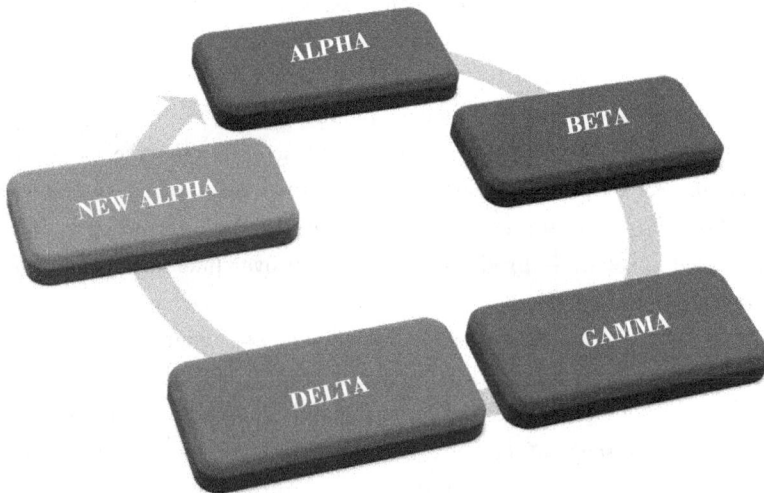

Figure 11.1   Don Beck's States of Change, Viljoen (2013, p 3)

Each of the states of change in Figure 11.1 above will be discussed briefly. The Change State Indicator includes 10 scales: Alpha, Beta, Gamma, Delta, New Alpha, First- and Second-order Change, Flex, and Order and Chaos.

A good metaphor might be flying through a complex weather system. There are safe passages with clear, stable conditions (Alpha). However, there can also be turbulence (Beta) and even wind shears (Gamma). At the transitional areas are tipping points (Delta) that can either cause us to turn back or move on to clear skies once again (New Alpha).

Alpha is a condition where individuals, organisations or societal human niches successfully address the problems of existence. An individual 'has it together' in the real world. The company is doing well in its niche. Society is meeting the needs of its citizens in an effective way, Beck explains.

Beta, Beck says, arises with doubts. Something is wrong. It is the early-warning signs of something that is not right. The old ways of working no longer work; the boat is rocking. Successful living may have introduced new and unforeseen elements into the environment. Maybe we are just bored because we are no longer challenged. We may have personal problems, companies may show evidence of decline; communities might experience stress, conflict and discord. We do not really understand yet what is happening. So three strategies may apply:

- We try to do more of the same because we do not believe that something is wrong in the bigger system. It is only our implementation or enforcement that can improve. Individuals recommit to their tasks and organisations 'get on with the programme'.

- We may look for ways to reform, fine-tune or adjust. The system will keep its main features. We experience nostalgia for 'the good old days' when everything seemed to work. We forgot why they did not. This is called first-order change.

- Alternatively, we recognise that the system is just a system; there are others as well. A window opens for a transition through the evolutionary option into a new alpha. This is called second-order change.

Gamma is a time of growing frustration, feelings of being trapped and an entire array of antisocial, self-destructive and acting out behaviours. The anger comes from first knowing what is wrong and why, second from understanding what will relieve the tension and create a new alpha, but third, fearing that powerful and often punitive barriers stand in the way. These barriers can be internal to the person or the group.

Gamma may lead to violence, destructiveness, strikes and revolt against the *status quo*. This becomes the revolutionary option as individuals and movements literally or symbolically throw themselves against the barriers. In milder cases, it's a time of wanting to escape, run away, break out and be free of the bonds that entrap us.

Gamma is often seen in people experiencing the panic of a mid-life crisis or when going through a major personal trauma where the future looks hopeless. Since forward movement seems blocked at gamma, we may experiment with a regressive search. We explore old ways of thinking, dust off solutions, revive the 'tried-and-true' and believe the 'old time way was good enough for those that came before me and therefore for me.'

Delta is a period of excitement and rapid change where the barriers are overcome and precious restraints drop away. People take care of their own destinies. The delta energy surge is often raw, enthusiastic and unrestrained, according to Beck (2013). Old ways of living give way to fresh solutions as unexpected different structures begin to emerge in a swirl of activity. This exuberance ignites creativity, resourcefulness, and dedication to the task of designing a new future or reality. The thrill of liberation mobilises people in search of the new utopia.

Delta often brings stress into relationships, and may even trigger negative reactions from those left behind. Too much delta, too soon, too emotionally displayed, can produce a serious backlash that actually reinforces the old barriers.

The new alpha is the consolidation of the ideas and coping systems that emerged during the delta state into new systems, paradigms and arrangement. The individual returns to a steady state as the world is once again in sync. The organisation is congruent to its market place or within its professional niche. Society itself appears to be in stride with the environment. Many come to believe the ultimate has been reached; the world will stay this way forever. Over the horizon, around the corner or up the road lies a new beta.

The 'prefer order' and 'thrives on chaos' scales indicate where the people see their personal pendulum to be. Since CSI is a composite instrument, this data reflects a general self-appraisal and may not apply equally to each human niche in the profile.

The human niche within us ebbs and flows or brightens and dims as conditions – both internal and external – change. Thus, the world-in-motion and the brain-in-motion are constantly moving through stages, in and out of steady states (alpha and new alpha) through transitional phases (beta, gamma, delta). The flex-scale indicates the relative ease with which these changes occur. For some people, shifts are fairly easy. For others, they are crisis points that consume vast energy. In figure 11.2 the scales of order, chaos and flex are presented.

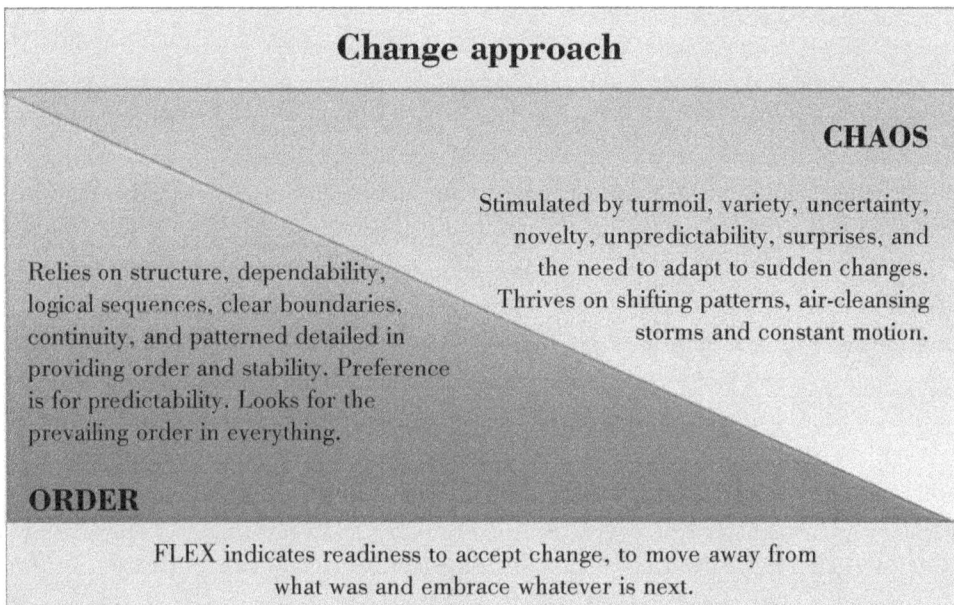

Change approach

CHAOS

Stimulated by turmoil, variety, uncertainty, novelty, unpredictability, surprises, and the need to adapt to sudden changes. Thrives on shifting patterns, air-cleansing storms and constant motion.

Relies on structure, dependability, logical sequences, clear boundaries, continuity, and patterned detailed in providing order and stability. Preference is for predictability. Looks for the prevailing order in everything.

ORDER

FLEX indicates readiness to accept change, to move away from what was and embrace whatever is next.

Figure 11.2   Don Beck's order, chaos and flex diagramme, Viljoen (2013, p. 4)

Finally, the theory proposes that every solution produces new problems, so the cycle continues to repeat itself at progressively higher levels of complexity. Because this progressive change is through different human niche terrain, you must understand that for example, orange gamma is different from green gamma or red gamma. Thus, the behavioural manifestations of the change states will differ depending upon the operating human niche. The alpha state is that of balance, but the kind of thinking (human niche) will determine just what that balanced condition is like.

The CSI also gives an indication of the individual, the group's, the organisational or the societal change paradigm. Two change paradigms are identified which can be described by to themes namely: more of the same or reframing.

Change paradigm	
First order change	**Second order change**
Change occurs within a system which, itself, remains unchanged. Restore balance. Improve within givens. Rooted in past decisions. Renew, Refurbish, Reform. Work harder and Smarter.	Mega-systems shift to new paradigms, new assumptions and new consolations. Generated by outside events/influences. Driven by perceived future. Puzzling, Unexpected, Paradoxical. New wine; new wineskins.
Basic theme: MORE OF THE SAME	Basic theme: REFRAMING

Figure 11.3   Don Beck's change paradigms, Viljoen (2013, p. 8)

A systemic interplay of human niches, questions of existence and coping mechanisms available to deal with the multiple combinations of external and internal challenges posed to the individual, the group, the organisation or the society, will lead to the change option that emerges. This change option can be described either as evolutionary or revolutionary. These options are described in the Figure 11.4 below.

Change options	
Evolutionary option	**Revolutionary option**
Previous problems solved	Demands fundamental change in structures/systems
Potential in the brain	Unrelenting "All or Nothing" assault on barriers/obstacles
Access to new systems	Defends actions by finding noble purpose for "the cause"
New models and patterns	Prototyping the new
Available resources	New realities emerging
Consolidation and support	Insitutionalising

Figure 11.4   Don Beck's change options, Viljoen (2013, p. 8)

The CSI provides valuable information for the individual. Further, it can inform OCD strategy at group or organisational level. The importance of change resilience in the new world of work is critical. This instrument provides systemic insights into the phenomenon of change in the system. As a person's change resilience changes, he or she moves through the change curve and new change states may manifest. In our music metaphor, the CSI studies how an individual plays when things change, and how open he or she is to adapting.

Emotional intelligence

Not everyone, however, possesses the skill, the competency, the capability or the will to play the preferred instrument effectively. Emotional intelligence, as defined by Reuven Bar-On (2005a) is the ability of an individual to cope with environmental demands. These abilities can develop. The Bar-On EQ-i measures this ability of an individual. It is possible that intelligence such as emotional intelligence may be developed. The higher the emotional intelligence of an individual, the more gifts caused by personality and intelligences manifest for the bigger good.

As emotional intelligence as described by Reuven Bar-On (2005b) is the only aspect of the psyche described in this manner that can change, it makes sense to use this instrument as a diagnostic tool for executive coaching and personal development. The ability to do pre- and post-tests on emotional intelligence development makes it possible to quantify personal growth statistically.

Emotional intelligence is a critical skill that must be developed in order to deal with diversity, as it encompasses the ability of a person to deal with environmental demands. Emotional self-awareness, which is one of the intra-personal skills, measures the extent to which a person reflects on and allows emotions and, then, acts accordingly.

It is argued throughout this book that awareness is a critical skill in the new world of work. Awareness and other emotional intelligence constructs, such as empathy (the ability to place yourself in someone else's shoes), interpersonal relationship skills (the ability to initiate, continue and enjoy relationships with others) and social responsibility (social awareness) may be enhanced through personal development.

An increase in interpersonal skills will result in enhanced cross-cultural relationships. Increased reality-testing (the ability to see things as they really are), flexibility (emotional adaptability) and problem-solving ability (the ability to deal with the situation) may also assist in intercultural relations.

The inclusion of stress management constructs (impulse control and stress tolerance) and general mood (optimism and happiness) differentiates the Bar-On EQ-i from other emotional intelligence measurements. This instrument can be instrumental in identifying future intervention. Further, it can quantify growth at individual and collective levels.

The Benchmark of Engagement

The BeQ™ measures the interplay between assumptions and perceptions in organisations around constructs that contribute to the unleashing of individual voices, contributions and gifts. At any point in time, a company should be able to measure the capacity within its system to perform (culture) in order to determine the essence of where it might be, how its members perceive its goals, objectives, leadership and culture and how this is all informed by the interaction between individuals, teams, the organisation itself, and the greater political, societal and situational context in which it operates.

Depending on how OCD practitioners roll out strategic initiatives and engage members in decision-making, an inclusive, accountable, transparent and consistent culture that encourages engagement can be constructed. The amount of human energy in the system can be determined. The level of energy in the system will dictate the type of OCD intervention that is needed in the particular system.

No company can ever see itself in isolation, since the micro- and macro-environment it forms part of will have a direct impact on its functioning. Changes within these environments are always systemic in nature, implying that direct/intended and indirect/unintended actions, impacts, perceptions and resultant behaviours will always be present in an organisation. Gaining insight and understanding into the various systemic and dynamic impacts will assist leadership in developing sustainable initiatives, co-created by all, that will contribute to the unleashing of individual engagement and, hence, increased commitment to the company's strategic drivers.

The BeQ™ stemmed from the extensive research conducted and documented in the author's doctoral thesis (2009). The BeQ™ has been conducted in 42 different countries, and more than 55 000 people participated in the ethnographic, multi-cultural research on engagement. Basically, it was found that inclusivity could be used to achieve sustainable business results on triple bottom line.

In order to create engagement, different outcomes must be achieved on different domains, namely:

Individual domain

Individuals must ensure that they have the ability to engage by:

- Self-development

- Optimising leadership behaviour

- Formal development efforts

- Managing the self

- Self-mastery and personal purpose work

Group domain

Engagement in groups must be enabled by:

- Optimising group dynamics
- Clarifying roles and responsibilities
- Understanding group stages and unconscious patterns

Organisational domain

Organisational culture (how things are done in a specific organisation) should be conducive to:

- Inclusivity
- Openness
- Valuing diversity
- Allowing voice

It is the task of leaders on all levels in the organisation to optimise engagement on individual, group and organisational domains. As Carl Jung (1954) said: "*As within, so without*". Customers as external stakeholders will soon sense the transformation that engagement unleashes from within. The BeQ™ also has an external measurement that can compare internal human capacity with external customer experience.

The author (2009) defined engaged commitment as "the trait of sincere and steadfast fixity of purpose, a person of energy and commitment" and "the act of binding oneself to a course of action". In the model that will be presented, the terms 'commitment' and 'engagement' will be used interchangeably. Employee engagement, thus, is a concept that is generally viewed as managing discretionary effort, that is, when employees have choices, they will act in a way that furthers their organisation's interests. An engaged employee is a person who is fully involved in, and enthusiastic about, his or her work.

The BeQ™-model measures the interplay between assumptions and perceptions in organisations around constructs that contribute to the unleashing of individual voices, contributions and gifts. Since the organisational and the country climate, as well as the employees' worldview, influence these perceptions, they are also explored.

In figure 11.5 below the constructs of the BeQ™ are displayed. It should be noted that these constructs can be viewed as the pre-requisites for sustainable business performance.

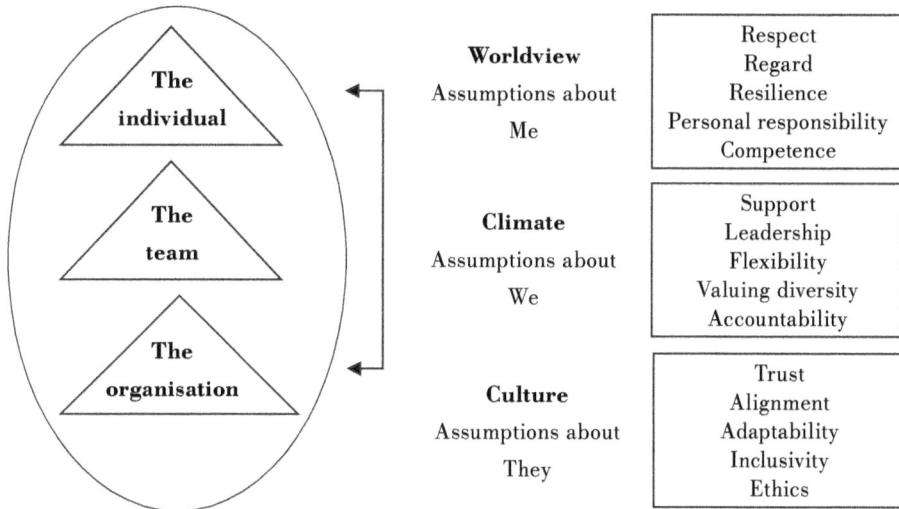

Figure 11.5   Benchmark of engagement™ constructs, Viljoen (2015, p.57)

Scientific correlations have been found between people having "voice" and levels of engagement. The questionnaire is customised to measure the unique business needs that present themselves to the management of the organisation, as well as to include dynamics unique to the country in which the organisation operates. The BeQ™ is unique in that:

- It is construct based.

- Systems thinking principles are applied.

- It is multi-culturally sensitive.

- It is diagnostic.

- Reports are interpreted by hand to ensure that fine subtleties are recorded.

- It incorporates spiral dynamics enabling a human niche distribution of the organisation or group.

- The I-engage, we-engage, org-engage and society-engage can all be used separately.

- The I-engage almost has psychometric properties (r = 0.78 where 0.4 is acceptable for a perception study and 0.8 is psychometrics).

- Line management can co-design up to 50% of the questionnaire.

- Specialised OCD practitioners interpret the results.

There are direct business outcomes that correlate with the feeling of human energy in the system to perform. The benefits of engagement are visible in figure 11.6.

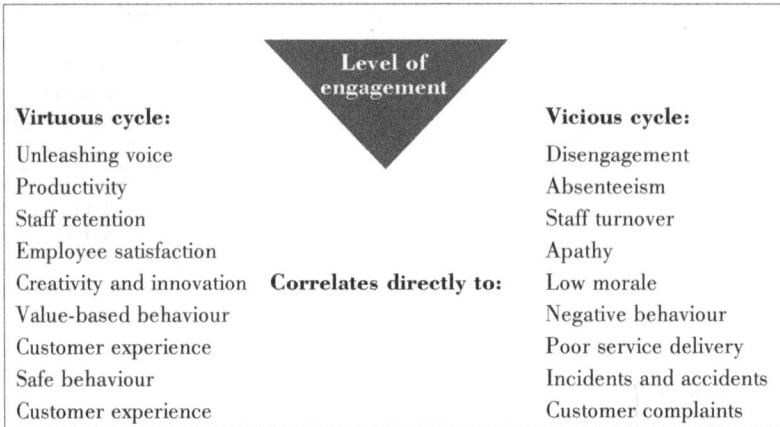

Figure 11.6 Benchmark of engagement™ constructs, adapted from Viljoen (2015, p. 54)

A typical BeQ process is planned and project managed as indicated in Figure 11.7.

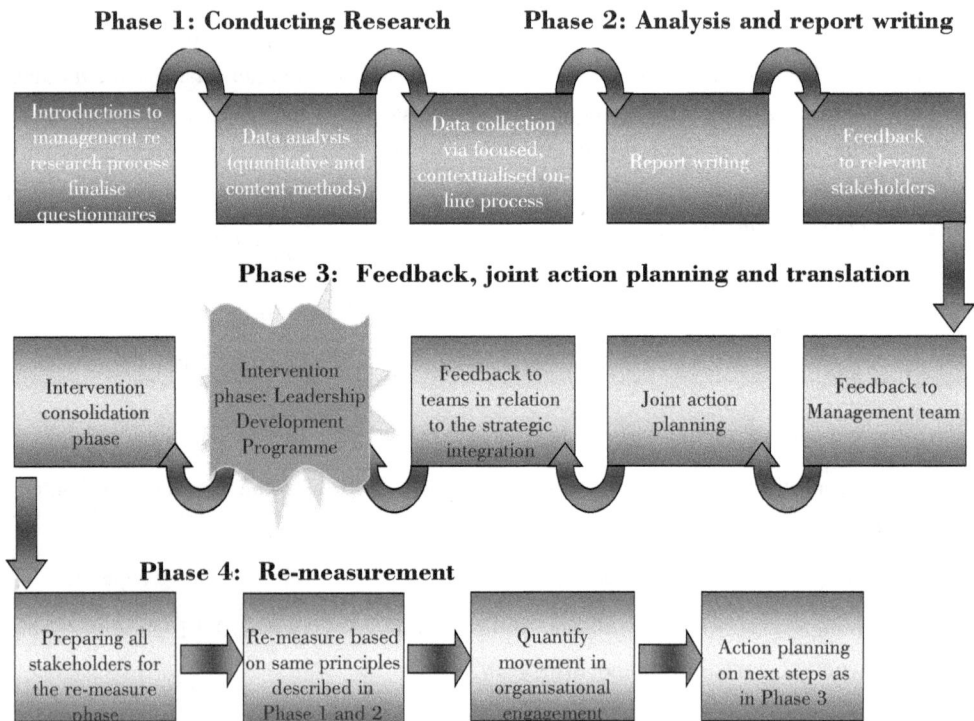

Figure 11.7 Benchmark of engagement™ process, Viljoen (2013, p. 15)

It is important to structure a BeQ™ process effectively as indicated in Figure 11.6 above. The BeQ™ is not a quick fix, nor is it a loose-standing measurement. It is organisational transformational philosophy. Dawie Strydom (2014), in a lecture to master's students, says that this instrument has in the nature more of a business study than a culture study.

11.3 An OCD approach towards assessments

In Figure 11.8 below, the complexity of ensuring optimal individual, group and organisational behaviour is displayed. All these aspects should be addressed from an OCD perspective to ensure congruence.

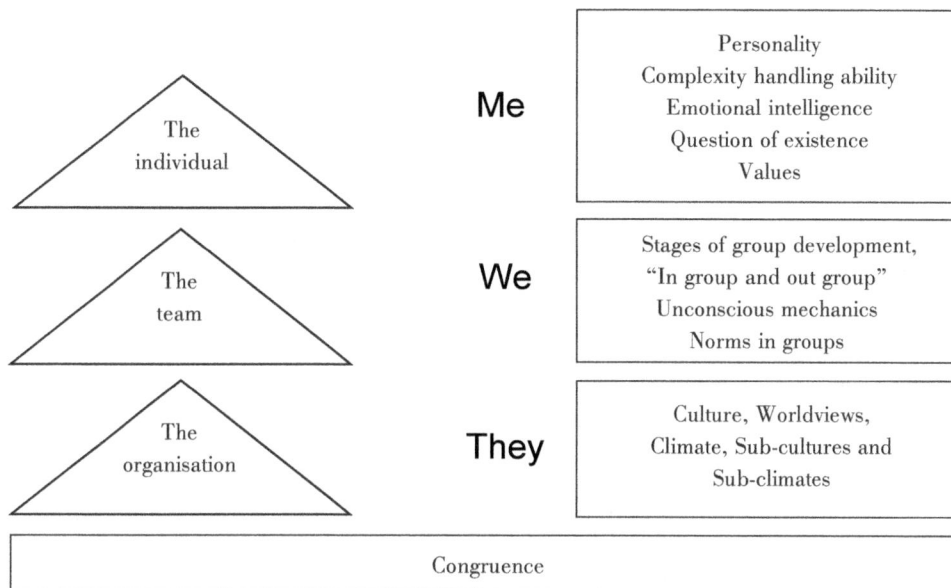

Figure 11.8 OCD approach to assessments

Figure 11.8 clearly shows the integral, comprehensive nature of an OCD approach towards assessments and interventions. It is not a quick fix, nor are they loose-standing interventions. Further, OCD practitioners seldom do 'fun'. They are deeply concerned with human behaviour in organisations and how to rekindle the individual and organisational spirit that will result in soulful organisations and purposeful, mindful leadership that manages functional social systems.

11.4 Finding your voice

> *"The world will not be destroyed by those who do evil, but by those who watch them without doing anything."*
>
> Albert Einstein

OCD consultants can assist leaders to crystallise their unique voices. This can happen if they:

- Gracefully accept the gifts presented by their personality preferences.

- Own up to the impact thereof (in terms of the music metaphor because they play the piano, and, by implication, not the drums).

- Develop the skills needed to do this, and are aware of what is required in the relevant context.

- Become aware of their own level of complexity ability.

- Understand their own human niche and change states.

- Develop their emotional and/or other intelligences and, thus, become self-aware, develop solid, interpersonal relationship skills, adaptability, and, lastly, problem-solving ability.

- Individualise, as Carl Jung (1954) described.

Understanding how the person's question of existence is congruent with the organisational and national culture can be very helpful in understanding the manifested dynamics. However, a specific organisational culture, namely a culture of inclusivity, is needed if individuals are to show willingness to bring their unique, diverse gifts and their voices to the organisational table. It is the task of leadership to create such a climate. This culture should be conducive to unleashing individual voices and gifts.

11.5 Conclusion

From the previous discussion it is clear that diversity factors such as diversity of thought form an integral part of the unique quality of an individual. It makes business sense to create opportunities for individuals to explore who they are, what their unique contributions are and ways to optimise these unique contributions, while simultaneously minimising the impact of their individual growth areas. Measurements and assessments should account for these differences.

Although each individual perceives and makes decisions on the basis of diverse factors such as personality, this process is uniquely different for everyone. An awareness of an individual's unique style, preference and skill is important for growth on an individual level.

Awareness of the self is situated within the boundaries drawn by culture, worldview and the individual habits of attention that contribute to cultural fluency. This awareness is an essential complement to the understanding of cultural dynamics. As awareness filters through the understanding which, in turn, increases and informs, individuals are able to apply themselves with increasing fluency.

Unless leaders develop an awareness of divergent cultural starting points and insight into own dynamics, miscommunication and frustration may negatively influence interpersonal relationships. OCD interventions may enable leaders, first, to optimise individual strengths, second, to manage the unintended implications thereof, and, last, to understand and optimise the strengths and development areas of others.

In this chapter, we dealt with the *being*. In the next chapter the organisational *doing* is discussed.

12

STRATEGY AND ORGANISATIONAL CHANGE

Co-authored by Dr Adri Drotskie

"I knew that in finding the Mandala as an expression of the Self, I attained what was for me the ultimate."

Carl Jung (1954)

12.1 Introduction

Strategy is an integral part of an organisation, irrespective of its size or nature. Strategy is about positioning an organisation for the future. In the rapidly changing, complex and uncertain environment in which an organisation has to grow and survive, strategy is a given.

In this chapter the focus is on the relationship between strategy and organisational change and their interdependency. The chapter starts with the latest approach in strategy, and moves to the relationship between strategy and organisational behaviour. The interdependency between strategy and change will then be investigated, and the chapter will be concluded with the important aspect of strategy implementation and the role of change. The link between strategy and structure was omitted as it forms part of the field of organisational design, and not OCD per se.

12.2 Strategy approach in the 2000s

Strategy is a well-established concept that was initially created within a military or war context. It was all about making plans to outperform the enemy. Strategy evolved over time, and in the 1960s the first definition of strategy within an organisational context, namely, "a set of decision-making rules for guidance of organisational behaviour" was developed by Igor Ansoff (1980). He identified the following distinguishing characteristics of a strategy:

- The process of strategy formulation does not result in immediate action.

- Strategy is used to generate projects through a search process.

- Strategy becomes unnecessary when the historical dynamics of an organisation takes it where it wants to go.

- Successful use of strategy requires strategic feedback.

In the 20th century, markets in the western world underwent significant changes in structure and behaviour. Strategy became a primary concern for business managers when competitors gained market power. Strategic planning came to the scene in the mid-1960s through the work of Minsberg. He worked with the concept of a way of separating thinking from doing, and created a new specialist function in organisations with people known as strategic planners.

During the 1960s to 1980s 10 schools of thought about strategy came about, namely, a prescriptive approach that included a design school, a planning school, a positioning school, and a strategy formulation approach comprising entrepreneurial, cognitive, learning, power, cultural and environmental schools, as well as a configuration school.

The 1990s was characterised by the difference between strategic planning and strategic thinking, and here Senge (1994) played a very important role through his approach to systems thinking. In 1996 one of the most classic articles on strategy was written by Michael Porter in the Harvard Business Review: "What is strategy?" This article emphasised that strategy was not about operational efficiency, but rather about occupying a unique positioning.

Against this brief background of the evolution of strategy, the focus in the 2000s shifted towards competitive strategy, as the role of competition became the most prominent environmental factor for organisations to survive and be profitable. Today strategy is about obtaining and maintaining a sustainable competitive advantage within a very complex external market and internal environment. An organisation achieves a sustainable competitive advantage when a niche in the market is established or when services and products are preferred above others.

Within an organisational architecture the role of strategy also changed over time. During the 1960s to 1980s strategy departments or units were established in large organisations with specific focus on strategic planning. Planners focused on the development of the strategies of the organisation.

When the focus shifted towards strategic thinking in the 1990s, these planning units started to focus on facilitating a strategy process within the organisation, and influenced leading people to think strategically. Emphasis was no longer on the actual plan, but it was about the thinking process leading to the plan. During this time more people from different functions and units and at different levels of the organisation were also involved in developing strategy. It moved away from being an exclusive activity done by the top management of the organisation.

In the 2000s the approach moved further towards the people. Strategy departments or units were decentralised, and strategy became a function of management within the organisation. Strategic thinking is now a competence and priority of every manager, and strategic conversations should take place continuously in management meetings. The vision and direction of the organisation, as well as the core or grand strategy, are still functions of the top executives and owners of the organisation, but the strategic approach and thinking, as well as the execution of the strategy, are everybody's responsibility.

A very good example of an organisation that followed the evolution of strategy and applied it with great success over time is Sanlam, a financial services organisation in South

Africa, which was established in 1918. This organisation is one of the best examples of accomplishing a sustainable competitive advantage over almost 100 years. Research showed that one of the key reasons why this organisation still exists after 100 years, is their focus on strategy and the application of strategic planning and thinking over time.

12.3 Strategy and organisational behaviour

Strategy has to do with people; it is totally dependent on people. People create strategy, people implement strategy. According to Gareth Jones and Jennifer George (2014:53) organisational behaviour as an area of management is about, "the study of factors that have an impact on how individuals and groups respond to and act in organisations".

Strategy is applied in organisations through a strategic management process, which includes the creation of the vision and grand strategy, development of strategic goals or objectives, strategy implementation and the monitoring and control of the strategy. All of these components are dealt with by people within a certain behavioural context and culture of the organisation.

Jones et al (2014:319-320) say, "culture influences the work behaviours and attitudes of individuals and groups in an organisation because its members adhere to shared values, norms and expected standards of behavior" . So the organisational behaviour impacts directly on the way the organisation deals with strategy, and the strategic management process is influenced directly by the behaviour of the organisation.

It is clear from the above that strategy plays an integral role in organisational behaviour and change. The important realisation is that strategy, organisational behaviour, organisational change and culture are all interrelated and part of a bigger system referred to as the organisation. The organisation functions within a changing environment as depicted in figure 12.1.

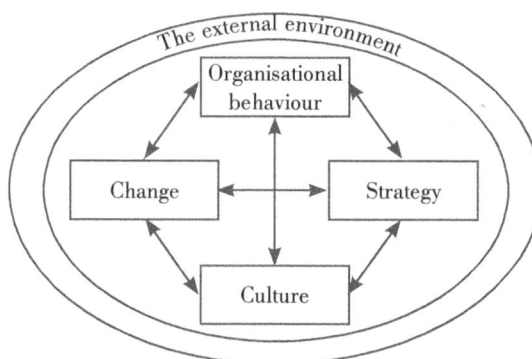

Figure 12.1   The organisation and its environment, Adri Drotskie (2015)

A practical way of understanding this impact is to measure the organisational behaviour or culture during the strategic management process as understanding the internal environment. It is very valuable to have a realistic view of the readiness of the organisation for the strategy implementation. By doing a climate study, while understanding the changes in the external and market environments of the organisation, the picture is completed, as the organisation also understands its internal environment and the readiness of its people.

12.4 Strategy and OCD

Organisational change is, according to Gareth Jones and Jennifer George (2014:355), "the movement of an organisation away from its present state towards some preferred future state to increase its efficiency and effectiveness". Strategy, as mentioned in previous sections of this chapter, is about creating the "preferred future state". The relation between strategy and change is very direct, and totally interrelated and interdependent.

Strategy and change go hand-in-hand. If an organisation applies a strategic management process, change interventions will be needed to execute the strategy successfully, as the strategy implies changes in the organisation and its people. If an organisation needs to change for whatever reason, a strategy is needed to plan the impact of the change and its consequences.

According to Ann Coulter (2013) a critical success factor of any organisation within the complex current environment, is the ability to embrace change. She continues, (2013:39), "in any type of change effort, the quality of strategic leadership can spell the difference between success and failure".

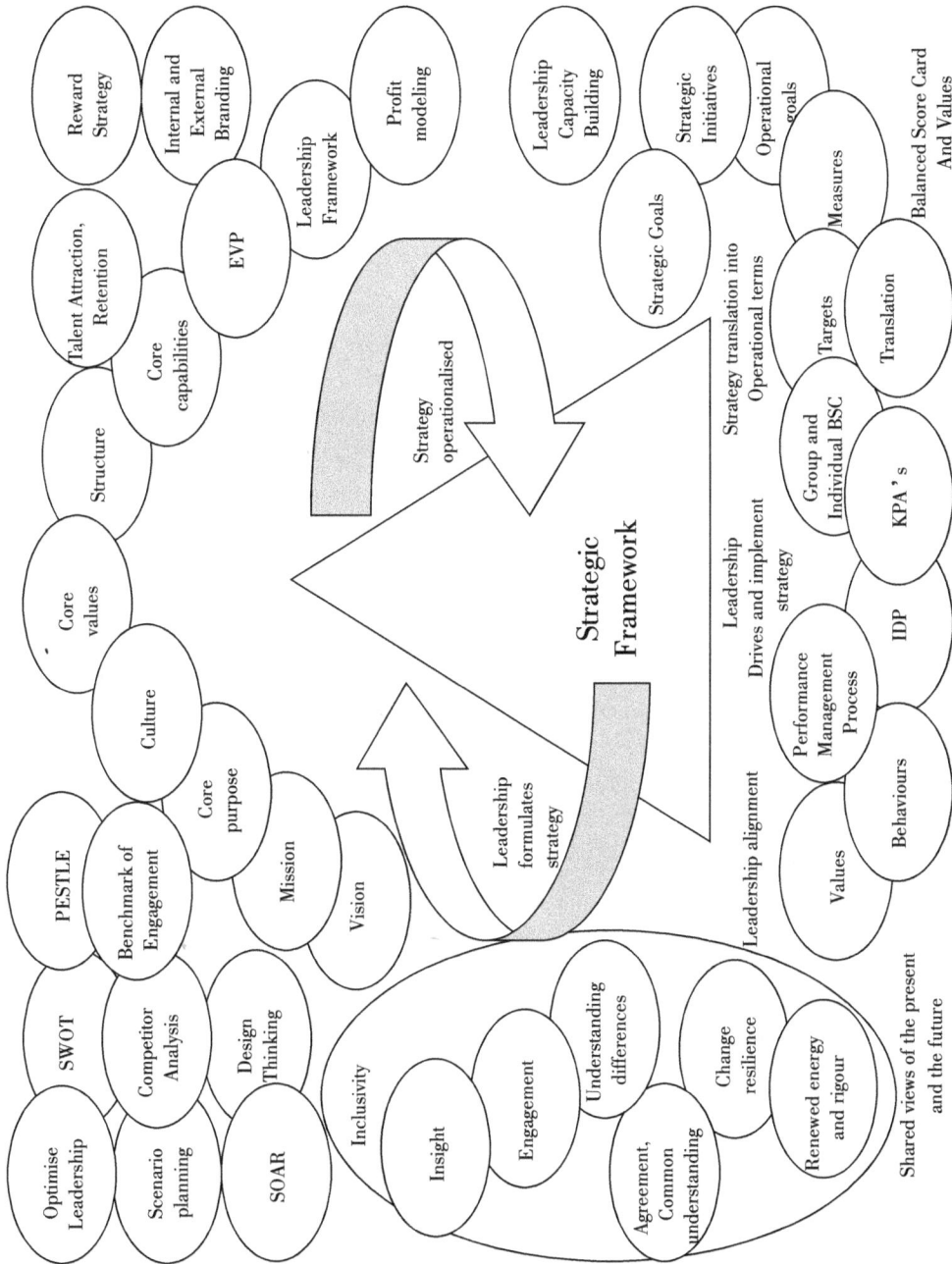

Figue 12.2   Integral strategic process, adapted from Viljoen (2015, p227)

In Figure 12.2 above it is clear that facilitating strategy in an organisation is an integrated, systemic approach. The author (2009) argued that the first step of a full strategic cycle is to ensure that the dynamics of the decision-making team are optimised. OCD interventions can be used to ensure effective decision-making at this level in the organisation.

At the top left-hand corner, the typical diagnostic tools that can be used to create shared understanding of the future are introduced. Through focused OCD interventions scenario planning sessions, a PESTLE analysis and competitive analysis can be facilitated. A climate study like the BeQ™ can provide valuable information about the underlying beliefs in the system as it pertains to the status quo and dynamics at individual, group and organisational level. The multi-cultural capability of this tool also provides insight into the social system of the organisation, namely the human niche distribution.

Design thinking as explained by Russell Ackoff (2003) and Johan Strümpfer (2001) and adapted by the author, can assist teams to map their current reality through causal diagrams and causal loops, to identify the most probable future and design the ideal future. A SOAR analysis or a SWOT analysis that is co-created by a group during a facilitation session can assist greatly in determining the gap between what is supposed to be happening and what is actually taking place. The whole organisation can be invited to participate in the diagnostic phase.

During the next phase top management teams construct strategic architecture. Typically, organisations will identify a vision, a mission, a core purpose and core values. Strategic OCD consultants can, however, assist top management teams to co-construct the culture – often an area of business that is left unattended to develop by itself.

A congruent structure should follow strategy. Core capabilities should be identified. How talent is attracted and retained, as well as remuneration should be constructed. An employee value proposition, internal and external branding, leadership capability development capability and profit modelling (how do we make money?) should be designed. OCD consultants should facilitate this process to ensure that line management has a voice, and can participate in the process without running the risk of being viewed as pushing their own agenda.

The strategic architecture should be designed at levels of Work 4 or at strategic development level (refer to stratified systems thinking of Eliott Jaques (1997). In Figure 12.3 below, the process of constructing strategic architecture from the themes that were identified during the diagnostic phase is displayed.

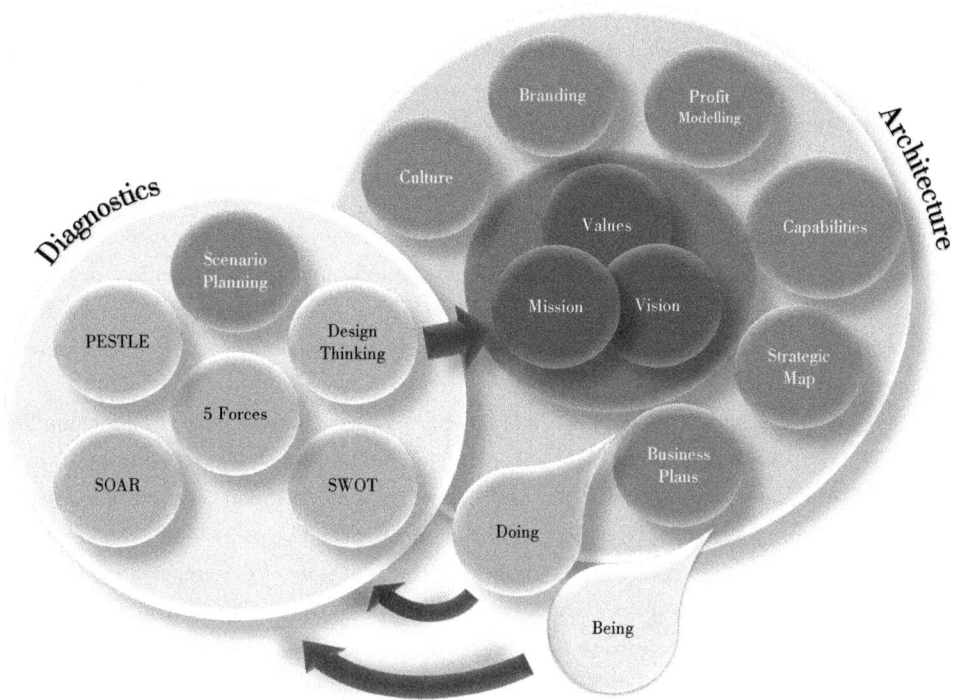

Figue 12.3   Constructing strategic architecture
Adapted from the author (2014) by Ross Saunders (2015, p.12)

A strategy map should then be co-created by focussing on the following questions a la Robert Kaplan and David Norton (2006):

- In what should we invest today to achieve our goals?

- At what processes should we excel at to achieve our goals?

- How should we appear to our customer?

- How should we appear to our shareholders?

OCD consultants may ask an additional question, namely, "How can we enable the system to execute strategy?" A one-pager is co-created that displays a virtuous cycle of strategic goals. Everyone in the organisation will plan around the same goals.

Typically, the strategy map is constructed at levels of Work 4 or at strategic development level. The strategic goals are supported by strategic initiatives, broken down into operational goals with a shorter time frame of discretion and operational initiatives. Level 3 and Level 2 business plans are created. It is critical that an individual leader has a balanced scorecard or an individual business plan, but also has a plan for the group in which he or she operates.

Measurements are linked to the strategic or operational goals. Targets are set at Level 1 in accordance with stratified systems theory (SST). The different goals are measured by key performance areas (KPAs) and key performance indicators (KPIs). A personal development plan (IDP) is contracted during the performance conversation with the focus on developing the behavioural and technical aspects needed to execute the task at hand. Organisational values are translated into behaviours through facilitated OCD sessions and also measured in the KPAs and KPIs.

Insight into business challenges is created by ensuring that everyone who is impacted by a decision forms part of the strategic process that determines the future outcome – a process of inclusivity. Engagement increases as meaningful interaction is facilitated. During the co-creation process employees learn to develop viewpoints that are different from their own. This is not only due to diversity of thought but also as a consequence of inter-departmental conflicts.

As agreement on strategic and operational objectives is achieved, shared understanding that again leads to significant and ultimately commitment, increases. By involving employees in decisions that are important to them, and impact directly on them, awareness increases and ultimately this has a positive impact on change resilience. The process releases renewed energy and rigour as shared views of the future and current state of the organisation become clear. OCD consultants may play a critical role in the whole translation of strategy process.

As an example of this, during the integration of the various defence forces such as APLA (Azanian People's Liberation Army) and MK (Umkhonto WeSizwe) into the integrated SANDF (South African National Defence Force), two generals had a conversation on the importance of strategy translation.

The first general said that in the defence force there is no time for sitting around and chatting about standard operating procedures. Soldiers must simply execute, and not think and speak. The other general wisely responded that if they were doing war strategy he truly would like to hear input from each of his foot soldiers, that strategy should be shared, and everyone should know exactly what to do.

However, when an army vehicle is under attack, it is important not to form a circle and have a dialogue on what to do – then we execute according to standard operating procedure. In the case study of ABSA below, strategy was co-created and translated throughout the organisation with lasting, sustainable results.

12.6 The ABSA case

Absa, a financial services organisation and member of the Barclays Group, implemented a process of combining strategy and change during the late 1990s and early 2000s. This led to the successful execution of strategy across this large organisation.

A revolutionary strategy was developed by the top management of the organisation, which would lead Absa into the 2000s as a sustainable and competitive financial services organisation. The decision was taken to communicate the strategy to all employees of the organisation, which at that time comprised about 32 000 people across South Africa.

The strategic management process that was used started with the vision and grand strategy and objectives being communicated to the top 100 managers in the organisation.

Each business unit and provincial management team then embraced this strategy, and translated it into tactical and operational plans per unit and province, leading to key performance areas (KPAs) for each individual in the organisation, aligned with one strategy.

In order to make this process a reality, top management in conjunction with the human resources management team, decided to implement a strategic management process and a change management process simultaneously. The process was facilitated by a team consisting of OCD consultants and strategy consultants.

Adri Drotskie and Rica Viljoen headed the facilitation team, with the unique focus on the integration of strategy facilitation and transformational OCD efforts. A methodology called a Big Systems Event or a Large Group Intervention (LGI) was used and that led to groups of up to 200 people going through the strategic management and change process together.

Griffin and Purser (1997) explain in a chapter of *The Handbook of Organisational Development* edited by Cummings, that LGIs are used in organisational change efforts across a variety of applications such as organisational development, organisational redesign, restructuring, strategic planning, visioning, values and principles clarification and process improvement. The authors of this chapter applied this methodology in the Absa case with lasting effect.

The LGI approach is based on systems thinking. The essence of systems thinking, says Peter Senge (1993) is that an organisation is a whole system that cannot be reduced to independent parts. This approach is based on the assumption that when viewed collectively, the pieces provide a more holistic understanding of the system and its potential for change.

Through this approach Absa successfully facilitated the total organisation – every single employee – to understanding the strategy, how to implement it, what each person's role was and dealing with the change that it implied. The organisational *doing* and *being* were incorporated during the facilitation process, and ultimately shared understanding of the strategy (the what), but also which leadership behaviours should accompany it (the way).

12.7 The PPS Namibia case

The beginning of 2010 was earmarked by a few big challenges for PPS Namibia. The total sales force was negative, and trust in the business process was at an all-time low. The challenge was to re-establish trust in the process, and to change the general perception of the reality.

Adri Vermeulen, chief executive (CE) of the company in Namibia, succeeded in turning around both challenges by building up a committed team with sound support coming from the holding company and management, and through implementing strategy.

As a successful executive, Vermeulen has 35 years' experience of brokerage. Before 2010, he was heading an insurance company in the biggest province in South Africa. Vermeulen continued with his success story in Namibia. He believes in applying strategy in an integrated and focused manner. He applies the inclusivity strategic approach as indicated in figure 12.2. Particular care is taken to ensure that understanding is shared in his team in terms of the strategic diagnostic tools identified in this figure. Strategic architecture is constructed. A strategic map is agreed upon. Business plans support this map. Vermeulen focuses all his attention on the implementation of the strategy map.

The business results achieved are staggeringly positive. For the last five years Vermeulen and his team achieved a 25% total asset growth year after year. The operating profit grew by 20% year on year since 2010. Investment return increased by 38% per year since Adri took over this business. Not only does the business result look promising, but staff members trust each other, and every member of the total sales force is engaged and committed.

Vermeulen lives a soulful life. Long ago, he adopted the bateleur eagle as a symbol for remarkable leadership. Sometimes, not often, he rewards a leader who shows exceptional characteristics with a lovely hand-crafted statue of the eagle as a gesture of honour. One of the senior business leaders in Windhoek wrote the following letter to Vermeulen on receiving this special award:

> Dear Adri
> (Unaltered)
>
> *This is just a short note to thank you most sincerely for the gift of your time and company in Windhoek the Friday morning before last, and more especially for the magnificent gift of the Bataleur Eagle sculpture – and all that it goes with! It's looking at me right now as I write these lines, and its steady stare is like a reminder of what it represents. You have a particular talent for symbolic gestures and your idea of an eagle group within your personal circles is a beautiful powerful one. I am very privilege to have been included – and I feel that I have been place under an obligation to live up to something. That's where the eagle's steady, challenging stare comes in!*
>
> *Your practical, generous gesture has also invited me to reflect on the important a valuable people in MY world. I have always tried to express appreciation freely and our conversation has strengthened my resolve to this.*
>
> Yours sincerely

Vermeulen shows remarkable leadership. Through the co-creation of the *doing*, and through inspiring and solid *being*, he wires the energy of people that work with him around carefully designed milestones derived from his strategic plan. Vermeulen himself is a bateleur for sure. Adri is currently writing the story of his colourful and successful career, and shares personal stories and practical advice that can be inspirational to all.

12.8   Implementation and the role of change

In most organisations the biggest challenge in strategy lies with the implementation or the execution of the strategy. To execute a strategy successfully, the organisation needs to focus on eight components (Thompson, Strickland & Gamble, 2010), as depicted in Figure 3.

Figure 12.4   Strategy execution process, Thompson et al. (2010, p. 330)

OCD practitioners should assist line management throughout the strategic formulation, the strategic architecture, the strategic translation and the strategy execution process. This is done, first, to create shared understanding of the what; second, to ensure that there is significance for the individual to apply his or her human energy to the task at hand and lastly, to ensure commitment. Only then can the traditional business planning, project scoping and execution happen.

One of the business leaders in the Absa case study, Johan Reyneke, used to say that time spent in strategic conversation was cheap time. The more shared understanding, significance and commitment we have, the fewer comebacks and conversations about what really should have been done will occur later.

As mentioned before in this chapter, all the components of the strategic management process, and therefore also the execution part of the process, have to do with people and their ability to deal with change. It is mentioned in the centre of Figure 12.4 that "The action agenda for implementing and executing strategy" is about "what to **change** or improve". All eight components are of equal importance for the successful execution of an organisation's strategy, but 'instilling a corporate culture' and 'exercising strong leadership' have the most direct impact on the change process. OCD consultants can play an important role in all eight components.

12.9 Conclusion

OCD does not only focus on the *being* side, the soft stuff, in organisations. As Leidler (1999) correctly stated, the soft stuff is the hard stuff. By ensuring that strategy is co-created and translated in an inclusive manner, the benefits of inclusivity are unleashed and the chance that strategy will be implemented in a sustainable manner increases exponentially. An integral approach towards strategy may align employees in the organisation around the *doing* and *being* with benefits to all parties involved. A multi-disciplinary approach, where OCD consultants support strategic consultants in wiring human energy around business goals, is highly advisable.

13

ANCHORING OCD IN CONSULTING PSYCHOLOGY

Co-authored by Dr Anna-Rosa le Roux

13.1 Introduction

This book concludes with a chapter on the importance of OCD practitioners anchoring themselves in the field of consulting psychology. The effective consultant psychologist adopts a scientific practitioner stance. This stance is explored here. The chapter concludes with ethical considerations that must form an integral part of the consulting psychologist. By complying with these requirements, the field of OCD will not only be professionalised, it will also ensure the credibility of individual practitioners and the discipline at large.

13.2 OCD and other fields of study

This book integrates OD and OC. This integration is purposeful as it deals with the same phenomenon, namely organisational change. Organisational change, as the larger field encapsulating the change phenomenon, is defined by Chris van Tonder in Roodt and Van Tonder (2008a, p2.) as " ... a non-discrete yet context bound process of energy movement that is reflected in an empirical difference in the state and or condition of the system over time".

Richard Beckhard and Rubin Harris (1987:vii) refer in their preface of *Organisational transitions: Managing complex change* to organisational change as a body of knowledge and technology that was historically understood by academics, applied by OD practitioners and generally not understood by the management of the organisation. This premise has now changed, and what was abstract matter to organisation management a decade ago, is now everyday management practice.

Chris van Tonder (2004b) further explains that both OD and change management are interventionist approaches. Managers and practitioners are concerned with how to introduce change or how to deal effectively with it. Traditionally change management focuses on planning, directing and control, whereas OD, on the other hand, is a social philosophy of change. It (OD) is thus more concerned with the social context and immediate social setting in which the change is engaged, than the change per se.

David Bradford and Warner Burke (2006) argue that OD is a subset of the larger field of the organisational change phenomenon, and has a clear value proposition as a separate focus area. Gert Roodt and CL van Tonder (2008) reviewed contemporary definitions of OD and found that these definitions supported the main components, highlighted in the classical definition of Burke, namely that OD is a process (or effort or strategy) for dealing with change, is generally of a planned nature, has organisation-wide (system-wide) application, relies on behaviour-based technology, in pursuit of improved organisational and individual functioning, is collaborative in nature, long-term oriented, involves top management and focuses on cultural change.

OCD is closely interrelated with all organisational functions and business units. This is due to its strategic positioning. Furthermore, it is also concerned with the optimisation of individuals, groups and organisations. It thus overlaps with individual and organisational (IO) psychology as it studies human behaviour in organisations. However, IO psychologists often use psychometrics during assessments and placements, and are often involved in talent management.

Talent management in turn overlaps with HR as succession pipelines, and performance and reward form part of HR's domain. The strategic HR function should be involved in constructing strategic learning architecture, organisational culture and reward strategy and in particular, focusing on the people perspective of the balanced scorecard.

The interrelatedness of OCD becomes clear – the OCD practitioners also concern themselves with strategy and culture. The important differentiator between HR and OCD, is that OCD focusses on integral, systemic interrelatedness of the organisation and the space between business units. Human Resources on the other hand focus to optimise the human resource capacity across organisational functions.

13.3 Critique of OCD

In general, the field of organisational change is not without its critics. Chris van Tonder (2004a) notes that our contemporary view and treatment of change is far too general (such as acontextual and non-specific) resulting in difficulty in implementing change management processes and interventions and its ultimate failure. He suggests that change is viewed as part of the "organisational fibre", creating the complex and infinitely variable terrain of organisational change.

The specific field of OD is also criticised from within its own ranks, as well as by those external to the discipline, Anna Rosa le Roux notes. David Bradford (2005:xxiv) voices the concerns of fellow OD practitioners, thought leaders, academics and OD consultants in the OD field when he states that OD has had its 'heyday' (late 1960s, 1970s, into the 1980s):

> "But those heydays appear to have passed. Even though the number of people who call themselves 'OD Consultants' has continued to increase, they are rarely in the top layers of organisations. Instead, if they exist at all within the Institution, they are relegated to the deepest bowels of the organisation, usually being part of HR (not

enjoying the highest status level itself). Chief Executive Officers rarely call in OD consultants. Instead, they typically rely on major consulting firms, many of which have taken on the rhetoric (if not the practice) of the OD field."

Joan Gallos (2006:xxiii) asserts that internal and external critics label OD as " ... foundering, lost, stuck at the organisational margins, failing to honour and practice its values". Often business leaders do not consult internal HR functions, but rather go to consulting firms. It is important to realise that OCD initiatives should be supported from the top for them to have the optimal impact. Although external consultant firms may add value due to the objective voice of an external person, they may not understand the business realities, and sometimes miss the finer power dynamics in the organisation. OCD interventions are often needed to ensure that the behavioural aspects in the organisation are functional.

As discussed in chapter 1, OCD as a profession has become fragmented in South Africa. The boundaries are becoming blurred between strategic HR and psychology, A haphazard, mechanistic approach towards the field of study, as currently manifesting in most organisations in South Africa and Africa, can lead to even further disintegration. To enable OCD to flourish, it must be mandated from the top, and must be concerned with the whole system and integral.

13.4 The role of OCD in future business

Due to the changing nature of the world of work, the implications of systems thinking and rising levels of consciousness (as discussed in chapter 2) OCD practitioners can play a significant role. Joan Gallos (2006: xxi) says that OD is poised for a renaissance. There is considerable room for improvement in the effectiveness of organisations in areas that organisational leaders consider critically important to the sustainability of their businesses. The field of OD offers some of its greatest strengths in these very areas. These areas include:

- Becoming global and multi-cultural

- Developing productive, performance-based work environments

- Building talent and organisational capabilities to fulfil future needs

- Accommodating new and changing external regulation

- Leveraging and integrating new technologies to support the business

- Meeting increasing expectations for socially responsible and sustainable business practices

The authors of this chapter add the following areas:

- Integration of insights and practices form individual/organisational psychology, industrial psychology, strategic human resources and anthropology into an integral practice.

- Integration of diagnostic tools from various fields of study, such as systems thinking and strategic architecture.

- Transcending OCD specialist into becoming strategic business partners in an attempt to address systemic dynamics.

- Integration of various intervention methodologies into an eclectic, dynamic facilitative approach.

- Integration of alternative organisational methodologies into a responsive, self-organising attempt to enable systemic dynamics to become functional (rather than dysfunctional).

- Designing OCD interventions from yellow – thus inclusive and functional.

OCD concerns itself with the functioning of individuals, teams and organisations. Due to the changing lie of the land, especially the important implications of the dynamic interplay of societal challenges on business, the role of the OCD practitioner is becoming increasingly important.

13.5 The emerging field of consulting psychology in South Africa

The multi-cultural nature of the new world of work and the increased diverse settings of organisations of the future ask for higher levels of complexity-handling ability, systems-thinking ability and the ability to be authentic. The OCD practitioner, as well as the consulting psychologist, is faced with scenarios that require problem-solving that is holistic, integrated, synergistic and value-adding to individuals, groups, organisations, and which is sustainable in communities.

These scenarios should be addressed from a multi-disciplinary perspective taking into cognisance the contextual drivers that define them. We are thus moving towards approaches and frameworks where the psychologist will be challenged to apply skill-sets that are beyond the traditional registration categories of psychology, namely industrial, educational, research, clinical and counselling.

Paul Thomas and Anthony Naidoo (2006:50) say:

> "The notion of consulting psychology as a distinct entity involves the incorporation and amalgamation of certain conceptual knowledge and competencies, from inter alia community, counseling, clinical, research, etc. under one umbrella concept with more inclusive divergent boundaries."

Rodney Lowmon (2002:1) positions consulting psychology as

> "...the field of consulting psychology borrows heavily from other specialities in psychology and beyond, (but) ... it declares independence, the right to stand on its own, to flourish and prosper, or shrivel and wither on its own terms."

Leo Strümpfer (2006:5) pleads for a more synergistic relationship between IO psychology, for example, and its root discipline, psychology:

> "Perhaps one can find an analogy in osmosis through a semi-permeable membrane; some 'thin' organisational boundaries should protect each of the domains of practice but these should be at their most permeable around the core areas of the parent discipline... There should be assurance that IO psychologists learn about the organisational context in which work is done and managed; additionally, they should become grounded in business/management disciplines too."

Consulting psychology is born out of necessity for solutions aligned with the application context of the world of psychology. The application of skills is driven from a broader psychological base, an in-depth understanding of the particular context, as well the practical modality of skills application, namely consulting.

The psychologist in consulting should be able to advise as well as create and implement holistic solutions through approaching these from an individual, group organisational and community context, feeding from a knowledge base that is relevant and supportive to the problems at hand.

13.6 Definition of consulting psychology

On an international level the Society of Consulting Psychology (SCP), Division 13 of the American Psychological Association (APA), has contributed significantly to both the clarification, as well as methods used by consultants.

Consultation helps individuals and organisations to become more efficient and effective. Consultants develop a climate for interdependent problem-solving and share expertise in solving a specific problem. Edgar Schein (1995) added the notion of systems thinking to the consulting process and highlights a systemic approach.

The APA Division 13 embraces the following definition of Consulting Psychology:

> "The function of applying and extending the special knowledge of a psychologist through the process of consultation to problems involving human behaviour in various areas ... a psychologist who provides specialist technical assistance to individuals or organisations in regard to psychological aspects of their context"

IO psychologist and qualified OCD practitioners in South Africa and Africa at large must align closely with the field of consulting psychology. A lot of value can be gained by involvement with the APA Division 13 conferences, activities and journals.

13.7 Principles of work

Consulting psychology is an emerging field within psychology and also draws from different knowledge bases outside of traditional psychology. Consulting psychology is still new in

South Africa, specifically regarding its differentiation from or positioning amongst other fields in the organisational change and transformation domain. Principles driving the establishment, growth, stakeholder buy-in, as well as promoting the discipline's value-add could be supportive of the following concepts:

- Holistic and integrated – consulting psychology promotes solutions that address clients' specific needs, as defined by the client-specific context.

- Multi-disciplinary teams – consulting psychology embraces the diversity represented in the dynamics and knowledge bases of different psychology registration categories.

- Learning orientation – consulting psychology promotes an attitude that demonstrates a willingness to learn, to grow and share knowledge that is stimulated by boundary-spanning thinking.

- Systems thinking – consulting psychology supports the synergistic interaction between the different psychological disciplines.

- Scientist-practitioner model – consulting psychology insists on an evidence-based approach to professional practice where the knowledge base of psychology is translated to the problems at hand and combined with judgement gained from experience.

- Values driven – consulting psychology is ingrained with an approach of authenticity, with the consultant modelling these behaviours in a client context.

These principles of work can be incorporated into OCD practices.

13.8 A scientist-practitioner approach

Rodney Lowman (2012) stated in his article, "The Scientist-practitioner Consulting Psychologist" that our concern with the scientific basis of our practice is more than something that is expected: it is an ethical obligation. The code of ethics of the APA (2002) specifically states in section 2.04 that Scientific and Professional Judgements of Psychologists' work is based upon established scientific and professional knowledge of the discipline (p.1064).

Furthermore, psychologists are also ethically obliged to **minimise harm** associated with their interventions (refer to section 3.04 of the code of ethics of the APA). Third, an evidence-based approach to professional practice can **differentiate** practitioners by ensuring that their work is based on what is reliably known, Lowman states. He continues to explain that in a world flooded with commodity tools, offered by vendors that claim that they can offer these more cheaply, the responsibility rests with the practitioner to educate the client in terms of reasons why a scientist-practitioner approach is more likely to result in desired outcomes.

In ensuring the ongoing relevance, differentiation and value-add of the profession, there is a distinct role to play on the sides of both scientists and practitioners alike. We need to be much more disciplined in the *practical implementation* of our scientific-practitioner approach, to create science that is more practically relevant whilst simultaneously applying the science and research to our practices. There is an equally important opportunity for practitioners and researchers to add value on both sides of the hyphen of 'scientist-practitioner'.

Due to the complexity of our organisational life, which is characterised with variables that are more abstract and only measurable over time, it is not a simple task to relate knowledge/research into practice. Lowman (2012:153) argues that for the science of psychology to make its research more relevant to practice, there needs to be an engagement with practice in assessing variables that are of central importance to organisational life.

Practitioners, on the other hand, are well-positioned to build theory from the rich basis of organisational life with which they are working: the problems they are trying to solve, the variable practice scenarios, rich context of multiple stakeholder involvement, change and impact or cost-benefits on the ground. Practitioners can contribute to the knowledge base substantially if they write up their practice-based findings, whether that is in the form of case studies or testable hypotheses.

Case studies from Africa are scarce, and should be documented. Integral research as described by Ronnie Lessem and Alexander Schieffer (2010) and other methodologies that allow for individual story-telling like auto-ethnographic work, oral histories, engaged theory and life histories, can be used to document stories that traditionally remain untold.

"We will not be taken seriously as a profession until we accelerate our attention to practicing explicitly on the basis of science and research and to creating science and research that are practice relevant," Lowman says (2012:155).

13.9 Ethics

We live in an era of "un-ethics" where the daily crashing of individual livelihoods and pension funds are recurring themes, entering our lives and resulting in concerns with ethical extremes. However, it is not only about not doing the bad things, but also about doing the good things.

At a recent APA Conference workshop in San Diego on ethics Rodney Lowman and Cooper (2015)[10] cited the four thinking frames that inform our lenses when we approach ethics in consulting. These are: i) Is this practice good for the organisation? ii) Is this practice good for the client practice? iii) Is this practice legal? iv) Is this practice in compliance with risk management frameworks in the particular consulting context?

Code of conduct

Important ethical issues for the consulting psychologist can be clustered around themes such as (refer to the Ethical Principles of Psychologists and Code of Conduct 2002, Modified in 2010, APA):

---

10 The American Psychological Accusation Division 13, Consulting Psychology, 2015 Midsummer Conference, San Diego, 3-8 February 2015

- Informed consent (3.10) – When psychologists conduct research or provide assessment, therapy, counseling, or consulting services ... they obtain the informed consent of the individual or individuals.

- Avoiding harm (3.04) – Psychologists take reasonable steps to avoid harming their clients, patients, students, supervisees, research participants, organisational clients and others, and others with whom they work, and to minimise harm where it is foreseeable and unavoidable.

- Protecting the rights of the participant in research and with clients (8.05) – Practitioners may dispense informed consent only when the study of factors related to job or organisation effectiveness conducted in organisational settings for which there is no risk to participants' employability, and confidentiality is protected.

- Boundaries of competence (2.01) – Psychologists need to provide services, teach and conduct research with populations and in areas only within the boundaries of their competence based on their education, training, supervised experience, consultation, study or professional experience.

- Avoid multiple relationships that can harm others (3.05) – Refrain from entering into a multiple relationship if the multiple relationship could impair the practitioner's objectivity, competence or effectiveness in performing his or her functions, or exploit or harm the other person with whom the relationship exists.

- Respect for the rights of the individual with whom we work (Principle E) – Psychologists respect the dignity and worth of all people and the rights of individuals to privacy.

An ethical code usually contains a set of guiding principles that are aspirational with the intent to guide and inspire practitioners toward the very highest ethical ideals of the profession as well as a set of ethical standards that are enforceable and present the standards of the profession. The latter becomes a professional judgement in a court of law and presents the standard of the service that could be expected by a reasonable, competent professional and is also therefore applicable to the non-registered psychologist. Many professional societies also publish guidelines that are developed by experts in the field that are not necessarily enforceable but present the 'collective wisdom' of the profession.

On a practical note, practitioners could ask what are the areas that should be considered in ethical decision making? Mark Duffy and Jonathan Passmore (2010) used a grounded theory approach to build a decision framework for coaching psychologists that include ethical principles such as those presented in professional codes and relevant literature. Key elements that informed practitioners' ethical decision-making were included as part of the model. With coaching positioned under the overall umbrella of consulting (psychology), we cite these elements as an example that can be translated to other areas of consultation.

Ethical awareness

Practitioners who are ethically aware are more likely to translate this awareness into practice. Active participation at a professional society is one vehicle that the responsible practitioner can use in creating a more ethically mindful approach. Professional societies each publish their ethical codes for members to comply with. Engaging in activities associated with continual professional development where ethical thinking is encouraged and practical ethical dilemmas are revisited in a peer related fashion is advised.

A personal ethical code

It is important of not only being aware of the ethical codes of professional societies, but also being aware of one's own ethical code and how personal values and beliefs can be used as a guide to inform ethical decisions. Practitioners need to map their own values and beliefs onto ethical codes and published literature, thus developing, enhancing and owning their own ethical principles.

Particulars of situation to be identified

Duffy and Passmore (2010) furthermore underline the role that the context plays in understanding and resolving ethical dilemmas, and advise that a thorough identification or fact-finding of the situation particulars is necessary. The same labelled dilemma may necessitate a different resolution depending upon the context, such as the organisation, the individuals involved and where the work is taking place.

Peer coaching, supervision and consulting significant others

The important role played by significant others, such as supervisors and peers, in helping coaches resolve dilemmas, should be acknowledged, say Duffy and Passmore (2010). Ethical choice is often not a matter of black and white, but one of grey that requires the dedicated thinking and answering questions around what is good for the self and the other.

Reflection and journal entry

Ethical decision-making is a cognitive process that requires reflection time by the practitioner. Reflection and thinking are an important part of the ethical process in order to avoid hasty or rushed decisions which had not been thought through.

Assess options

As in all good decision-making models, the value of exploring options and the risks and benefits associated with each course of action are underlined. Assessing options would provide the practitioner with the opportunity to be more thoughtful in their chosen course of action.

Evaluate process and outcome

Evaluation is an important part of the ethical decision-making process. This evaluation should include not only assessing and learning from the entire process undertaken and the consequences of one's actions, but also feeding these learnings back into the process of continual professional development.

Multi-culturalism and ethics

Ethics can be interpreted differently from different thinking systems as discussed in chapters 5 and 6. To maintain the integrity of the profession, and to ensure that the sacredness that is required when work with humans is conducted, OCD practitioners must adopt consulting psychological ethical conduct. By integrating these ethical standards into OCD practices, the individual practitioner, and by implication the field of study, will gain credibility.

Acting in accordance with the ethical guidelines of the profession requires a lifelong commitment and personal effort to act ethically. We have a duty to encourage ethical behaviour from all our students, our supervisors, our employees and our colleagues. Furthermore, we are encouraged to consult with others to ensure that what might have started out as a grey ethical dilemma is turned into a black-and-white decision in alignment with the relevant ethical codes and guidelines that are available.

13.10 Conclusion

Whether an OCD practitioner is a qualified psychologist or not, the principles described here are crucial to creating a sustainable practice. By aligning practices with international standards, and by being involved with applicable professional bodies, the individual OC practitioner can ensure continuous development, relevance and currentness of interventions.

It becomes increasingly important that the untold stories be documented. This is particularly true for South Africa, and the African continent, as traditionally, stories have only been shared orally here. The hidden wisdom and ways of Africa may well be able to inform the world. In Africa, sitting in a circle, sharing age-old wisdom is common practice. OCD practitioners can access this wisdom by introducing circular seating structures during group sessions and allow for the story to find the participants.

Anticipated outcomes are not reached for economic, political and societal challenges, in terms of spiral dynamics. Purple feudal systems, red autocracy, blue democracy, orange capitalism and green socialism, all failed in an attempt to solve societal needs. New attempts are required. OCD consultants must determine, design, deliver and delineate outcomes in a multi-cultural sensitive inclusive manner – as from yellow. Yellow is an integrative thinking system – it looks for causes and syntheses rather than mechanistically breaking down the whole into pieces.

This no longer makes sense philosophically. OCD as a field of study is facing the same risk – if it is not tackled from an integral philosophical stand, the haphazard approach from individual practitioners will not result in the optimisation of individual, group, organisational and societal behaviours.

This book on inclusivity, integral theory and OCD was aimed at stimulating the reader to enquire, and even to do research on the various topics integrated here. By no means do the author and co-authors claim that this is a complete description of the field of study. The *Handbook of Organisational Development* by Thomas Cummings (2008), the *California School of Organisational Studies Handbook* edited by Carson and Lowman (2003), *Organisational Development: Theory and Practice* by Gert Roodt and Chris van Tonder (2008), *The NLT Handbook of Organisational Development and Change: Principles, Practices and Perspectives* by Brenda Jones and Michael Bruzzel (2014) come closer to this aim.

Here, an effort was made to interweave integral theory, inclusivity theory, spiral dynamics theory, OC and OD, various methodologies, modalities and interventions into an eclectic, systemic field of practice. By adapting a scientific-practitioner's stance, OCD consultants can simultaneously satisfy the needs of their clients while contributing to the body of knowledge. By adapting the ethical principles described here, the OCD practitioner can build a sacred, satisfying and sustainable practice while leaving an impactful legacy of growth in the people and organisations they touch.

---

11 Spiral Dynamics theory is discussed in Chapter 5 and 6.

Only gradually did I discover what the Mandala really is:
'Formation, Transformation,
Eternal Mind's eternal creation' (Faust, II).
And that is the self, the wholeness of the personality,
which if all goes well is harmonious,
but which cannot tolerate self-deceptions.

Carl Jung (1954)

EPILOGUE

After connecting on the theory of spiral dynamics, the following piece was written by Tina Countryman, an American with Cherokee roots.

The Richness of PURPLE ... Spiral Dynamics
February 15, 2015 at 1:17pm
Tina Countryman

In honour of Loraine Laubscher and Rica Viljoen

To be truly touched; where spirit sits ... and is spirited ... by that touch ... the soul of hope ...

How amazing it is; that moment; an instant before you had given up. Everything just dropped; the heaviness of the weight of sadness. Your heart broken and dead. Sitting alone in the death of your silence; mourning what was; what is; what might have been; having to embrace and embody this darkness of being; no choice really because you have no wind beneath your wings. And then, a miracle occurs; you are in a new moment; everything shifts something stirs in the deepest spaces of your being. Time starts to dance you alive again; space opens and invites you into the sacredness of life; this miracle becomes your beating heart; your soul of being and you are consumed by joy and the wonder of life once more ... To be truly touched; where spirit sits ... and is spirited ... by that touch ... the soul of hope ...

If we are to have any hope of survival, and not just as a species or human beings, but if our humanity is to survive and flourish amidst the richness of the land that fashioned it, it is imperative that we re-connect to that very sacred soil that nourishes its roots and nurtures its being.

For too long now we have been living separated from our soul; our very heart of being. The gradual but devastating demise of the precious pearl of our existence, the essence of our presence, has reached an overwhelming state of crisis.

As a race, we are all suffering in immeasurable ways. We have misplaced the ability to empathise; we have become numb to the atrocities we inflict upon one another, our beloved planet and our universe. Our humanity, what makes us compassionate and responsible beings has been drained from our bodies in the same ways we have systematically depleted the natural resources of our divine Mother.

Somewhere along the journey of humankind, we began to think of ourselves as being superior to all other creations. How could we possibly have ceased being aware of the devotion and love that our earth and universe continually bestows upon us? Everything we need to sustain our lives has been freely gifted by this wonderful living, breathing organism that we are of. In it, we move and have our being. Time for us to reclaim our lives, our home and our humanity by remembering the richness of our roots.

Are you not exhausted? Do you not feel the heaviness and the hurtful emptiness of your ways of living? Can you not see all that is there to be cherished and treasured? For free? Take a moment to really see and experience the lilac; is it not exquisite? Does it not bring healing to your mind and body? How can your heart help from being filled with joy as you open your senses to the many medicinal wonders of the flowering lilac hanging in gravity; there in the aliveness of time, filling her space with beauty.

What about the mountain? Is it not majestic? Worthy of respect? Does it not inspire awe just by its magnitude alone? The rain forest; how many plants has it brought into existence? How many cures have been found? How many human lives have been made better because of it?

Have you ever just sat outside, maybe on a porch, maybe in a swing, on a cool crisp day, drifting with the clouds as the sun shared it colors with you and the sky before it dipped beyond the horizon? Maybe you were enraptured by the soft melodic sound of an evening rain as the cool of the breeze kissed against your skin. How can you continue to ignore these wonders of nature? To connect to their energies, ever so softly would bring such calmness and peace of being. Don't let these opportunities continue to pass you by for the restoration of your humanity depends upon this reconnection to life.

I love the mornings; the serenade of the birds outside my window; the gentle rays of light streaming through reminding me that I have been gifted another day; another chance to experience the wonderment of being human in a more than human world.

I suppose though, my favorite is the night sky. Let the stars dance for you! If ever you feel low on energy, the stars will happily share theirs and you will be restored; replenished with joy and wonder and awe ... allow the moonbeams to bring you silver bliss ...

Have you ever thought about the experience of a butterfly in its cocoon? How wonderful it must feel to fly free; you can fly free too if you wish. I love rainbows; how they dance and scatter their color across the blue sky; just as magical as the stars splash themselves in infinite numbers.

Let us reclaim our humanity. Beauty and wonder is our inheritance as human beings. This amazing planet is our home. She caresses us with all her wisdom and divinity. Let us take back our sacredness of being. Let us re-establish a healthy relationship within the spaces we live and breathe. Let us make sure our rivers will run wild and not poisoned so that we can play underneath the waterfalls with no cares. Spirit sits in the house Life built. Let us free spirit so that she can once again fly in the soul of a compassionate and responsible humanity... Let us celebrate our wisdom and honor our roots and dance in the richness of PURPLE...

May the OCD interventions that you facilitate, mandate or attend, unleash the same spiritedness in you.

REFERENCES

Ackerman L. 1997: Development, transition or transformation: the question of change in organisations. In *Organisation development classics*. San Francisco CA: Jossey-Bass.

Ackoff, R. (1994) *The Democratic Corporation: a radical prescription for recreating corporate America and rediscovering success*. Oxford Univ. Press: New York.

Ackoff, R. (2003) Redesigning Society, with Sheldon Rovin. Stanford Univ. Press: Stanford, California.

Adger, WN. (2000) Social and ecological resilience: Are they related? *Progress in Human Geography*. 24(3) p.347-364.

Allan, P. (1997) Minimizing employee layoffs while downsizing: employer practices that work. *International Journal of Manpower*. 18(7) p.576-597.

Altschuler, IA. (1948). A psychiatrist's experience with music as a therapeutic agent. In: Altschuler I. (ed.) *Music and Medicine*, New York, NY: Books for Libraries Press. p.250-265.

American Psychological Society (2010) *Ethical Principles of Psychologists and Code of Conduct 2002* (Modified in 2010).

Andrade, G, Mitchell M & Stafford E. (2001) New evidence and perspectives on mergers. *Journal of Economic Perspectives*. 15(2) p.103-120.

Ansoff, HI. (1980) Strategic issue management. *Strategic Management Journal*. 1 p.131-148.

Ansoff, HI. (1987) The emerging paradigm of strategic behaviour. *Strategic Management Journal*. 8(6) p.501-515.

Ashton, L. (2007) *Custodian training workshop guide of Bioss related technologies*, 4. Johannesburg: Bioss.

Atherton, JS. (1999) Resistance to learning: a discussion based on participants in in-service professional training programmes. *Journal of Vocational Education and Training*. 51(1) p.77-90.

Bar-On, R. (1997) *EQ-i Bar-On Emotional Quotient Inventory: technical manual*. Toronto: Multi-Health Systems.

Bar-On, R. (2005a) *EQ-I Bar-on Emotional quotient inventory: technical manual*. Toronto: Multi-Health Systems.

Bar-On, R. (2005b): *The Bar-On Model of Emotional-Social Intelligence, special issue on emotional intelligence*. http://www.eiconsortium.org. Accessed on 02/02/2015.

Barrett, R. (2000) Achieving strategic facilities management through strong relationships. *Facilities*. 18(10) p.421-426.

Beck, D. (2013) The Master Code. Spiral Dynamics Integral Accreditation. Course notes. Santa Barbara: Adizes Business School.

Beck, DE & Cohen, CC. (1996): *Spiral dynamics: mastering values, leadership, and change*. Cambridge: Blackwell.

Beck, DE & Linscott, G. (2011) *The crucible: forging South Africa's future*. 2nd reprint. Sandton: New Paradigms Press.

Beckhard, R & Harris, RT. (1987) *Organizational transitions: Managing complex change*. Reading, MA: Addison-Wesley.

Bercelli, D. (2007) *Evaluating the Effects of Stress reduction exercises*. Unpublished Ph.D thesis. Arizona State University. 12/2007.

Bercelli, D. (2012) *The revolutionary trauma release process: Transcend your toughest times*, 5th ed. Vancouver: Namaste Publishing.

Blom, T. (2015) *Fusing organisational change and leadership into a practical roadmap for South African organisations*. Unpublished Doctor of Business Leadership. Graduate School of Business Leadership. University of South Africa.

Bloom, H. (2010) *The Genius of the Beast. A radical re-vision of capitalism*. New York: Prometheus Books.

Bohm, D. (1998) *On dialogue*. London: Brunner-Routledge.

Bradford, DL. (2005) OD, A promise yet to be realised. In W.J. Rothwell & R. Sullivan (Eds.), *Practising Organisational Development A Guide for Consultants*. (p. xxiii-xxvii). San Francisco: Wiley.

Bradford, DL & Burke, WW. (2006) The Future of OD. In JV. Gallos (ed.). *Organization Development* (1st ed.). San Francisco: Wiley.

Braverman, H. (1995) *American Socialist*. Archive in ETOL. p. 6 .

Brown, JS. (1991) Research that reinvents the corporation. In JS Brown (ed.). *Seeing differently*, Boston: Harvard Business School Publishing. p. 216 .

Brown, J & Isaacs, D. (2005) *The world café: shaping our futures through conversations that matter*. San Francisco: Berrett-Koehler.

Burke, WW. (1994) *Organizational development: a process of learning and changing*. Massachusetts: Addison-Wesley.

Burke, W & Litwin, G. 1992: A causal model of organisational performance and change. *Journal of Management*. 9(18) p.523-545

Bushe, GR. (1990) *Advances in appreciative inquiry as an organization development technique*. Reading, MA: Addison Wesley.

Cahn, R. (2006) 'Polich J. Meditation states and traits: EEG, ERP, and neuroimaging studies'. *Psychology Bulletin*. 132. P.180-211.

Carson, AD & Lowman, RL. (2002) Individual-level variables in organisational consultation, in RL Lawman (ed.). *The California School of organizational studies handbook of organizational consulting psychology: a comprehensive guide to theory, skill and techniques*. San Francisco: Jossey-Bass. p.5-26.

Celes, C. (2009) *Map of Consciousness: A powerful framework for your personal growth* [online]. Available from: http://personalexcellence.co/blog/map-of-consciousness/. Accessed 29/06/2014.

Champy, J. (1995) *Reengineering management*. New York: Harper Business Books.

Charman, RA. (2006) Has direct brain to brain communication been demonstrated by electroencephalographic monitoring of paired or group subjects? *The Journal of the Society for Psychical Research* 60. p.1-24.

Cilliers, F. (2000) Team building from a psycho-dynamic approach. *Journal of Industrial Psychology*. 26(1) p.18-23.

Coetzee, A. (2013). Spirituality and leadership through transcendence. Unpublished Masters degree. Available at the University of Johannesburg.

Colinvaux, PA. (1980) *Fate of Nations*. New York: Simon and Schuster.

Collins, J. (2001) *Good to great*. New York: HarperCollins Publishers, Inc.

Cooperrider, D, Whitney, D & Stavros, J. (2003) *Appreciative inquiry handbook*. San Francisco: Berrett-Koehler.

Coulter, M. (2013) *Strategic Management in Action*, 6th Ed. Boston: Pearson.

Covey, SR. (2004) *The 8th habit*. London: Simon & Schuster.

Cummings, TG. (2008) *The Handbook of Organisational Development*. Southern California: Sage.

Darling, JR & Heller, VL. (2011) The key for effective stress management: Importance of responsive leadership in organisational development, *Organisational development Journal*, 29(1). p.1-26.

D'Aveni, RA. (1989) The aftermath of organizational decline: longitudinal study of the strategic and managerial characteristics of declining firms. *Academy of Management Journal*. 32(3) p.577-605.

Dawson, P. (1996) *Organisational Change: A Processual Approach*. London: Paul Chapman.

De Geus AP. (1997) The living organization. *Harvard Business Review*. 3. p.52-59.

De Jager, W. (2003) *Change leader workbook*. 1. Johannesburg: Absa.

Deming, WE. (1993) *The new economics for industry, government, education*. Cambridge, Mass: Massachusetts Institute of Technology, Center for Advanced Engineering Study.

Dentor, M & Bouwer, E. (2003) Entrenching change and high performance through the Beehive Model of organizational renewal. Global Conference on Business and Economics. 7. p.5-7. London: Unpublished.

Diamond, J. (2001) The Therapeutic power of music, In: Shannon, S. Ed. *Handbook of complementary and alternative therapies in mental health*, Academic Press.

Du Plessis H. (2004) Stories and drama: Are they useful as value adding business partners? http://www.learningtheatre.co.za/feature.htm Accessed on 07/06/2014

Duffy, M., & Passmore, J. (2010) 'Ethics in coaching: An ethical decision making framework for coaching psychologists' International Coaching Psychology Review, 5 (2) pp.140-151.

Drucker, PF. (1987) Management: the problems of success. *Academy of Management Executive*. 1(1) p.13-18.

Dubois, HFW. (2002) Harmonization of the European vaccination policy and the role TQM and reengineering could play. *Quality Management in Health Care*. 10(2) p.47-57.

Edwards C, Robinson O, Welchman R & Woodall J. (1999) *Human resource management journal*. Blackwell Synergy and Oates.

Erikson, E.H. (1964). Insight and responsibility. New York: Norton.

Fischer R. (1971) A cartography of the ecstatic and meditative states, *Science*. 1164. p.896-904.

Fischer, R. (2006) Roland Fischer's cartography of ecstatic mystical states: A reappraisal. *Transpersonal psychology review*, 4(2) p.4-16.

Fischer, R & Boynton, A. (2005) Virtuoso teams. *Harvard Business Review*. 83(7). p.116-123.

Fisher, J. (2006) Process of personal change. Business Balls.com. http://www.businessballs.com/personalchangeprocess.htm#personal%20construct%20psychology. Accessed on 25/04/2014.

French, W.L. & Bell, C.H. (1999) Organizational development. New Jersey: Prentice Hall.

Freud, S.(1964) *Jokes and their relationship to the unconscious*, New York: Norton.

Galbraith J.K. (1978) *The new industrial state*. 3rd revised edition. New York: New American Library.

Griffin, T.J. & Purser, R. (1997) Large Group Interventions: Whole System Approaches to Organizational Change. In Cummings, T.G. (eds) The Handbook of Organisational Development. Southern California: Sage.

Grinberg-Zylberbaum, J., Delaflor, M., Attie, L., & Goswami, A. (1994) The Einstein Podolsky-Rosen Paradox in the brain: the transferred potential. *Physics Essays*, 6:422-426.

Gummer, B. & McCallion, P. (eds), (1995) *Total quality management in the social services: theory and practice*. Albany, NY: Rockefeller College Press.

Graves, C. (1974): Human nature prepares for a momentous leap. *The Futurist*, April. p.72-87.

Grove, C. (2005). Introduction to the GLOBE Research Project on Leadership Worldwide. http://ww.grovewell.com/pub-GLOBE-intro. Accessed on 25/04/2015.

Hagen, EE. (1962) On the theory of social change: how economic growth begins. Dorsey Press: Homewood, Illinois.

Hammer, M. (1990) Reengineering work: don't automate, obliterate. *Harvard Business Review.* 7. p.104-112.

Hamilton G. (1978) Pariah capitalism: a paradox of power and dependency. *Ethnicity Groups*, 2: 1-15.

Handy, C. (1995) The empty raincoat: making sense of the future. London: Arrow Books.

Harris S. nd. Good Read Quotes. https://www.goodreads.com/quotes/302666-the-only-thing-that-guarantees-an-open-ended-collaboration-among-human. Accessed on 15.4.2015.

Hawkins, DR. (2005) Map of the scale of consciousness, *Transcending the levels of consciousness.* UK: Veritas Publishing.

Heroldt, J., Ungerer, M., Pretorius, M. (2000) *Business planning: strategic business planning series*, Nuts & Bolts series. Randburg: Knowledge Resources.

Higgins, JM. (2005) The eight Ss of successful strategy execution. *Journal of Change Management.* 5(1). p.3-13.

Hill, S & Wilkinson, A. (1995) In search of TQM. *Employee Relations.* 17 (3). p.8-26.

Hofstede, G. (1999) The universal and the specific in 21st-century global management. *Organizational Dynamics.* p.34-43.

Hopson, B & Adams, J. (1976) Towards an understanding: defining some boundaries of transition dynamics. In Adams, J, Hayes, J and Hopson, B (ed.). *Transition: understanding and managing personal change.* London: Martin Robertson. Pages unknown.

Hunt, D. (2015) Science and non Duality. Available at http://www.scienceandnonduality.com/the-intimacy-of-silence/. Accessed on 15/02/2015.

Huss, A. (2006) *Leading change performance workbook.* Module in MOTI-degree. Johannesburg: Da Vinci Institute.

Hutchins, D.C. (2008) *Hoshin Kanri: the strategic approach to continuous improvement.* Burlington: Gower.

Iacoboni, M & McHaney RW. (2013) Applying empathy and mirror neuron concepts to neuroleadership, *NeuroLeadership.* Rock, D. and Ringleb, A. (eds.). p.369.

Jamieson, D & Worley, C. (2006) Pre-publication draft for the Handbook of Organization Development. California: Sage.

Janssen, JF. (1996) *The four rooms of change.* Boston, Massachusetts: Harvard Business School Press.

Jaques, E. (1975) Social systems and a defense against persecutory and expressive anxiety. In Klein, M (ed.). *New directions in psychoanalysis.* London: Tavistock. 478-409.

Jaques, E. (1989) *Requisite organization.* Arlington: Cason Hall.

Johansen-Berg, H: 2009. *Juggling enhances connections in the brain* [online]. *Nature Neuroscience.* 12. Oxford University Press. p.1360-1361. Available from http://www.ox.ac.uk/media/news_releases_for_journalists/. Accessed 24/06/2014.

Jolij, J. & Meurs, M. (2011) Music alters visual perception. *PLos ONE*, 6(4). DOI:10.1371/journal. pone.0018861.

Jones, BB & Brazzel, M. (2014) *The NTL Handbook of Organization Development and Change: Principles, Practices, and Perspectives*. 2nd Edition. San Francisco: NLT Institute.

Jones, B & Clark, P. (1976) *Psychological factors in regional economic development*. In Chatteryi, M (ed.). *Space location and regional development*. London: University Symposium on Regional Science.

Jones, GR & George, JM. (2014) *Contemporary Management*. 8th Edition. New York: McGraw Hill Education.

Jovanovic, B & Rousseau, PL. (2002) The Q-theory of mergers. *American Economic Review, American Economic Association*. 5(92). p.198-204.

Josipovic, Z. (2013) Freedom of the mind. *Frontiers in Perception Science*. 4. p.538.

Jung, CG. (1954) On the Nature of the Psyche. 1988 edition. In H. Read, et al. (eds.). *The Collected Works of C.G. Jung* (vol. 8). Princeton: Princeton University Press (original work published 1948).

Kaplan, RS. & Norton, DP. (1996) *The balanced scorecard*. Boston, MA: Harvard Business School Press.

Kelada, JN. (1996) Integrating reengineering with total quality. Wisconsin: Quality Press.

Kets de Vries, MFR. (1991) *Organizations on the couch: handbook of psychoanalysis and management*. New York: Jossey-Bass.

Kets de Vries, MFR. (2001) *The leadership mystique*. London: Prentice Hall.

Kets de Vries, MFR. (2005) *Lessons on leadership by terror: finding a Shaka Zulu in the attic*. UK: Edward Elgar

Kilmann, RH. (1989) *Managing beyond the organizational fix*. San Francisco: Jossey-Bass.

Kohlberg, L. (1973) The claim to moral adequacy of a highest stage of moral judgment. *Journal of Philosophy*. 70 p.630-646.

Kolb, DA & Frohman, A. (1970) An organizational development approach to consulting. *Sloan Management Review*, 12(1). p.51-65.

Koortzen, PY & Cilliers, F. (2002) The psychoanalytical approach to team development. In Lawman, RL (ed.). *The California School of organizational studies handbook of organizational consulting psychology: a comprehensive guide to theory, skill and techniques*. San Francisco: Jossey-Bass. p.260-283.

Kotter, JP. (1990) *A force for change: how leadership differs from management*. Boston: HBS Press.

Kotter, JP & Rathgerber, H. (2006) *Our Iceberg is melting*. 1st edition. New York: St Martins Press.

Kotter, JP & Schlesinger, LA. 1979: Choosing strategies for change. *Harvard Business Review*. 57(3) p.106-114.

Kreitner, R & Kinicki, A. (2004) *Organizational behaviour*. 6th edition. New York: McGraw-Hill.

Krüger, W. (2005) Change iceberg. www.valuebasedmanagement.net. Accessed on 05/09/2015.

Kübler-Ross, E. (1973) *On death and dying*. New York: MacMillan.

Kuhn, T. (1996) The structure of scientific revolutions.,3rd edition. Chicago, University Press.

Laubscher, LI. (2013) *Human Niches: Spiral Dynamics for Africa*. Ph.D dissertation. Modderfontein: Da Vinci Institute. Available at http://www.mandalaconsulting.co.za/.../Thesis%20%20 Loraine%20Laubscher.pdf.

Lazar, S. (2009) Neuroplasticity: Your brain's amazing ability to form new habits, [online] 4 April 2009 Available from www.refocuser.com/2009/05/neuroplasticity. Accessed 12/07/2014.

Leaf, C. (2013) *Switch on your brain. The key to peak happiness, thinking, and health.* Michigan: BakerBooks.

Le Roux, A. (2009) *The development of a multidisciplinary organisational development model.* Unpublished Ph.D thesis. University of Johannesburg.

Lessem, R. (1993) Four worlds: The South African business sphere. In *African Management: Philosophy, Concepts and Applications.* Randburg: Knowledge Resources.

Lessem, R & Schieffer, A. (2010) *Integral Research and Innovation: Transforming Enterprise and Society.* Farnham: Gower Ashgate.

Lessem, R & Schieffer, A. (2015) *Integral Polity.* Farnham: Gower Ashgate.

LeBarOn, M. (2005) *Bridging cultural conflicts: a new approach for a changing world.* San Francisco: Jossey-Bass.

Leidler, RJ. (1999) *The ultimate leadership task: self-leadership. Career Mastery, Mastering the Art of Continuous Employability in the 21st Century.* Johannesburg: Absa p.183-201.

Levine, P. (1997) *Waking the tiger. Healing trauma. The innate capacity to transform overwhelming experiences.* Berkeley: North Atlantic Books.

Levine, P. (2010) *In an unspoken Voice: How the body releases trauma and restores goodness.* Berkeley: North Atlantic books.

Lewin, K. (1951) *Field theory in the social sciences.* New York: Harper.

Lifton, RJ. (1961) *Thought reform and the psychology of totalism.* Harmondsworth: Penguin.

Lippit, R, Watson, J & Westley, B. 1958: *Dynamics of planned change.* New York: Harcourt and Brace.

Lowman, RL. (2012) The Scientist-Practitioner Consulting Psychologist. *Consulting Psychology Journal: Practice and Research.* 64(3). p.151-156.

Luders, E, Toga, AW, Lepore, N, & Gaser, C. (2009) The underlying anatomical correlates of long-term meditation: larger hippocampal and frontal volumes of gray matter. *Neuroimage.* 45(3). p.662-668. [pdf] doi: 10.1016/j.neuroimage.2008.12.061

Marquardt, D. (1999) *Action learning in action: transforming problems and people for work-class organizational learning.* Palo Alto: Davies-Black.

Mayikana, M. (2003) Managing diversity: has there been any visible improvement? *Management Today.* 19(5). p.32-33.

Mbigi, L. (2000) Managing social capital. *Training & Development.* 1. p.36-40.

McCloskey, D & Klamer, A. (1995) One quarter of GDP is persuasion in rhetoric and economic behaviour. *The American Economic Review.* 85. p.195.

Mezirow, J. 1978: Perspective transformation. *Adult Education,* USA, XXVIII. 2. p.100-110.

Mihata, K. (1997) The persistence of 'emergence. In Raymond, E, Horsfall, E & Lee, ME (eds.). *Chaos, complexity & sociology: myths, models & theories.* Thousand Oaks: Sage. p.30-38.

Miller, FA & Katz, JH. (2002) *The inclusion breakthrough: unleashing the real power of diversity.* San Francisco: Berrett-Koehler.

Mohrman, SA, Finegold, D & Klein, JA. (2002) Designing the knowledge enterprise: beyond programs and tools. *Organizational Dynamics.* 31(2). p.134-150.

Nel, C. (2003) Leading the Absa Way course material. Johannesburg: Absa.

Newell, H & Dopson, S. (1996) Muddle in the middle: organisational restructuring and middle management. *Personnel Review*. 25(4). p.4-20.

Nohria, N, Joyce, J & Robertson, B. (2003) What really works. *Harvard Business Review*, 81(7). p.43-52.

O'Connor, CA. (1993) Resistance: the repercussions of change. *Leadership and Organization Development Journal*. 14(6). p.30-6.

Occelli, O. (2012) *Resurrecting Venus*. Carlsbad: Hay House.

Opie, P. (1951) Lewis Carroll Alice's Adventures in Wonderland. *The Oxford Dictionary of Nursery Rhymes*. Oxford: Oxford University Press. p.213-5.

Pennington G. (2003). *Guidelines for promoting and facilitating change*. www.ltsn.ac.uk/genericcentre/index.asp? Accessed on 03/01/2013.

Peters, TJ & Waterman, RH Jr. (1982) *In search of excellence*. New York: Warner Books Edition.

Planck, M. (1931) Consciousness matters. *The Observer*. January 25, 1931.

Radin, DI. (2004) Event-related eletroencephalographic correlations between isolated human subjects. *Journal of Alternative and Complementary Medicine*. 10 p.315-323.

Radin, D. (2013) *Supernormal. Science, yoga, and the evidence for extraordinary psychic abilities*. New York: Deepak Chopra Books.

Radin, DI & Nelson, RD. (1989) Evidence for Consciousness-related anomalies in random physical systems. *Foundations of Physics*. 19(12) p.1499-1514.

Rajhans, G. (2013) *The power of mantra chanting: why and how to chant*. Available from http://hinduism.about.com/od/prayersmantras/a/mantrachanting.htm Accessed 20/07/2014.

Ramose, MB. (2000) African renaissance. *A Northbound Gaze*. 19(3) p.47-61.

Reivich, K & Shatte, A. (2002) *The resilience factor: 7 essential skills for overcoming life's inevitable obstacles*. New York: Broadway Books. Rice, KE. nd. Integrated Socio-psychology website. Available at www.integratedsociopsychology.net/vmemes.htm. Accessed on 15/02/2015.

Rogers, CR. (1973): *Client-centered therapy*. London: Constable.

Roodt, G & Van Tonder, CL (2008). Central features: change, process, values and systemic health. In CL van Tonder & G Roodt (eds.), *Organisational Development: Theory and practice*. Pretoria: Van Schaik. p.39-59.

Roth, WM, Lawless, DV, Tobin, K. (2000) Coteaching /cogenerative dialoguing as praxis of dialectic method forum. *Qualitative Social Research*, 1(3) http://www.qualitative-research.net/fqs/fqs-e/submission-e.htm. Accessed on 06/10/2014.

Roth, G. (2011). *Four Shamanic Questions* [online]. Available from www.livingforaliving.org/post/40503287102. Accessed 17/12/2014.

Rudd, CE. (2013) *Developing a holistic, sustainable and transferable framework for learning*. Unpublished Ph.D thesis. Available at Da Vinci Institute for Innovation and Technology.

Saunders, R. (2015) Management of People Assignment. Available at the Da Vinci Institute for Innovation and Technology.

Schmidt, S. (2012) Can we help just by good intentions? A meta-analysis of experiments on distant intention effects, *The Journal of Alternative and Complementary Medicine*. 18(6). p.529-533.

Schutte, PC. (2004) Employee satisfaction and customer service: a literature perspective. Johannesburg: IGH. Unpublished.

Schein, EH. (1987) Process Consultation. *Journal of Applied Behavioral Science*, 23(2). p.255-262.

Schein, EH. (1995) *Organizational culture and leadership*. San Francisco: Jossey-Bass.

Senge, PM. (1990) *The fifth discipline: the art and practice of the learning organization*. New York: Bantam Doubleday Dell.

Senge, PM. (1993) *The fifth discipline*. UK: Random House.

Senge, PM. (2003) Creating desired futures in a global economy: reflections. *The SOL Journal on Knowledge, Learning and Change*. Cambridge: The Society for Organizational Learning.

Senge, PM, Scharmer, CO, Jaworski, J & Flowers, BS. (2004) *Presence: human purpose and the field of the future*. Cambridge: The Society for Organisational Learning.

Serres, M. (2012) Integral Post-metaphysics. Available at http://integralpostmetaphysics.ning.com/forum/topics/michel-serre. Accessed on 13/02/2015.

Shleifer, A & Vishny, RW. (2003) Stock market driven acquisitions. *Journal of Financial Economics*. 12(70). p.295-311.

Siebert, A. (2005) *The resilience advantage: master change, thrive under pressure and bounce back from setbacks*. New York: Practical Psychology Press.

Smeltzer, LR. & Zener, MF. (1994) Minimizing the negative effect of employee layoffs through effective announcements. *Employee Counselling Today*. 6(4). p.3-9.

Schmidt, S. (2012) Can we help just by good intentions? A meta-analysis of experiments on distant intention effects. *The Journal of Alternative and Complementary Medicine*, 18(6): pp. 529-533.

Smulyan, L. (2000) *Balancing acts: women principals at work*. Albany: State University of New York Press.

Stacey, R. (1996) *Strategic management and organizational dynamics*, 2nd edition. London: Pitman.

Strümpfer, DJW. (2003) Resilience and burn out: a stitch that could save nine. *South African Journal of Psychology*. 33(2) p.69-79.

Strümpfer, DJW. (2007) Lest we forget that industrial and organisational psychology is psychology. *SA Journal of Industrial Psychology*, 33 (1), pp. 1-7

Strümpfer, J. (2001) Complex problem solving. Course presented at Absa. Johannesburg: Absa.

Sultanoff, BA. (2001) The environment. In Shannon, S. (ed.) *Handbook of complementary and alternative therapies in mental health*. Academic Press, a Division of Harcourt, Inc.

Strydom, D. (2014). Lecture on Organisational Behaviour. MCOM. University of Johannesburg. November.

Swanepoel, B, Schenk, H, Van Wyk & Erasmus, B. (2003) Change: making the environment more complex. *Management Today*. 19(5). p28-31.

Thomas, L & Harri-Augstein, ES. (1985) *Self-organized learning: foundations of a conversational science for psychology*. London: Routledge.

Thomas, PN & Naidoo, AV. (2007) Psychological consulting in South Africa: The emergence of a new practice modality and its implications for training. *New voices in psychology*. 2(1). p.46-64.

Thompson, AA, Strickland, AJ & Gamble, JE. (2010) *Crafting and Executing Strategy*, 17th Edition. McGraw-Hill International: Boston.

Ulrich, D. (1997). Human Resource Champions: The Next Agenda for Adding Value and Delivering. Boston: Harvard Business School Press. Van Heerden, HK. (1985) Handbook of values management thinking: for practical application in facilitating values management problem solving workshops. Cutting Edge Series. A Cutting Edge Series Publication.

Van Tonder, CL. 2004a: The march of time and the "evolution" of change. *SA Journal of Industrial Psychology.* 2004, 30(3). p.41-52.

Van Tonder, CL. 2004b: *Organisational change: Theory and practice.* Pretoria, South Africa: Van Schaik.

Van Tonder, CL. (2009) Personal discussion with the author. April 2009.

Viljoen, RC. (2012). Africa is not for sissies. *Da Vinci Institute for Innovation and Technology Newsletter.* December. Modderfontein.

Viljoen, RC. (2013) Change state indicator. Available at Mandala Consulting. Randburg.

Viljoen, RC. (2014) *Inclusive Organisational Transformation: An African Approach.* Farnham: Gower Ashgate.

Viljoen, RC & Laubscher, LI. (2015) Spiral dynamics integral. In Lessem, R, Schieffer, A (eds.). *Integral Polity* Farnham: Gower Ashgate.

Viljoen, RC & Laubscher, LI. (2015) African spirituality. Insights from the cradle of mankind. In Spiller, C & Wolfgramm, R (eds.). *Indigenous spiritualties at work: Transforming the spirit of business enterprise.* Charlotte: Information Age Publishing.

Weick, K. (1995) *Sense making in organizations.* Thousand Oaks: Sage.

Weick, KE & Quinn, RE. (1999) Organisational Development. *Annual Review of Psychology.* 50. p.361-86.

Wheatly, M. (1992) *Leadership and the new science.* San Francisco: Berrett-Koehler.

Wheatly, M. (2005) We can be wise only together, in Brown, J & Isaacs, D (eds.). *The world café.* San Francisco: Berrett-Koehler. p.ii-vi.

Wilber, K. (2010) AQAL Glossary. Introduction to Integral Theory and Practice: IOS Basic and the AQAL Map, vol. 1, no. 3. Available at www. humanemergence.nl/uploads/2011/03/IOS-Basic-Intro-to-Integral.pdf. Accessed 07/01/2015.

Wilkins, AL & Patterson KJ. (1985) You can't get there from here: what will make culture-change projects fail. In Kilmann, MJ (ed.). *Gaining control of the corporate culture.*

Wyker, J. (2001) Spiritual Psychotherapy. In: Shannon, S (ed.). *Handbook of complementary and alternative therapies in mental health.* Ann Arbor: Academic Press, A Division of Harcourt, Inc.

Zohar, JD & Marshall, I. (2000) *A spiritual intelligence.* London: Bloomsbury.

ADDITIONAL RESOURCES

Cooperrider, D. (1990) Positive image, positive action: the affirmative basis of organizing. In Srivastva, S & Cooperrider, DL (ed.). *Appreciative management and leadership*. San Francisco: Jossey-Bass. p.91–125.

Cooperrider, D & Srivastava, S. (1987) Appreciative Inquiry in organizational life. In Woodman, RW & Pasmore, WA (ed.). *Research in organizational change and development*. Greenwich, Conn: JAI Press.

Cooperrider, D & Whitney, D. (2000) Exploring appreciative inquiry. *Journal of the World Business Academy*. 14(2) p.69-74.

Harris, MM & Fink, LS. (1987) A field study of applicant reactions to employment opportunities: does the recruiter make a difference? *Personnel Psychology*. 40. p.765-783.

Hölzel, BK, Carmody, J, Vangel, M, Congleton, C, Yerramsetti, SM, Gard, T & Lazar, SW. (2011) Mindfulness practice leads to increases in regional brain gray matter density. *Psychiatry Research: Neuroimaging*. 191(1). p.36-43.

Jaques, E. (1997) *Requisite organization: a total system for effective managerial organization and managerial leadership for the 21st century*. Arlington: Cason Hall.

Jung, CG. (1961) *Psychological Types*. A revision by RFC Hull of the translation by HG Baynes. London: Routledge & Kegan Paul.

Jung, CG. (1962) *Symbols of Transformation: An Analysis of the Prelude to a Case of Schizophrenia*. (2) trans. RFC Hull. New York: Harper & Brothers.

Jung, CG & Jaffé A. (1962) *Memories, Dreams, Reflections*. New York: Random House.

Trompenaars, F. (1994) *Riding the waves of culture: understanding diversity in global business*. Burr Ridge: Irwin.

Wolcott, HF. (1995) The art of fieldwork. Alta Mira. Press, Walnut Creek. *Conscious Femininity: Interviews with Marion Woodman*. Inner City Books.

INDEX

E

eagle group 172
Economic Freedom Front (EFF) 58, 67, 76
economies, emerging 8, 9, 13, 22, 64, 69, 71
ecstasy 114
efforts 10, 12, 14, 18, 20, 23, 29, 41, 52, 70,
    72, 77, 133, 176, 185
  difficult organisational transformation 101
  strategic 19
elders 56, 65, 76
election 58, 75–76
emotional containment 16, 108
emotional intelligence 20, 50, 126, 129, 156
emotional states 110, 111
emotions 7, 13, 44, 45, 48, 49, 51, 77, 104–
    106, 112, 114, 115, 130, 156
  negative 104, 105
empathy 77, 110, 126, 128, 129, 150, 156
employees 14, 30, 31, 48, 51–52, 54, 64, 67,
    70, 71, 74, 93, 95, 120, 134, 135, 158,
    170
energy 10, 13–15, 22, 25, 29, 43, 66, 68, 88,
    92, 102, 106, 107, 139, 154, 157, 158
  red 67, 80
  renewed 167, 170
energy field-awareness 73
engagement 8, 13, 15, 16, 21, 25, 49, 71, 89,
    99, 125, 147, 150, 157–160, 167, 170
  employee 69, 158
  individual 157
enhanced levels of interpersonal skill 102, 115,
    117
enlightenment 112
entertainment 93, 94, 140
environment 14, 21, 83, 94, 108, 121, 125,
    153, 154, 157, 163, 165, 166
  external 5, 16, 22, 29, 45, 50, 75
  internal 24, 29, 164–166
essence 15–17, 19, 24, 25, 34, 56, 59, 80,
    83, 101, 157, 171
ethical codes 182–184
  decisions 182, 183
  principles 182, 183, 185
ethics 181, 184
  code of 180
evaluation 67, 184
events 57, 66, 70, 104, 108, 121, 123, 127–128

large group 108, 123
large-group 9, 123, 125, 127
large-group facilitated 123
psycho-analytical 52, 126, 127
small-group 127
excel 4, 27, 59, 87, 169
exco 91, 131
execute 29, 166, 170, 173
execute organisational strategies 69
execution 32, 36, 164, 173
existence 7, 51, 57–60, 62, 64–67, 69, 71,
    72, 74, 75, 77, 84, 107, 151, 152, 155,
    162
experiences 23, 53, 65, 77, 84, 94, 99, 104–
    107, 110, 111, 113, 117, 118, 171, 180
experiential education 117
  learning 9, 21, 117–118
exploration 32, 45, 47, 89, 126
external world 14, 19, 23, 29, 58

F

facilitation 4, 6, 8, 49, 70, 74, 118, 120, 122–
    124, 127, 128, 130–132
  group process 122
  approaches 9, 131
  process 171
  types, following 120, 124
  psycho-analytical 20, 21, 130
facilitative approach, dynamic 178
facilitators 20, 90, 91, 97–99, 118–119, 123–
    125, 128–131
  group process 2
factors 17, 20, 24, 25, 34, 37, 43, 162, 165,
    182
factory 134, 143, 144
fear 43, 46, 49, 51, 57, 72, 84, 89, 102, 103,
    108, 112–113
feedback 5, 50, 51, 92, 98, 124, 139, 144,
    160
  strategic 163
femininity 24
field 1–4, 7–8, 10, 12, 29, 39, 47, 51, 59, 75,
    92, 106, 175–180, 182, 184, 185
  emerging 178, 179
fight 14, 63, 65, 106, 107, 126
financial services organisation 164, 170
  competitive 170

ENDORSEMENTS

Individuals, organisations, communities and societies are facing a significantly new world order. Their playing field has become one of discontinuous, radical change, heightened complexity, snowballing chaos, growing diversity, deepening ambiguity, and widening seamlessness (or boundarylessness). Ever-shifting goal posts regarding critical success criteria, the rules of the game, of co-operation/ competition, responsiveness, innovation, speed, flexibility, value-add, quality, and cost effectiveness are forcing all to make the seemingly impossible possible if they wish to perform and succeed. At a deeper level, all need to shift their view of the world by seeing it as an interconnected, systemic dynamic whole, manifesting successive states of chaos and order, finding expression in virtuous or vicious cycles. In our endeavour to understand and intervene sustainably in an inclusive manner in this new world, Rica's timeous book provides an invaluable way of thinking about and acting upon and in the new world order.

Prof Theo H Veldsman, Department of Industrial Psychology and People Management,
Faculty of Management, University of Johannesburg

In the dynamic world of today, where organisations must continuously adapt to a range of internal and external challenges and where change is a constant, competence in organisational change and development is necessary for survival, competitiveness and growth. The simplistic remedies of the past no longer work and Dr Rica Viljoen's book is both practical and inspiring in its academic groundedness combined with useful models and methodologies for finding the right solution to complex problems in organisations. She helps organisations formulate a blueprint to establish the conditions for the reliable delivery of the company's business strategy on an ongoing basis – and in a manner that shapes and reinforces an organisational culture and capability consistent with the reliable delivery of the company's long-term vision of driving superior returns together with sustainable outcomes.

Italia Boninelli, Executive Vice-President People and Organisation Development
AngloGold Ashanti

This is not just another treatise on organisational change and development (OCD). Dr Rica Viljoen presents the reader with an extensive grounded body of relevant knowledge to challenge and guide the leader, manager and professional along the complex networks of paths and hedges to understand the intricate dynamics of the real world and human behaviour relative to OCD. Through her insights and grasp of the confusing complexities and the multi-dimensional facets, she skilfully integrates and challenges conventional knowledge and creates new understanding. This will stand the practitioner in good stead in this very important and unique Africa.

Dr George Lindique gflin@absamail.co.za

The real meaning and contribution of OCD are demonstrated when theories are applied in practice, and when the processes and interventions that are introduced assist and enable organisations to adapt to the rapid, ever-changing environments to ensure that we sustain and improve our business models. Our company is fortunate to have had Rica as its OCD consultant since 1997 and many of the interventions and techniques mentioned in this book have been applied over the years in our company. This book will help future generations to understand the value of different human thinking patterns and their contributions in building prosperous enterprises.

Henk Van Zyl, Director: Human Resources, Interstate Bus Lines

My connection with Rica goes back for almost 15 years. This book and the content from her perspective made my life in leadership so much easier. It's relevant and to the point, but also very practical to implement in business.

Adri Vermeulen, Chief Executive, PPS Namibia

www.ingramcontent.com/pod-product-compliance
Lightning Source LLC
Chambersburg PA
CBHW082032230326
41599CB00056B/6266